Black, Coppe
The District of Columbia's
Black Civil War Regiment

By

C.R. GIBBS

With a Foreword by
Frank Smith, Founding Director,
African American Civil War
Memorial Freedom Foundation
Washington, D.C.

Three Dimensional Publishing
Silver Spring, Maryland

First edition

Printed in the United States of America

ISBN: 1-877835-81-1

Contents

Foreword

When the Civil War started in 1861, there were about 4.5 million blacks living in the United States. Four million of that number were enslaved blacks living in the agricultural regions of the South. As one contemporary observer noted these men, women, and children were surrounded by a "hellish institution... unparalleled in its mode of evil treatment by the master to the slave." But the great national strife that was the war between the states gave thousands of enslaved young men of African descent an opportunity to help end the rebellion and gain their liberty.

Approximately 150,000 of the soldiers listed on the Wall of Honor of the African American Civil War Memorial were enslaved when the war started. Approximately 50,000 of the men listed on the wall were free blacks. These free men were mostly laborers, farmers, waiters, craftsmen, and mechanics.

We find the largest number of formerly enslaved soldiers coming from the state of Louisiana, with approximately 24,000. The state of Kentucky was second with approximately 23,000. Tennessee was third and Mississippi was fourth with each supplying about 20,000 black men to the Union forces. There are more than 209,000 men listed on the wall. They hailed from all over the United States, Canada, South America, the Caribbean, and Africa.

In comparison with the figures above, the number of black soldiers credited to the District of Columbia, 3,265, seems small. And yet this number is equal in size to three regiments and demonstrates that African Americans in the nation's capital sent a larger percentage of their population to war-time service than the number - 13,265 - credited to whites in the city who comprised a far larger number of eligible citizens. It is this commitment, courage, and sacrifice that C.R. Gibbs recounts in *Black, Copper, and Bright: The District of Columbia's Black Civil War Regiment*. This book tells us the largely forgotten story of the First Regiment, United States Colored Troops organized in the District of

Columbia in the spring and summer of 1863. There was tremendous opposition to the organization of this regiment from the very beginning and Mr. Gibbs weaves a masterful and exciting story of the unit's travails and triumphs. He rescues this story from the dust of history and reminds us all of the struggles that occurred here on the streets we walk today and climaxed on the battlefields of Virginia and North Carolina.

We must challenge ourselves to do all we can to correct the great oversight in history by telling the story of the service and courage of these soldiers. As we honor them, we honor the best in our country and ourselves as we prepare the next generation to be more noble and patriotic.

Frank Smith, Ph.D.
Founding Director,
African American Civil War Memorial
Freedom Foundation

Introduction

This is the story of the First Regiment, United States Colored Troops. The unit was organized and trained in the District of Columbia in the Spring and Summer of 1863 and was the first such organization of its kind formally mustered into the federal service. The regiment was also the first of its kind organized in the Middle Atlantic states. Led by white officers, the regiment drew men of African descent not only from the District but also from Maryland, Virginia, the Carolinas, New England, Canada, and the West Indies. The regimental chaplain was the famed Henry McNeal Turner who pastored Israel Bethel African Methodist Episcopal Church at the foot of Capitol Hill.

The regiment distinguished itself in combat in Virginia and North Carolina, participating in some of the Civil War's most famous battles including: Chaffin's Farm, Fair Oaks, and Fort Fisher. At the battle of Wilson's Wharf, the regiment participated in the only battle in Virginia, possibly the only one in the entire Civil War in which nearly all the Union troops were black. The battle proved once and for all that black troops would fight on their own without extensive support from white soldiers. During the war, the regiment lost five officers and 180 enlisted men to death, wounds, and disease. The regiment was cited for its bravery by several Union officers including Generals Benjamin Butler and W.F. Smith. The regiment was mustered out on September 29, 1865, with most of the men returning to the District for a first of its kind meeting with President Andrew Johnson. In addition, after the war, many of the enlisted men became leaders in local churches and community organizations.

Although the regiment earned an undeniable place in history, it has seldom been the object of serious study. This is the first book devoted solely to the First Regiment United States Colored Troops.

The title "Black, Copper, and Bright" is taken from the title of Chapter 12 of Margaret Leech's 1941 Pulitzer Prize winning examination of the Civil War in Washington, D.C., entitled *Reveille In Washington.* The chapter discussed, among other things, the African American community in the city at that time. My book is a tribute to the regiment, to its officers, but particularly to the enlisted men of the regiment and their boiled beef, hard tack and coffee existence. Using primary sources, I have tried to describe their sacrifices, heroism, and humanity, warts and all. The book is divided into five chapters covering the regiment's recruitment, service, its chaplain, and its homecoming. There is also a chapter tracing the life of one soldier down through his descendants today. And unlike some regimental histories, I have listed important biographical data - more than what is available on the Internet at present - on each officer and enlisted man who served in the First Regiment, USCT in an appendix with over 1200 entries. A complete listing of all who served in the regiment has been an awesome task. Mistakes, particularly with the names, are unintended and due to a plethora of factors including: limited spelling ability of the soldiers, cultural phonics, other alternate spellings, or the oversight or inattention of military clerks. I regret any errors or omissions, and solicit any corrections.

I hope my book will add important historical and genealogical information to a crucial era in the history of the nation's capital. In my researching, I have met fewer than a dozen descendants of these soldiers. My great hope is that the book will kindle fresh genealogical inquiry and the discovery of more descendants. This general history is not the final word on the regiment, but serves as the first significant step on the road to more detailed work. There are 1200 individual stories that should be told as well. I recall the words Christian Fleetwood used to end his brief 1895 pamphlet, *"The Negro As Soldier."* "There is no need for panegyric, for rounding phrases or rounded periods. The simple story is eloquent with all that is necessary to make the heart swell with pride."

C.R. Gibbs
Washington, D.C.
May, 2002

Acknowledgements

This work has been enriched by the efforts and support of many people. Among the most outstanding have been Frank Smith, Asa Gordon, Terence Lindsey, Peter Hanes, Lawrence Jackson, Charisse Fagins, Joy Kinard, and Pamela Smith, who prepared the manuscript. I am particularly indebted to Donna Welles and Leida Torres of the Moorland Spingarn Research Center at Howard University; Alice Robinson and Janette Graham of the Black Studies Division, Martin Luther King Library, D.C. Public Library System; Mary Haynes, U.S. Army Center for Military History; Michael Meier of the National Archives; Dennis Northcott, Missouri Historical Society; and William T. Stolz of the Western Historical Manuscript Collection, University of Missouri. I am also grateful for and acknowledge my reliance on Warren A. Innis's unpublished master's thesis on the First and Seventh regiments, USCT; it was an important source of information on the regimental letterbooks and muster rolls.

Most of all, I deeply appreciate the patience and encouragement from my wife Bettie who put up with me throughout the inconveniences and difficulties of researching and writing.

CHAPTER I

HOUR OF DESTINY

"The Colored Regiment - Recruiting Commenced"

Washington *Evening Star*

Black, Copper, & Bright

Rally Song for 1st Regiment of Colored Volunteers, DC
written and dedicated to the same May 25, 1863

Let the North rally forth
In resistless might.
Let her send her legions forth
For liberty and rights!

CHORUS Hi rally! Ho rally! To the war we'll go
And we'll show those traitors south the courage of their foe!
How can we silent be
In this stormy strife!
For we'll stake for liberty
The friendly boon of life!

CHORUS Hi rally! Ho rally! To the war we'll go
And we'll show those traitors south the courage of their foe!
Come what may - now's the day
The year of jubilee!
Dawn is nigh with freedom's ray
Mankind must now be free!

CHORUS Hi rally! Ho rally! To the war we'll go
And we'll show those traitors south the courage of their foe!
Let us trust, cause so fair
Can suffer no defeat.
Oppressors yet shall lick the dust
Beneath our conquering feet!

CHORUS Hi rally! Ho rally! To the war we'll go
And we'll show those traitors south the courage of their foe!

John H. Holman Papers
Western Historical Manuscript Collection
Columbia-University of Missouri

From the first, black men in the District of Columbia sought to fight for the Union.

The news of the rebel attack on Fort Sumter struck the nation's capital with trip hammer force. As word reverberated along the city's rainswept streets that fateful Friday, thousands of residents, irrespective of color, had to choose allegiances that sharply affected their lives for the next four years.

President Lincoln's Proclamation the following Monday, April 15, 1861, declaring a state of insurrection and calling out 75,000 militia, transformed the initial confusion and distress into grim resolve. And yet, incongruously, because of the city's strong economic, political, and social ties to the South, it was known as a hotbed of secession and was widely believed filled with residents of "doubtful loyalty." Neighbor to two slaveholding states, Maryland and Virginia, the defenseless city now daily received reports of the activities of groups of southern sympathizers: bridges down, northern troops attacked, and telegraph lines cut. Many pro-southern white males crossed the Potomac to Alexandria to enlist in units like the Washington Volunteers. Even the District's Mayor James E. Berret, it was whispered, supposedly had secessionist sympathies. He was later briefly arrested, detained, and then exonerated.

In those first days of alarm, additional units of the Washington militia and then other local volunteer forces were mustered into federal service for 60 or 90 days to protect the city, and a few later served longer periods in the Union Army.

African Americans in the city were well aware of the immediate danger facing the besieged capital in that critical period (April 10 - April 24) before sizeable reinforcements from northern states arrived. They were eager to show their martial spirit in helping to subjugate the rebellion and serve in a struggle that most believed would turn into a war for the extirpation of slavery.

On April 23, 1861, Jacob Dodson, a black resident of the city, sent the following note to Simon Cameron, Lincoln's Secretary of War:

> Sir: I desire to inform you that I have some three hundred reliable colored free citizens of this City, who desire to enter the service for the defense of the City.
>
> I have been three times across the Rocky Mountains in the service of the country with Fremont and others.
>
> I can be found about the Senate Chambers, as I have been employed about the premises for some years.[1]

Dodson had been one of several blacks to accompany Major John Charles Fremont, the "Pathfinder," on his famous series of expeditions during the 1840s. Fremont then described Dodson as "...a free young colored man of Washington City, who volunteered to accompany the expedition and performed his duty manfully throughout the expedition and voyage." Dodson was 18 years old in 1843 and is believed to have been a servant of Fremont's father-in-law, Senator Thomas Hart Benton of Missouri. Also described as "...strong and active and nearly six feet in height... expert as a Mexican with a lasso, superior to a mountain man with a rifle, equal to either on horse or foot, and always a lad of courage and fidelity," Dodson served as one of the Major's privates and later petitioned Congress for the same pay, land, and other allowances received by Fremont's white California adventurers.

Dodson shared a number of dangers and hardships with Fremont on the Oregon Trail and in California during the Bear Flag Revolt, which helped bring that state into the Union. As Major General Fremont during the Civil War commanding the Western Department in Missouri, his advocacy of emancipation as early as 1861 may have been influenced by his service with African Americans.[2]

Dodson's note was in spite of existing local and federal laws reflecting a 1792 act of Congress that limited militia service to able-bodied white males, except in Louisiana, and an 1820 Army general order that read: "No Negro or mulatto will be received as a recruit." The following year the Army restricted enlistments to "all free white male persons."[3] Largely forgotten outside the black community were the services of black soldiers from Maryland and Virginia during the American Revolution, or that black sailors under Commodore Joshua Barney had dragged cannons from the Washington Navy Yard to the Battle of Bladensburg Heights during the War of 1812.

On April 27, 1861, Cameron sent Dodson the following response: "In reply to your letter of the 23rd instant, I have to say that this Department has no intention at present to call into the service of Government any colored soldiers."[4]

Black men across the country made similar overtures to the government during the first year of the war and all received similar rebuffs. "What upon earth is the matter with the American government and people?" asked Frederick Douglass. "Do they really covet the world's ridicule as well as their own social political ruin?" "Ask the President," he said, "if this dark and terrible hour of the nation's extremity is a time for consulting a mere vulgar and unnatural prejudice.... This is no time to fight with one hand when both are needed.... This is no time to fight only with your white hand, and allow your black hand to remain tied."[5] The sole bright spot was that because of severe manpower shortages, the Union Navy began accepting black enlistments in September, 1861. As bleak as prospects seemed for wider participation in the war, individuals and events were conspiring to cause change beginning in the spring of the following year.

There was substantial resistance to the war becoming the lever of black deliverance. Throughout the North, and in the national capital in particular, the sentiment that this was a "white man's war" solely for the preservation of the Union was often reflected in the pages of the *National Intelligencer*. On October 8, 1861, from its perch at 7th and D Streets, N.W., the conservative, pro-southern and pre-eminent local newspaper proclaimed: "The existing war has no direct relation to slavery. It is a war for the restoration of the Union under the existing Constitution." The paper's position on emancipation had been made clear the previous month. On September 23, an editorial had mused: "Even if the liberation of slaves were an avowed object of the war, it could be accomplished only in the track of a liberating army, as mere edicts of emancipation would be utterly powerless except so far as they are carried into effect by the law of force, against the wishes and interests of the parties concerned as slaveholders...."

Against the wishes and interests of "thin-souled" slaveholders the inexorable link between slavery, war, and emancipation remained a fixture in Washington papers if for no other reason than the rivulet of fugitive bondsmen who began to appear day and night at the city's edges looking for freedom. Although subject to apprehension by soldiers whose camps ringed the capital or policemen who prowled its alleys and roads, field hands and house servants nevertheless risked time in the dank "Blue Jug" the city jail at Judiciary Square. The prison was painted with the gloomy tint that gave it its name. The luckless bondsmen who were caught were usually returned to slavery. Newspapers in Maryland and Virginia dripped with reports of absconding slaves and the reward notices that followed in their wake as they trudged to freedom following liberty's lodestar.

Many, like the three unnamed slaves on the bridge over the Anacostia River, were seized by members of the 71st New York Regiment. Two more were held at the Navy Yard until they were claimed by a Mr. Reeder of St. Mary's County. Numberless others arrived safely and were absorbed into a black community which - in 1861 - still retained many vestiges of its pre-war character.

The society of which African Americans like Jacob Dodson was part was marked by self-reliance, enterprise and pride.

In an 1871 special report to Congress on the "condition and improvement of the public schools in the District of Columbia," the Commissioner included the following statement:

...Another fact important to be considered is that the colored people, who first settled in Washington, constituted a very superior class of their race. Many of them were favorite family servants, who came here with congressmen from the South, and with the families of other public officers, and who by long and faithful services had secured, by gift, purchase, or otherwise, their freedom. Others were superior mechanics, house servants, and enterprising in various callings, who obtained their freedom by their own persevering industry. Some, also, received their freedom before coming to this city...[6]

Blacks generally lived throughout the city but there were concentrations north of K Street, above P Street and west of New Jersey Avenue; on the fringes of the marshlands at Tiber Island or in Foggy Bottom. And African Americans both owned and rented all over Capitol Hill. In Georgetown, a checkerboard residence pattern began to appear with black and white blocks alternating with each other. The aspirations and movements of these African Americans were made difficult by a series of onerous local laws. As one historian has related:

The severe black code derived from the old Maryland statute books, was the law of the District, never modified by Congress. Under its provision that an unclaimed fugitive could be sold to pay for his imprisonment charge, the District had had an unsavory early history of the kidnaping and sale of free men. Although slave trading had been abolished there in 1850, the participation of magistrates and constables in the fees paid by the runaways' masters continued to degrade the courts and corrupt the police; while it was to the financial interest of the jailers to detain fugitives as long as possible. Slaves who wandered farther than the legally prescribed distance from home were liable to be thrown into jail, even though they had had no intention of escaping. No free Negro, without a certificate of freedom on his person, was safe from arrest. Since his testimony could not be received as evidence against a white person, he was without redress. The city police and the District marshal's deputies gave almost their entire time to hunting and seizing colored people, while unofficial slave catchers were attracted to this business, in which there was much to gain and nothing to lose.

The black code had at an early date been supplemented by repressive city ordinances. Lashes were prescribed for pathetically childish offenses - for setting off firecrackers near a dwelling, for bathing in the canal and for flying a kite within the limits of the corporation. More important, in the resultant oppression and extortion practiced by the police, was the regulation that Negroes found on the street after ten o'clock at night could be locked up until morning, and fined as high as ten dollars.[7]

Undeterred by these obstacles, District blacks resisted these oppressive laws, built strong social institutions, and engaged in diverse skilled trades, service occupations, and small businesses. Moreover, the city drew unto itself an imposing class of black leaders, male and female, who often were intellectuals doubling as ministers, business persons, and tradesmen. The year before the war began the census reported:

	Free	Slave
Males	4,702	1,212
Females	6,429	1,973
	11,131	3,185[8]

Free blacks outnumbered slaves. Women outnumbered men. This would make the recruiting of a regiment comprised solely of black male city residents extremely difficult in 1861. Nevertheless, African Americans in the District and across the country initially clamored for the right to enlist. Whenever the opportunity presented itself, Frederick Douglass and others hammered home the theme: "Let the slaves and free

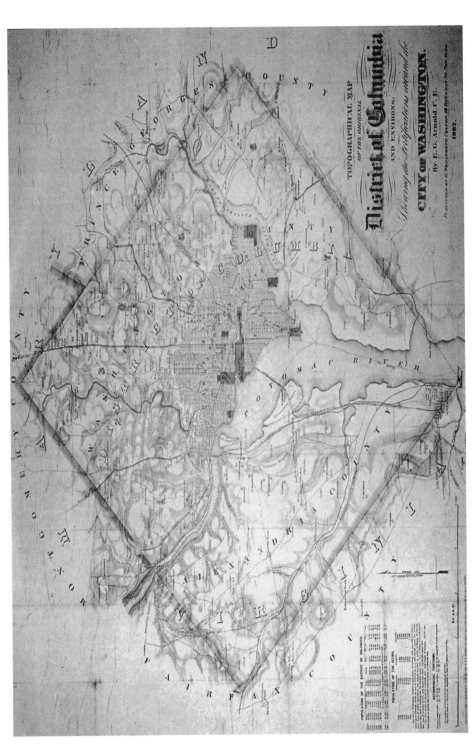

The District of Columbia in 1862.

colored people be called into service, and formed into a liberating Army."
And they had a small group of farsighted and determined allies on Capitol
Hill.

In September 1861, Republican Senator Charles Sumner of
Massachusetts said, "It is sometimes said that this war ought to be carried
into Africa. There is something better; carry Africa into the war. Careful
calculations demonstrate that of this number there are upwards of one
million of an age for military service; that in Virginia alone there are
121,564 male slaves of an age for military service. Can we afford to reject
this national alliance, inspired by a common interest and consecrated by
humanity."[9]

On January 12, 1862, Congressman Thaddeus Stevens of Pennsylvania,
another advocate of emancipation and the use of black troops, presented
a bill urging the enlistment of 150,000 such men. He helped shove the bill
through the House, but it died in the Senate. Again on July 5, he raised
the issue in the House saying: "I would raise a hundred thousand of them
tomorrow and have them drilled."

Congressman Robert Mallory of Kentucky objected raising the prospect
of servile insurrection and the "indiscrinate slaughter of men, women, and
children" and then added that "one shot of cannon would disperse thirty
thousand." Stevens reported in a voice tinged with irony: "Why then
object to them as a savage and barbarous race, if one gun will disperse an
army.... History tells us that they make the best and most docile soldiers
in the world. They are not barbarians in nature. They are a people as well
calculated to be humanized as any other."[10]

For a short time, however, the use of African American soldiers was
swept off the front pages and to the back of popular consciousness by the
battle over emancipation; its epicenter was the nation's capital.

Petitions, memorials, resolutions, propositions, and bills seeking to end slavery in the nation's capital had flooded Congress for decades. Partisans on both sides squared off for seemingly endless debates in the House and Senate.

The imposition of the gag rule, a pro-slavery measure, in the House of Representatives in the 1830's and 1840's, which choked off debate over slavery, was a response in part to concern over attempts to free District slaves. An unexpected result of the gag rule, finally repealed in 1844, was perceptively revealed by Philip Hone, a New York politician, in the January 28, 1840 entry in his *Diary, 1828-1851*:

> William Cost Johnson, of Maryland, has been speaking two days on the never-ending, still-enduring, and ever-exciting subject of abolition petitions. He is a fine fellow and a true Whig, but an out-and-out anti-abolitionist from principle, - not as Bynum and other such fellows are, to turn it to party purposes and make it a vehicle of personal abuse against their political opponents; and so he told them in the plainest, straightforward manner, and rebutted in his person, and by flat contradiction, that the Whigs, as a body, are inimical to the interests of the South. A resolution offered by Mr. Johnson as a standing rule was adopted after an animated contest by a majority of six in a full house. It goes farther than any former action upon this vexatious subject. It forbids the reception of any petition against slavery in the District of Columbia or elsewhere, or the entertaining of anything by the House which relates to slavery. It strikes me as an unfortunate measure. It is the very thing to please the abolitionists; the cry of persecution strengthens their cause. It is unjust, and I am inclined to think unconstitutional, and this apparent triumph of obstinacy over fanaticism will redound, I fear, to the benefit of the latter.

I spent a few minutes this morning in the Supreme Court. What a contrast between the gravity and decorum of that hallowed sanctuary of the laws, and the levity and disorder of the House of Representatives! - the quiet, subdued tone of the former, and the noisy declamation of the latter; and the reverend black-silk gowns of the judges, and the piebald costume of the people's representatives.

In 1849, then Congressman Abraham Lincoln had offered a District abolition bill "subject to the consent of the free white people and with compensation to owners." Essentially a political sham because it contained no provisions for immediate freedom, the measure was a compromise move to block bills favoring direct emancipation from coming to the House floor. The bill does forecast Lincoln's preference for gradual emancipation with compensation and reveals his true pro-slavery roots by extending the fugitive slave law into the District. Thirteen years later, events forced Lincoln to revisit the controversial subject. This bill was introduced by Senator Henry Wilson of Massachusetts (who also fathered the bill abolishing the District's Black Code).

Mayor Wallach, whose brother owned the *Star*, and the city council made plain their objections to District emancipation. The chief one being that the city would become an "asylum for free Negroes, a population undesirable in every American community."

On April 16, 1862, Lincoln signed into law "An Act for the Release of Certain Persons held to Service or Labor in the District of Columbia." Although the word slavery was omitted from the title, everyone understood the law's spirit and letter. Not only was emancipation immediate, slaveowners who were loyal Unionists were compensated up to $300, and each newly freed African American who consented to voluntary emigration outside the United States could receive up to $100. Within the next nine months, the government paid several hundred claimants nearly a million dollars for the "release" of approximately 3,100 "persons held to service or labor within the District of Columbia by reason

MAY 3, 1862.]   FRANK

Federalists have produced the largest, and, according to Dr. Russell, the finest army in the world; that the Government pays its way; that comparatively there is no distress; that there is no discontent; that there are no mobs; that the people act as one man in support of the Government; and that the Government is acting strictly in obedience to the Constitution; *that the lesson taught to Europe is a most important and a most valuable one—first that an efficient army can be improvised in a few months out of volunteers; that soldiers so improvised can fight like or better than veterans; that standing armies are therefore no longer necessary with nations enjoying constitutional governments;* that volunteers are armies when wanted; that next the fight between the Merrimac and the Monitor demonstrated that naval warfare as hitherto conducted must now cease; that wooden men-of-war should either be cut up or converted into merchant ships: that iron-clad steamers henceforth will rule the ocean; that very few of these will be required, and that of course, our navy estimates, after the few are built, will gratify even Mr. Bright; that these are great and glorious discoveries, that they hand over civilization to the protection of science; that wars will be few, because without uninterrupted trade nations cannot resist immediate misery; that all civilized peoples have now clearly one interest; that not one of them can drop out of the market without entailing on all others the evils of bad trade; *that the Americans have secured for themselves an eternal exemption from external wars; that all other nations will let them alone, because a conflict with them would be ruinous;* that the Yankees, by this war, have made themselves masters of the position; that their produce is essential to the prosperity of the civilized world; and that, consequently, the civilized world will always keep on friendly terms with them."

Emancipation in the District of Columbia.

THE President having signed the bill abolishing Slavery in the District of Columbia, communicated the fact to Congress in the following Message:

Fellow-Citizens of the Senate and House of Representatives:

The act entitled " an act for the release of certain persons held to service or labor in the District of Columbia," has this day been approved and signed.

I have never doubted the constitutional authority of Congress to abolish slavery in this district, and I have ever desired to see the National Capital freed from the institution in some satisfactory way. Hence there has never been in my mind any question upon the subject except the one of expediency, arising in view of all the circumstances. If there be matters within and about this act which might have taken a course or shape more satisfactory to my judgment, I do not attempt to specify them. I am gratified that the two principles of compensation and colonization are both recognized and practically applied in the act.

In the matter of compensation it is provided that claims may be presented within 90 days from the passage of the act, but not thereafter, and there is no saving for minors, *femes covert*, insane or absent persons. I presume this is an omission by mere oversight, and I recommend that it be supplied by an emendatory or supplemental act.

ABRAHAM LINCOLN.

Washington, April 16, 1862.

Published text of emancipation decree in the District of Columbia (from *Frank Leslie's Illustrated Weekly*).

of African descent." There is evidence that Lincoln "regretted" emancipating District slaves. Lincoln's longtime friend Orville H. Browning confided in his diary that the President was concerned that freedom in the nation's capital would create a shortage of servants.

The response in the African American community was, on the other hand, instantaneous and deeply felt. One black District citizen wrote to a friend in Baltimore, "This indeed has been a happy day to me sights have I witnessed that I never anticipated."

He then described how he gave the happy news to two female friends of his, one of whom had a slave son:

> When I entered, they perceived that something was ahead and emmediately [sic] asked me "What's the news?" The District's free says I pulling out the "National Republic" and reading its editorial. When I had finished the chambermaid had left the room sobbing for joy. The slave woman clapped her hands and shouted, left the house saying, "let me go and tell my husband that Jesus has done all things well." While the cook who is free retired to another room to offer thanks for the blessing sent. Should I not feel glad to see so much rejoicing around me? Were I a drinker, I would get on a Jolly spree today, but as a Christian I can but kneel in prayer and bless God for the privilege I've enjoyed this day.... Would to God that the Law applied also to Baltimore but a little patience and all will be well.[11]

The *Anglo-African,* a black newspaper published in New York, placed the event into a national perspective with an editorial that included the following words.:

> It was a fitting celebration of the anniversary of Fort Sumter, that Congress should pass a bill to emancipate the capital from

the thrall of slavery forever. Henceforth, whatever betide the national, its physical heart is freed from the presence of slavery....[12]

The April 26, 1862 issue of the *Christian Recorder,* the official organ of the African Methodist Episcopal (AME) Church, exclaimed:

Here in Washington, the heel of Providence stamps on the head of the serpent - the serpent in our political Eden, - the accursed corrupter of those who once bore the image of God, but seem now to have lost it, almost utterly, if not forever. No wonder, the head being thus trampled under foot, that the loosened and squirming coils of the monster, writhing through all the South, manifest so strongly the spreading pangs of death. All hail the day of emancipation here! All hail the day of prospective emancipation everywhere! Aha! Thou rattle-snake, slavery! And art thou at last humbled in the dust? Would thou couldst suffer as thy victims, both white and black, have suffered!

....FREEDOM - ALL HAIL!

All hail the sixteenth day of April, 1862! - the first day of freedom in the District of Columbia, in the Capital of our Republic! All hail, with thanksgiving to God, and gratulations to mankind! All hail, with special gratulations to those who now stand up, "redeemed, regenerated, and disenthralled!" "Fair shines the morning star!"

Sunrise is not far behind. If, taking "the wings of the morning," you can poise yourself in the shadowy rim of the horizon, and look over and downward a little, you will start back, dazzled by the near approach of the greater glory. O, thou King of glory? - shall not all be day very soon? Amen. So be it, a thousand times over. Let the angels of history and prophesy sit down side by side, and each make her record.

HISTORY, thus: - "April 16th, 1862. President Lincoln announced to Congress that he had signed the bill for the immediate emancipation of slaves in the District of Columbia. Blessed be the name of the Lord forever!"

April 16 remained a special day in the hearts of the District's black residents. On the first District emancipation day anniversary after the end of the Civil War, the city's black community organized a huge parade. The District emancipation day parade became an annual event that continued into the early years of the twentieth century. The parade was revived in 2002. There are plans to make it an annual event again.

The press of events, however, gave scant opportunity for celebration. What had been a trickle of freedmen now reached floodtide. Elizabeth Keckley, an African American dressmaker who had only recently begun making gowns for Mary Todd Lincoln, the President's wife, observed the flow of humanity with these words:

In the summer of 1862, freedmen began to flock into Washington from Maryland and Virginia. They came with a great hope in their hearts, and with all their worldly goods on their backs. Fresh from the bonds of slavery, fresh from the benighted regions of the plantation, they came into the Capital looking for liberty, and many of them not knowing it when they found it. Many good friends reached forth kind hands, but the North is not warm and impulsive. For one kind word spoken, two harsh ones were uttered.... Poor dusky children of slavery, men and women of my own race--the transition from slavery to freedom was too sudden for you! The bright dreams were too rudely dispelled; you were not prepared for the new life that opened before you, and the great masses of the North learned to look upon your helplessness with indifference--learned to speak of you as an idle, dependent race. Reason should have prompted kinder thoughts. Charity is ever kind.[13]

First reading of the Emancipation Proclamation before the cabinet.

Moved by the suffering of her people, Keckley founded the Contraband Relief Association. She described it as "a society of colored people to labor for the benefit of the unfortunate freedmen." Mrs. Lincoln, one of the group's earliest supporters, contributed $200. Many other black women involved themselves in such work in the city. Maria W. Stewart arrived from New York in 1863 and established a school for the children of the newly arrived freedmen. She also taught Sunday school and immersed herself in church work.

By 1871, Stewart had raised $200 to purchase a building for her school where she taught reading, writing, spelling, mental and practical arithmetic, and whatever other studies were needed for 50 cents a month. She later became a head matron at Freedmen's Hospital. Born free in Hartford, Connecticut, in 1803, Stewart was the earliest known American woman to lecture in public. As early as 1838, she had publicly called for abolition in the District, and several of her speeches and writings were printed in William Lloyd Garrison's anti-slavery periodical *The Liberator.*
Her themes of female empowerment and racial pride have marked her as a proto-feminist by many modern black feminist scholars.

Sojourner Truth came to Washington and dedicated herself to bettering conditions for African American freedmen and soldiers. She often spoke at the 15th Street Presbyterian Church to raise funds for the Colored Soldiers Aid Society. In December 1864, the National Freedman's Relief Association appointed her "counsel to the freed people" at Arlington Heights. For over a year she taught and preached there at Freedman's Village. Some whites aided in forming various freedmen's relief groups. Swelling numbers - perhaps 40,000 at war's end - required Army intervention in the forms of shelter, food, and employment until the Freedmen's Bureau took over.

In the meantime, the "white man's war" bred carnage of unprecedented extent and savagery. Through the Summer and Fall of 1862, the war dragged on. Driven to stalemate or defeat by southern arms, many northern whites grew discontent and seemed increasingly reluctant to enter the Army. Some began to sing a tune entitled "Sambos' Right to be Kilt."

Governor Kirkwood of Iowa put it bluntly. Before the end of the war he wanted to see "some dead niggers as well as dead white men."[14]

Added to this was the still widespread Unionist distaste for making emancipation a war aim. But what was unthinkable in 1861 must be considered in 1862. With the clarity that desperation and military necessity brought, Lincoln now saw emancipation as a measure that "...would shorten the war, and thus lessen its expenditure of money and blood... In giving freedom to the slave, we assure freedom for the free - honorable alike in what we give, and what we preserve," so reported the *Star* on December 1, 1862 from its vantage point at 11th and Pennsylvania Avenue, N.W. Unionist in sentiment, it had the largest circulation of any paper in the city.

The District's black folk were ecstatic as well over Lincoln's signing of the Emancipation Proclamation. There were watch night church services, day long prayer and thanksgiving sessions, and spontaneous eruptions of praise and prayer. The service at Israel Bethel African Methodist Episcopal (AME) Church, soon to be the District's main black regimental recruiting center, was particularly memorable (see Chapter Three). African Americans in the city understood the synergy between freedom in the District and the Emancipation Proclamation, and many had relatives, friends, and loved ones in the grip of the Confederacy. What was equally clear was the sentiment best expressed by Frederick Douglass that nothing was "...more certain than that the speediest and best possible way open to us, manhood, equal rights, and elevation is that we enter the service." The war that he had once characterized as a simple struggle between the "beautiful truth and the ugly wrong" had been transformed.

Though unlettered and with manners rough-hewn, the waves of contrabands, who rolled like eddies around the District, also understood their responsibilities in the great contest between liberty and slavery. At a meeting at a contraband camp in the city, just before the Emancipation Proclamation took effect, George Payne, a former slave, addressed his fellow freedmen:

Friends, don't you see de han' of God in dis? Haven't we a
right to rejoice? You all know you couldn't have such a
meetin' as dis down in Dixie! Dat you all knows. I have a
right to rejoice; an' so have you; for we shall be free in jus'
about five minutes. Dat's a fact. I shall rejoice that God has
placed Mr. Lincum in de president's chair, and dat he wouldn't
let de rebels make peace until after dis new year. De Lord has
heard de groans of de people, and has come down to deliver!
You all knows dat in Dixie you worked de day long, an' never
got no satisfacshun. But here, what you make is yourn. I've
worked six months; and what I've made is mine! Let me tell
you, though, don't be too free!. De lazy man can't go to
heaven. You must be honest, an' work, an' show dat you is fit
to be free; an' de Lord will bless you an' Abrum Lincum.
Amen![15]

There were scattered unofficial attempts by a handful of Union officers
in South Carolina, Kansas, and Louisiana to raise black regiments prior to
the Emancipation Proclamation. These units now, with official sanction,
became the first to engage the enemy. But the Proclamation, even more
so than the preceding Confiscation Acts, made evident the specific use of
blacks as soldiers by including in its language the provision that "...such
persons of suitable condition will be received with the armed service of
the United States...." The proclamation was implemented as War
Department General Order No. 1 the following day.

The first northern state to take the lead in recruiting black troops was
Massachusetts. As early as the Summer of 1862, the Bay State had passed
legislation to prepare military enrollment lists including the names of all
male citizens, "white or colored" between the ages of 18 and 45. The
Governor, John Andrew, had long been an advocate of the use of black
troops, and in January 1863 as soon as the proclamation took effect he
began to raise funds and recruit men for what would become one of the
most famous black units in Civil War history: the 54th Regiment of
Massachusetts Volunteers of African descent. Along with the sons of
Frederick Douglass and Martin Delany, men from the District enlisted in

"Union Jim."

this soon to be storied organization eager to strike at the vitals of the "peculiar institution" and when the establishment of a similar regiment from the city was still uncertain.

Two members of the 54th who enlisted from the District were privates assigned to G Company. Their names were William Myers, a 22 year-old waiter, listed as missing in action after the assault on Fort Wagner depicted in the movie "Glory" and William Washington, an 18 year-old farmer, who was mustered out of the regiment in August 1865. A third man was Corporal Samuel Stevenson of Company K. He was a 27 year-old laborer who was wounded at the Battle of Honey Hill in November of 1864 and mustered out in August 1865.[16]

Another 10 black native Washingtonians were reported enlisted in the 55th Massachusetts Volunteer Infantry, the 54th's sister regiment. Both units trained at Readville outside Boston, and both withstood the bloody furnace of battle and acquitted themselves with courage and skill.[17] District papers, as might be expected, had divergent views on these events. The *National Republican*, the white daily most supportive of and interested in the African American community, praised the happenings in Massachusetts. The *National Intelligencer* mocked these efforts and was skeptical of black military ability until later in the war.

Another example of the willingness and ability of the city's black men to fight was reported in the March 28, 1863, *Harper's Weekly* in a story entitled "Jim Williams." The article described him as being "...of small compact stature, twenty-six years of age, was born in the District of Columbia, from whence he was sold about six years ago to Benjamin Barber, of Carroll Parish, Louisiana." Williams escaped from slavery and became a cook in the 95th Illinois Regiment. And, *Harper's* continued:

> On Tuesday, the 10th of February, learning that a scouting party had just gone out to make a reconnaissance in the neighborhood of his home, Williams determined to join them; and, borrowing a mule and musket, followed and overtook the party about five miles distant, and just before they fell into a

rebel ambuscade of guerillas, numbering about two hundred and fifty, who had left their horses in the rear, and, under cover of canebreaks and bushes, were reserving their attack until our advanced-guard of about forty infantry should be fairly within range. At this, a volley was discharged by the rebels which prostrated one quarter of our men; the remainder charged bayonets and drove the rebels from their shelter. Now commenced a running fight. Jim Williams dashed to the front and swept on about one hundred and fifty yards in advance. When under cover of a tree he commenced firing; this started up three guerillas a short distance from him. The wily scout, observing them rise, leveled his musket and demanded their surrender, upon which two threw down their arms; the third, at the same instant, fired at Williams, the ball cutting off his belted knife. Williams returned the fire, sending a ball through the head of the rebel and killing him instantly. He then brought in his two prisoners with their guns, one of which he was allowed to keep as a proof that Negroes can fight. The little party of forty succeeded in dispersing the rebels and taking thirty-one prisoners before the remainder of the troops arrived.

On returning to camp, a guerilla scout was observed by the quick eye of Williams a quarter of a mile off. He darted after him like a hound for his prey. The rebel waited the onset, when Williams, coming within about fifty yards, delivered an off-hand shot which sent the foe reeling on his horse's neck, crying "O God! I'm shot."

Williams is very anxious to raise a company of Negroes for scouting service, and said to the writer of this, on leaving him a few days since "I am willing to work, but would rather fight." General M'Arthur, who appreciates true bravery without regard to color, holds him in the highest estimation, and freely gives him the post of honor in scouting the swamps of Louisiana.

In an editorial entitled "The Afric-Americans And The Union War," the May 1, 1863 *New York Tribune* reviewed the changes of the past two years some of which applied to the District as well:

> Even one year ago, it would not have been safe for the patriotic blacks to assemble for military drill and parade within the limits of our City. Today there is no serious objection, save on the part of a few venomous sympathizers with the Slaveholders Rebellion to any amount of arming, drilling, enlisting, and fighting on the part of the blacks...every regiment of blacks organized to fight for the Union will diminish by so many the numbers of whites to be drafted into our armies by conscription.... God gives men opportunity - a gift to which little can be added. In the history of every people, of every race, there comes an hour decisive of their destiny. It rests solely with them to improve it and be saved, or neglect it and perish. That hour for the Afric-Americans is striking today.

Striking too were the early reports of the successful use of black troops on the battlefields of the Midwest and South that began to surface about this time. Black soldiers skirmished with and killed rebels, drove in their pickets, took prisoners, destroyed equipment, captured livestock, and liberated scores of blacks banishing forever for them the taste of slavery's griefs. The nagging question of whether the black man would fight was being answered with a powerful affirmative. The merits of their employment for military service were being proven through their valor and steadfastness (see *Frank Leslies Illustrated Newspaper* for March 7, 1863 and *Harpers Weekly,* March 14, 1863). Pressure was building for the raising of more African American regiments in the Spring of 1863 when two ambitious former hospital chaplains, J.D. Turner and W.G. Raymond, approached President Lincoln about organizing a regiment of black men in the District of Columbia.

Both men wrote to Lincoln, together and separately, about their plan. They asked influential friends to provide written introductions and recommendations. On April 8, 1863, Phineas D. Gurley, the pastor of the New York Avenue Presbyterian Church, which Lincoln attended, wrote to the President. A former chaplain of the Senate, Gurley described Raymond's service as a chaplain and then noted that he "...wishes to be assigned to duty elsewhere. He is a working man who will go where you send him with a mind and heart devoted to his appropriate duties. I hope, in view of his successful experience, you will retain him in the service and assign him to a post of importance."

On April 23, 1863, Preston King, a New York Republican, who had left the Senate the previous month to resume the practice of law, wrote Edwin Stanton, the Secretary of War, on Raymond's behalf calling him "...faithful and zealous... and devoted to the cause of his country." King's letter contained endorsements by four officials in the Office of Indian Affairs and a captain in the provost marshal's office.

Two days later, both men penned letters directly to Lincoln. Raymond told the President that he was "...anxious to put down this rebellion," and that he wanted "to command a regiment of colored men in the District of Columbia and vicinity." To add heft to his proposal, he affixed a resolution by Washington Council No. 4 of the Union League, a Republican political group, pledging its cooperation, and the names of other supporters including Republican Senator Ira Harris of New York, Preston King, several officers and senior enlisted men in the local provost marshal's office, the chaplain of the Judiciary Square Army Hospital, a colonel in the 86th New York Volunteers, and several others.

Raymond also reminded the President that his and Turner's plan was on the desk of the Secretary of War and that it was strongly endorsed by Governor Alexander Ramsey of Minnesota and former Republican Congressman John Covode of Pennsylvania, which was also Turner's home state.

Raymond wrote a second letter to the President that same day. This time he mentioned his wife and four children, his brief service as a commissioned officer which he gave up to become a chaplain, his desire to remain in the city and his "zealous" support for the Lincoln administration. "Many of the intelligent colored men of this city" had signed a petition in favor of his plan he asserted and this along with the help of "his many influential friends who have promised to assist him" would make the venture a success. He ended this letter by telling Lincoln "I am nearly forty-five years of age and have been a Baptist clergyman for twenty-five years all of which I respectfully submit for your decision."

In his letter to Lincoln, Turner stated "I have always since my earliest recollection, sympathized with the oppressed colored race and have earnestly labored for their elevation not infrequently at considerable personal expense." Turner also wrote that he had tried unsuccessfully the previous fall to get "...an appointment in connection with the colonization movement...." Here he appears to be referring to Lincoln's disastrous attempt to colonize black Americans on Vache Island, off the coast of Haiti. The scheme had taken off in the Fall of 1862. By the end of December, the President had signed a contract with Bernard Kock, the governor of the island. Kock defaulted. Lincoln cancelled the contract and set up a new agreement with two of Kock's partners. Several hundred settlers arrived to find horrible conditions and had to be evacuated.

Turner went on to remind Lincoln of his long-time ties to the Republican Party. He also pointed out his 18 months of service as an army chaplain particularly during the bloody Peninsula Campaign in Virginia which was waged by the Army of the Potomac under General McClellan between the Spring and Summer of 1862.

In his conclusion, Turner observed that he felt he could be of "...more good both to my country and my race in command of a colored regiment. My motives are good. My experience is considerable in the Army. And my fitness in view of my sympathies I think admitted by all who know me, unquestionable. I have the confidence of the colored people here who are doing all they can to secure my appointment, and if your excellency will give me this favor, I will not abuse your confidence."

The following day, April 26, 1863, another letter arrived at the White House endorsing Raymond, Turner, and their ideas. Signed by John Landan, William Henry Channing, and William Y. Brown, prominent local Army chaplains, the letter extolled Raymond and Turner's "...moral and Christian character and integrity" noting as well their fitness for the position as men of judgment and discretion." The three chaplains "...expressed their earnest desire that your excellency may approve their application. And we would humbly suggest that in our judgment the sooner they have authority to commence operations the better for our glorious country."

Other letters not quoted here follow the same vein as those given above: long on platitudes and generalities and short on specifics and abilities. Despite the blizzard of endorsements, recommendations and references favoring both men, their actual qualifications for such an undertaking were slim. Union army chaplains were "ministers in uniform." Both men, whatever degree of personal valor they possessed, largely lacked the critical skills of command and tactics, training and an officer's combat experience required to make such an important and unique endeavor a success. Moreover, neither man provided precise examples of his contacts with or his work in the city's African American community.[18]

During the first week of May 1863, this circular began to appear from one end of the District to the other:

MEETING FOR THE
ORGANIZATION OF A
COLORED REGIMENT IN
THE DISTRICT OF COLUMBIA

The President has authorized Col. J. D. Turner, late Chaplain in the Army and Lieutenant Col. W. G. Raymond, late Chaplain in Trinity Hospital of this city, to raise a Regiment of Colored Troops in the District of Columbia. A meeting will be held in Asbury Chapel, corner of 11th and K Streets, on Monday evening next, May 4th, 7:30 o'clock, to organize, and make arrangements to visit the President and receive his orders.

All who desire to enlist in the 1st Regiment District of Columbia Colored Volunteers, and thus demonstrate their manhood, are earnestly invited to be present, and hear, consult, and decide.

By order of J. D. Turner, W. G. Raymond.[19]

Turner had been a chaplain in the 4th Pennsylvania Cavalry. He had enlisted on October 18, 1861 at Harrisburg, Pennsylvania. His unit came to the capital and served as military police before participating in campaigns in Virginia. He resigned from his regiment on January 25, 1863 because he could not fulfill his duties as chaplain. He stayed in the city.

Raymond was a first lieutenant in the 86th New York Regiment. He had been promoted to that rank on October 7, 1861. He had enlisted at Elmira, New York. He was appointed hospital chaplain on July 25, 1862. His regiment, also known as the "Steuben Rangers," was assigned to protect the city at about the same time as Turner's regiment. Raymond was honorably discharged on April 13, 1863.[20]

Turner's intent was to be colonel in the regiment with Raymond as lieutenant colonel, his second-in-command. They received assurances from Lincoln that the regiment they raised would be accepted for service when 640 men were present on the rolls. The establishment of black regiments presented vast opportunities for many whites to quickly gain officers' commissions or higher rank with attendant increases in pay and prestige. Horace Greeley, the abolitionist editor of the *New York Tribune* asserted:

> There are few, if any, instances of a white sergeant or corporal whose dignity or whose nose revolted at the proximity of blacks as privates, if he might secure a lieutenancy by deeming them not unsavory, or not quite intolerably so; while there is no case on record where a soldier deemed fit for a captaining in a colored regiment rejected it and clung to the ranks, in deference to his invincible antipathy to "niggers."[21]

Jacob Bruner, a quartermaster-sergeant, resigned from the 68th Ohio Infantry Regiment to take a commission with the 9th Louisiana Volunteers of African Descent. He wrote to his wife in April 1863: "Uncle Abe has at last sensibly concluded to arm the darkey and let him fight. They are not to be placed by the side of the white soldier but is to be organized into companies, regiments and brigades by themselves with white officers. This is considered a master stroke of policy and has produced a most cheering and beneficial revolt among the soldiers." He wrote his wife later that month to tell her that he had "...accepted a First Lieutenant position in one of the colored regiments: my wages will be one hundred and ten dollars and fifty cents per month: or thirteen hundred and twenty six dollars per year! I expect my commission in a few days. Now my dear what do you think of it I [sic] did I meet your approbation in accepting? I can serve in that capacity as well as in any other and if any of my friends turn up their noses never mind it I can buy [?] their favors with my wages. Tell me you are content and I do not care what the rest of the world may say." Perhaps warming a bit to his new responsibilities. Bruner informed his wife at the end of the month that the black men entering his regiment "...learn very fast and I have no doubt they will make as rapid progress as white soldiers."[22]

Undoubtedly, a substantial number of white officers in black regiments held severe and brutal racial prejudice which pointedly affected how they dealt with their men. Other whites who served came with abolitionist or egalitarian sympathies and experiences. Others were attracted to such a novel experiment and saw it as a personal challenge. Many saw their participation as yet another way to deliver a blow against the rebels. And there were some who were drawn by motives and passions unfathomable and unrecorded. Whatever their reasons, white men could obtain officer's shoulder straps; black men could not, until later in the war. At a time when most whites considered blacks little more than animals, when political, social, and racial equality was considered a frightful foolish fancy at best, the thought of blacks commanding whites was unpalatable in the extreme.

Even such a usually uncompromising ally of African Americans as Senator Stevens was forced by massive negative public and congressional reaction to the discussion of black officers to concede with these words:

> I do not expect to live to see the day when, in this Christian land, merit shall counterbalance the crime of color. True we propose to give them an equal chance to meet death on the battlefield. But even then their great achievements, if equal to those of Dessalines, would give them no hope of honor. The only place where they can find equality is in the grave. There all God's children are equal.[23]

On March 6, 1863, Frederick Douglass wrote to abolitionist Gerrit Smith: "it is a little cruel to say to the black soldier that he shall not rise to be an officer of the United States whatever may be his merits; but I see that though coupled with this disadvantage colored men should hail the opportunity of getting on the United States uniform as a very great advance."

The denial of officers commissions, unequal pay, and the execution or sale into slavery of black prisoners of war rankled some blacks and retarded recruitment efforts in portions of the black community.

RECRUITING BEGINS

The May 5, 1863 *Star* recounted Turner's and Raymond's initial foray into recruiting with an article captioned: "The Colored Regiment-Recruiting Commenced -." Turner and Raymond visited Camp Barker, a converted army barracks and depot teeming with contrabands at 12th and

Q Streets, N.W. They were joined there by a Reverend Mr. Jenkins, A. L. Sanborn, a clerk at Columbia Hospital, and Peter Clay, a camp assistant, all of whom, according to the *Star* "...are expecting to be officers in the new regiment." Potential recruits were invited to walk up and give their names. About 4 o'clock Sanborn, who had gone elsewhere searching for enlistees, returned with 15 men: 13 from the College Hospital - named for its affiliation with neighboring Columbia College, and two from Carver Hospital. Both hospices sat on Meridian Hill just north of the city limits and were two of over 50 facilities in the District that at one time or another, treated the torrent of sick, wounded, and injured soldiers streaming into the city. About 30 men were recruited that afternoon.

At what the *Star* reported was a large and animated meeting at the chapel - actually Asbury United Methodist Church - that night, the afternoon's recruits were on prominent display near the pulpit. Turner and Raymond opened with prayers and later gave speeches at the black church. One of Asbury's trustees, a Mr. Snowden, chaired the meeting. A number of blacks also spoke including George Hatton, a 21 year-old porter from Prince George's County, and Charles Tasco, a 25 year-old laborer from Fredericksburg, Virginia, both of whom later joined the regiment. Several white dignitaries and observers were present including J. C. Howells, private secretary to the Governor of Idaho and a Colonel Bingham of New York who hoped to raise "a colored brigade." All the speakers reinforced the reasons for enlistment. About 100 men enrolled that night.

Little could dampen the contagious enthusiasm crackling between the speakers and the audience. But the more thoughtful attendees could not help but notice that also present that night was a squad of soldiers from the 39th Massachusetts Regiment stationed there to prevent any trouble. Tension and violence between blacks and whites was growing. Contraband camps had been raided by slaveowners and bounty hunters searching for runaways. Contrabands, singly or in groups, were assaulted by pro-Confederate rowdies and thugs. A member of the city police force was reported to have said that he would put as many bullets through a nigger recruit as he would through a mad dog. Secessionist bullies in the

District picked fights with black enlistees and soldiers in uniform throughout the war.

Recruiting stepped into high gear with the appearance of Reverend Henry McNeal Turner, pastor of Israel Bethel AME Church at South Capitol and B Streets (now Independence Avenue) at the foot of Capitol Hill. His powerful charisma, oratory, organizational skills, and leadership of the second largest black church in the District (see Chapter Three) added new energy and manpower to the drive for enlistment.

Turner had been one of the first local black religious leaders to favor black enlistment. A correspondent for the *Christian Recorder,* Turner wrote in 1862 that so long as complete emancipation was the goal, African Americans would be willing to serve: "...unless freedom, eternal freedom is guaranteed to them, their children, their brethren. To talk about freeing only those who fight and should happen to escape the ball, is all gammon." Early the following year, Turner continued to encourage black participation: "The cry has long been, give us the opportunity; show us a chance to climb to distinction, and we will show the world by our bravery what the Negro can do, and then as soon as we are invited to stand on such a basis as will later develop these interior qualities, for us to deride the idea and scornfully turn away would be to argue a self-consciousness of incapacity."[24]

Turner turned his church into the city's major recruiting center for the regiment. One of his leading aides, Thomas H. C. Hinton, became a recruiting sergeant. At a meeting at the church on May 8th, Turner became part of a formal recruiting committee which also included Reverend John F. Cook, Jr., Pastor of the Fifteenth Street Presbyterian Church, Adolphus Winkfield, a Baptist pastor, and Anthony Bowen. Turner was a South Carolinian who had come to the city the previous year. Cook was a native Washingtonian, the scion of one of the District's leading African American families, who with his brother George also operated Union Seminary, a private school for blacks at 14th and H Streets, N.W. Winkfield was pastor of one of the city's four black Baptist churches. Bowen, who had run an Underground Railroad station from his home at 85 E Street in southwest, had also founded the first black YMCA in 1853, two church schools and was on the verge of being ordained an AME minister. The committee's purpose was to hold mass meetings, display posters, and visit homes of potential recruits. Each recruit was promised seven dollars a month and one blanket, one cap, one canteen, one haversack, one pair of overalls, two shirts, and two pairs of socks.

During the May 12 meeting at the 15th Street Presbyterian Church, then at 15th and I Streets, N.W., Dr. Theodore Cooper, one of the District's handful of black physicians, voiced uneasiness about continuing reports of rebel maltreatment and executions of black soldiers. He, nevertheless, promised to enlist.

Confederate War Department General Order, No. 60, August 21, 1862 had established the policy that black soldiers were nothing more than armed slaves in rebellion against the authority of the southern government and would not be considered prisoners of war. In addition, any commissioned officers employed in drilling, organizing, or instructing slaves, with a view to their armed service in the war could be executed as "outlaws." No distinction would be made for the black men in any Union regiment who were born free and knew nothing of whips and fetters.

In response to the preliminary Emancipation Proclamation (September 1862) and the final Emancipation Proclamation, the Confederate government underscored General Order No. 60. On May 1, 1863, Jefferson Davis approved and signed joint congressional resolution S.2 "on the subject of retaliation." The bill reiterated the policy that captured officers of African American regiments should be "put to death or be otherwise punished at the discretion" of a military court. Black soldiers were ordered to be "...delivered to the authorities of the State or States in which they should be captured to be dealt with according to the present or future law of such State or States" which meant execution or sale into slavery.

The resolution accused the United States government of trying to "emancipate," "abduct," "incite," and "employ" Negroes in war against the Confederate States and overthrow "the institution of African slavery" which would produce "atrocious consequences." These were actions so heinous, according to the rebels, that they should be "repressed by retaliation." The rebels wasted little time in carrying out their threats. In early 1863, two free Massachusetts-born black servants traveling with a regiment from their state were captured and sold into slavery. At the same time, 20 black Union army teamsters with General William S. Rosecran's command were captured near Murfreesboro, Tennessee, tied to trees by the roadside and shot. In May, two black soldiers on guard duty at Port Hudson were captured and hanged.

Within the next two months, after the battles of Port Hudson and Millikens Bend, in which black troops played major roles, there were confirmed reports of the murder of white officers attached to black regiments as well as more executions of black soldiers. News reports of the "magnificent behavior" exhibited by the black soldiers from Louisiana and Mississippi, however, would serve to increase enlistment in the First District of Columbia Colored Volunteers. The volunteers had to be examined before they were mustered in. This was done at Israel Bethel's lyceum next to the church. The physicals were administered by Major Alexander T. Augusta, a black physician who left a lucrative practice in Canada to return to the land of his birth for an army surgeon's commission. He was assisted by Dr. Theodore Seeley, surgeon at the Armory Square Hospital (7th and Independence Ave., S.W.) Seeley said he had never seen finer physical specimens than these recruits. He noted with satisfaction their "determined" looks.

The May 15, 1863, *Star* carried this item:

FIRST APPEARANCE OF THE NEGRO SOLDIERS - Company I of the colored regiment of this District made their appearance on our streets this forenoon. They numbered some forty or fifty and wore a red, white and blue badge. Some of them, however, in addition to the badge, wore also a cockade composed of the same colors. They seemed to bear their honors well, notwithstanding the derisive remarks they met with as they marched along - coming in several instances from those of their own color. Their drillmaster - as we presume - a colored man, seemed to appreciate the dignity of his position to the fullest.

On May 18, 1863, Turner held another meeting at Israel Bethel. This gathering is typical of the many held during the recruiting drives for the city's black regiment. Reverend David Smith, who had been instrumental in establishing an AME presence in the nation's capital, opened with prayers and the hymn, "Am I a Soldier of the Cross." Raymond gave a progress report on the pace of recruiting, saying that he had expected to have two companies mustered in that same day and quarters for them too. His request had been held up inexplicably inside the War Department. Turner hoped that the next day would shine on the page of history on account of the mustering in of two companies, at least, of colored men valiant and true. He ended his remarks by referring to a beautiful handmade flag draping the pulpit. The banner was made by Julia Henderson, a black woman, who wrote in a letter accompanying the flag that she hoped it might be the first to enter Richmond, the capital of the Confederacy. She received a vote of thanks and enthusiastic applause for her generosity.[25]

The next speaker, a Mr. Cooper of Michigan, told the crowd that the object of the evening's meeting should interest every black man and woman present. A great change, he predicted, was about to take place. There was not a man near his home in Chicago who was not ready to shoulder arms and fight for the ascendancy of his race. Why should not the people of the District do likewise? All that he had met with wherever he went were eager for the fray, and he hoped the colored men of Washington would not be behind. The fear that the colored soldiers will not be adequately protected by the government was without foundation, said Cooper. He assured the audience that the new Secretary of War Edwin Stanton had given a letter stating that no fear need be apprehended on that point. A soldier, black or white, is a soldier and must and will receive the protection of the government, notwithstanding "Jeff Davis and his infernal crew." Cooper ended, amid applause, with an invitation to the men to come forward and sign up.

A Captain Thoret of the British Navy was next. He testified to personally having seen the success of the African and West Indian regiments employed by England. "Their bayonets were never behind," he said. "Mister Lincoln has given you the opportunity and you must come forward and put your shoulder to the wheel." Reverend Turner followed up Thoret's remarks with another invitation for enlistment. He added that any coming forward could do without any fear of interrupting the speakers.

Henry Johnson, a black man from North Carolina, was then introduced. He was going to be a soldier, he said. He also expected them to kill him but let them. He only hoped that if the rebels did not get the field, his friends would bury his body. "While the men were fighting," Johnson drawled, "the women must fight too. They must fight the rebel women in the city and whip them too." His remarks brought a gale of laughter from the audience. Johnson said he was elevated at Lincoln's election and he predicted that after the war the black regiments were coming back to elect him again. Applause erupted. He noted that some folks had not wanted to go along with the contrabands. For his part, he joked he would have just as soon gone along with a contraband as any other sort of band. The fact was the contrabands were getting ahead. Johnson reminded the audience that a group of contrabands was marching around near the church with nothing on their shoulders but sticks. He believed, he added, that if they had enough guns they would shoot somebody. He recalled the time when black folks were spoiling for a fight - when they were ready and anxious to die for their race - but where are they now? They had this, that, and the other to say against going. "What do you want Mr. Lincoln to do," he asked mockingly," feed you ice cream?" Again and again Johnson appealed to their racial pride and with colorful taunts and infectious humor, the North Carolinian proved to be the hit of the evening.

LOCAL NEWS.

A COLORED SOLDIER IN TROUBLE.—Yesterday afternoon considerable excitement was raised in the neighborhood of the Northern Market by a muss between Wm. James, one of the first regiment D. C. Colored volunteers, and several white soldiers and citizens, during which the colored man was used pretty roughly. There are two versions of the affair, one of which is: that a white soldier met James and asked him what he was doing with the uniform on, when he replied with a curt answer and afterwards struck the white soldier, and the crowd at once jumped on him; but he managed to get hold of a hatchet, with which he was about to defend himself when he was arrested. Another story is, that a white man named Truman Drummond met James and demanded him to take the scales off of his shoulders, which he refused to do, and D. struck him with a stick, while another man used a brick. Officer Steele and Corporation officer O'Conner took the colored soldier in charge, as also Truman, and took the first named off to prevent a more general riot, as at the time he was using language calculated to incite a disturbance. They were taken towards Justice Thompson's, but on the way were met by Col. Raymond, who requested that the case might be heard before Justice Johnson, and forthwith both parties were taken before him, when the evidence went to show that James was the first assaulted, and he was dismissed. Drummond was held to bail to keep the peace.

Washington *Evening Star*, June 5, 1863.

Next, were brief remarks by a J. E. Greene of Michigan who said he was initially disappointed when William H. Seward (Lincoln's Secretary of State) failed to obtain the Republican presidential nomination in 1860. Greene told the gathering that since then he had switched and voted for Lincoln and was now to aid him in his great work.

Reverend James Reed, who had purchased his own freedom some years earlier, turned the mood solemn by saying that although legally free, he had never felt himself truly emancipated. Despite Lincoln's proclamation, black folks were still slaves in Reed's eyes. You boast that you are free but what guarantee do you have that it will not be taken from you? You are at the mercy of an army of whites, who can turn upon you and cause you to fall at their feet like a puppy. The white man will never acknowledge you as free if now that he has put a musket in your hand, you refuse to use it. Go forth then. Suffer and fight and prove yourselves men. And you, young women, who would keep these young men from going, you know if you were to get married you wouldn't be able hardly to get enough to eat but let them go, and after the war is over, they will hold important places, and if there is anything to be given by the government it will be given to them in preference.

Reverend Turner attempted to introduce Bingham the self-styled "Colonel" or "General" (depending on the newspapers) from New York. Already a fixture at these meetings, Bingham was shouted down in favor of a local black man, George Hatton. Hatton was emerging as a natural leader whose intelligence, eloquence and manliness rebuked those in Washington like Congressman William Allen. An Ohio Democrat, Allen was against the use of black troops. In a February 1, 1863 speech on the floor of the House of Representatives, Allen had prophesied dire events if the government put "...at its command half a million ignorant vicious Negroes...." Allen also said: "The proposition of raising those regiments of negro soldiers to fight the battle of the country is so absurd and ridiculous as a military measure that I cannot vote for its reference to the Military Committee."

On the night of May 18, however, as Hatton rose to the pulpit, he held the throng in the palm of his hand and his presence dismissed the words of doubters like Allen. Reluctant in his manner; Hatton said that he did not feel "in the kelter" for speaking. He stood to assure everyone that the story that he had signed the rolls but was now backing out was not true. He was going with Colonel J. D. Turner to do his first fighting - he hoped in the slave state of Virginia. As he looked out on the audience, he had spotted a great deal of stamping of feet and clapping of hands when the name of liberty was pronounced although a number of invitations had been given thus far, there had not been a single response. Hatton said that he thought that any man who would act this way ought to be sent across the lines into rebel-held territory. Hatton then described a fight that he and a compatriot had on their way to the meeting. They were attacked by three federal soldiers - whom he said they made to run. Time was when a negro dare not strike a white, Hatton added, but he is getting up in the world now.

Reverend Turner replaced Hatton at the pulpit with the remark that while he could not say with his Methodist colleagues that they were bound for the land of Canaan, they were bound for the land of Dixie where they had rich spoils to win. There are rich lands there, which we will go and possess. We will become substantial voters and revolutionize the government of Virginia he predicted, accompanied by applause. Bingham of New York finally got his chance to say a few words just before the meeting adjourned. No one joined that night but the next day two companies totaling over 130 men were mustered in at Israel Bethel and marched to No. 3 Barracks at Soldier's Rest, a huge transient soldiers camp at Delaware Avenue and C Streets N.W. (near what is now Union Station). They spent much of the next day drilling under "captains" Sanborn and Birdsall. They also received more recruits.

On the afternoon of May 21, one of the men drilling at Soldier's Rest was walking down Pennsylvania Avenue when a drunken white soldier told him to get out of the road, you damned "nigger!" The black man replied indignantly: "Look out what you say there. You can't call me a nigger. I'm a soldier too and there will be a fight if you insult me."

Further escalation was prevented by a passerby. The men were separated. Each went his separate way.

On May 22, the War Department issued General Order No. 143 which established the Bureau of Colored Troops. This bureau was placed under the Adjutant General's Office and Major Charles W. Foster was appointed chief, with the title of Assistant Adjutant General. The bureau was given responsibility for recruiting black troops, organizing their regiments, and maintaining records of these organizations once they were placed in federal service. With black troops now being organized on a large scale throughout the Mississippi Valley, in the northern states, and several units already in active service, the War Department sought to bring order to what was becoming an increasingly chaotic process. By centralizing responsibility and accountability and establishing clarity and consistency, the War Department would place over 200,000 black men under arms by war's end.

For the First District Colored Volunteers, one immediate effect of the army's more direct involvement was a change of scenery:

> When the two companies were at last mustered in, they were hurriedly taken from Washington to Analostan Island, opposite Georgetown. There, out of sight, they were clothed in the army blue. Their removal was a discouragement to the white recruiting officers, who wanted to use them to stimulate enthusiasm and reassure the doubtful. These officers were not permitted, under penalty of arrest, to visit Analostan Island. One of them said that the President himself did not know where the colored soldiers were encamped, but had been driving around Washington with Mrs. Lincoln, trying to find them. No criticism was made of the War Department, but there were hints of outside interference. One theory was that trouble had been caused by a desperate fight to have District citizens appointed as officers of the colored regiment. The strictness and secrecy of the seclusion on the island may have been prompted by a fear of race riots and bloodshed, once the

Negroes were armed, for civilians and soldiers continued their persecution of colored men. Early in June, a disorderly gang made an attack on the contraband camp, and seriously wounded several Negroes before a detachment of Massachusetts troops arrived to protect them. So numerous were the assaults on colored soldiers that a special military commission was appointed to examine the cases.[26]

CAMP GREENE

Analostan Island (now Theodore Roosevelt Island) is a 75-acre steak-shaped slice of rock in the Potomac River. Before the Civil War it had been the site of a Native American encampment and 18th century plantation with a causeway that connected it to the Virginia shoreline. At one point the land was owned by the wealthy planter George Mason, the author of the Virginia Declaration of Rights and American Revolutionary War leader. Mason deeded the island to his son John who used it as a summer home and farm until forced to sell in 1833 to cover his debts.

The island was home to commercial gardens, wharves, and a saloon until Union troops occupied it at the beginning of the war. The First District Colored Volunteers arrived to find land cleared and wooden buildings constructed for their use. There was a cook's shack, small infirmary, parade ground, rows of barracks, a building for the regimental band, officers' quarters, and a firing range. The Army called it Camp Greene. "Colonel" Turner and "lieutenant-colonel" Raymond were banished. During the first week of June the Army ordered Colonel William Birney to the island to complete mustering in and begin formal military training. Birney, the son of abolitionist James G. Birney, played a critical role in establishing black units that is virtually forgotten today. He was instrumental in organizing and training the First District Colored Volunteers, and also the 2nd and 4th Regiments, United States Colored Troops. He recruited black men from the Eastern Shore of Maryland to Fortress Monroe in Virginia and then fought alongside them in some of the war's bloodiest battles.

City Map showing location of Analostan Island (Site of Camp Green) opposite Georgetown.

Birney set up a hectic pace for the men at Analostan. Each day was full of the rigor and intricacies of drill and ceremonies and military courtesy: how to march, the manual of arms, when and whom to salute, respect for superiors, obedience to duty, caring for the uniform and equipment, and proper hygiene and deportment. While all soldiers have to learn such things, the urgency brought to the First District Colored Volunteers was that so many of the men were ex-slaves suffering from decades of dehumanization, and more than few of whom whose hearts, minds, and bodies bore slavery's deep, burning scars. The metamorphoses from slave and civilian to soldier and full citizen were helped by the unvarying schedule of each day with reveille at five a.m., followed by roll call, breakfast, sick call, clean up of the company area, guard or picket duty, and several hours of drill before lunch. There would be more drill in the afternoon, a training period for the corporals and sergeants, an afternoon or evening dress parade followed by supper. Between 6:30 p.m. and 9:30 p.m., the men had open time before the beating of evening tattoo summoned the men to their quarters for the night. "Taps," then a haunting new bugle call, signaled "lights out."

Recruiting continued. At a meeting at Asbury Methodist in early June, at which over 100 men signed the unit's rolls, a speaker fired the crowd with these words:

> When we show that we are men, we can then demand our liberty, as did the revolutionary fathers - peaceably if we can, forcibly if we must. If we do not fight, we are traitors to our God, traitors to our country, traitors to our race, and traitors to ourselves. (Applause.) Richmond is the place for us, and we mean to go there. (Applause.) Our friend, Jeff. Davis, says we shall go there (laughter), and we will go; but they won't be glad to see us.[27]

Men now flocked to the island: from Georgetown, came Eli Johnson, a married man with a family; Henry Green, whose father lived on the Island in southwest; Henry Fletcher from Prince George's County, with a sister living on K Street; Haitian-born Daniel Williams came, his arms tattooed "with India ink;" John Chen escaped slavery in Caroline County Virginia to enlist as did Henry Bailey from Suffolk. From slavery's bosom and from north of the Mason-Dixon Line, in fine broadcloth or tattered Osnaburg, African Americans took the ferry from Georgetown or walked to Analostan across the Aqueduct Bridge.

George Johnson also came to Analostan. He gave his age as 16 and was enlisted in Company H, until his parents found out. He had joined without their permission. They contacted the War Department and Johnson's three week military career was at an end. Dropped from the rolls, he turned in his uniform, and was sent back to the city.

A special time for the men was the day uniforms were issued. The basic suit of government clothing consisted of a loose-fitting navy blue wool sack coat with five brass eagle buttons down the front; soon to be polished to a mirror-like brilliancy. Next came a white or gray flannel shirt (regulations authorized three a year). The trousers were sky-blue kersey wool without cuffs and worn with suspenders. The sack coat, shirt, and trousers weighed six pounds by themselves and caused prolonged cursing and grumbling when worn in the hot and humid climate of the South.

The army issued flannel drawers which were so grievously uncomfortable many men purchased their own or had them made, rather than wear what the army provided. Also issued were thick socks and heavy square-toed black leather shoes or "bootees." Then came a blue forage cap, long blue frock coat, and a sky-blue overcoat. In sequence came the knapsack, haversack, tin canteen, tin cup and plate, waist belt, and metal buckle, leather cap pouch, bayonet and its scabbard, and cartridge box and sling with the federal shield on its center (with the rubber blanket, poncho, wool blanket, and shelter half the soldier carried about 50 pounds of equipment and clothing). When the recruit had donned the uniform, the effect was startling. Many of the men had never owned so many clothes. The uniform was the first solid sign of Uncle Sam's commitment and signaled manhood, honor, and freedom. Military service, despite its inequities, was the path to a higher destiny. Backs straightened, chins lifted. More potent still was the issuance of muskets.

With these, by the power of their own hands, black men could purchase justice, respect, and deliverance.

William Wells Brown recorded an example of the potent symbolism attached to the uniform in this story:

> A colored sentinel was marching on his beat in the streets of Norfolk, VA., when a white man, passing by, shouldered him insolently off the sidewalk, quite into the street. The soldier, on recovering himself, called out, -
>
> "White man, halt!"
>
> The white man, Southerner like, went straight on. The sentinel brought his musket to a ready, cocked it, and hailed again, -
>
> "White man, HALT, or I'll fire!"
>
> The white man, hearing shoot in the tone, halted and faced about.
>
> "White man," continued the sentry peremptorily, "come here!"
>
> He did so.
>
> "White man," said the soldier again, "me no care no cent 'bout this particklar Cuffee; but white man bound to respeck this uniform (striking his breast). White man, move on!"[28]

The uniform and musket solidified each man's personal sense of duty and dignity and welded together a group spirit of pride and honor shared by those engaged in the great mission of freedom and the privileges and protections that flowed from it. The degree of contempt for traitors and backsliders to their mission is shown by a tragic incident that took place in June 1863. Two brothers - Frank Gant, corporal, and William Gant, drummer, came to the city on leave. When it was over, the corporal returned but the drummer refused. Ordinary persuasion failed to induce him to return and his brother, the corporal, was sent, with two men, to take him. They went to his mother's house, in the alley between Ninth and Tenth and L and M streets, N.W. and found him. He was obstinate and refused to go. When the men approached to take him, he seized an axe to resist and was bayoneted by his brother. The bayonet entering his stomach, inflicting a deep and dangerous wound, from which he recovered.[29]

As Frederick Douglass expressed it:

> Once let the black man get upon his person the brass letters
> U.S.; let him get an eagle on his button, and a musket on his
> shoulder, and bullets in his pocket, and there is no power on
> the earth or under the earth which can deny that he has earned
> the right of citizenship in the United States. I say again, this
> is our chance, and woe betide us if we fail to embrace it.

Frederick Douglass told a group of Philadelphia blacks in July 1863: "The hour has arrived. Your place is in the Union Army. Remember that the musket - the United States musket with the bayonet of steel - is better than all mere parchment guarantees of liberty. In your hands that musket means liberty."[30]

The first shoulder weapons issued to the First District Colored Volunteers were old Model 1842 percussion muskets; flintlocks altered to percussion firing mechanisms, each with a .69 caliber, 42-inch smoothbore barrel and weighing about nine and a half pounds. They were ineffective at any respectable distance. Daily target practice proved frustrating but the men gamely kept at it while their officers complained to their superiors. It was the following year before the regiment received standard issue Model 1861 .58 Springfield rifled muskets. In any event, the mere sight of the volunteers marching in the city - to guard detail or church - with their buttons and barrels glinting in the sun was enough to muzzle a sizeable number of their critics and fill the hearts of their defenders.

The men learned to lift the walnut stocks of their weapons to their shoulders, stand in a double-ranked line of battle - elbow-to-elbow - and fire in mass to their front or rear. The soldiers were taught to fire their weapons as quickly as possible, usually that was about three times a minute.

George Seaton, an enterprising white businessman, obtained an appointment as regimental sutler. He followed the regiment selling it goods that the army did not provide such as cookies, candy, cheese, butter, milk, envelopes, stationery, canned fruits and vegetables, razor blades, thread, and tobacco. Army regulations officially barred Seaton and other Union sutlers from selling liquor, keeping their tents open after nine at night, before reveille or during Sunday church services. Sutlers' prices were high and the soldiers were often broke. Through tickets, tokens, cards, and other types of markers sutlers extended credit to officers and enlisted men. There was seldom a payday where Seaton was not close to the paymaster to collect his debts as soon as the men were paid. The compiled service records of numerous soldiers contain notations about various sums owed to the regimental sutler. He performed an important service and helped enliven perpetually tasteless army fare.

Heavy rains that summer frequently made Camp Greene a quagmire. Ankle-deep mud, soaked clothes, soggy salt pork or beef, bland beans, tasteless hardtack, gritty greens, and bad coffee discouraged all but the toughest and most committed. Conditions were unusually rugged. The training often risky and bone-wearying. But hunger and exertion gave them omnivorous appetites. In typical Army fashion they learned to be less than picky about their rations. A handful like Frank Whiting, Richard Jones, and Hezekiah Edwards deserted. Some others including Spencer Jackson, George Kinney, and Wyatt Beverly died of disease. Samuel Gallop died on July 22, 1863, of "acute inflammation of the peritoneum." He had enlisted ten days earlier. He did not live long enough to see his first payday as a soldier. William Carter drowned in the Potomac in late July.

Colonel John H. Holman.

By the beginning of the final week of June, six companies of volunteers had been raised and mustered in. The final complement of officers was received and assigned as follows:

> John H. Holman, Colonel; Elias Wright, Major; Myron W. Smith, Adjutant; Company A, W. Z. Bennett, Captain; E. C. Beeman, First Lieutenant; S. A. Bean, Second Lieutenant; Company B, H. S. Perkins, Captain; W. W. M. Houston, First Lieutenant; A. L. Sanborn, Second Lieutenant; Company C, Giles H. Rich, Captain; S. H. Birsdall, First Lieutenant; Nathan Barnham, Lieutenant; Company D, Albert Clark, Captain; H. M. VanWinkle, First Lieutenant; Marcellus Bailey, Second Lieutenant; Company F, W. D. Parlin, Captain; Clifford L. Eagle, First Lieutenant; H. M. Day, Second Lieutenant; Company F, John A. David, First Lieutenant; S. M. Stout, First Lieutenant.

These officers were selected and vetted by a special board of examiners established to appraise applicants for commission in black regiments. These boards also determined the rank each officer's candidate received. Unlike the arbitrary methods used to officer most white regiments, the Army established exacting standards of military knowledge and experience, deportment and moral character, literacy and physical fitness. Most of officers listed above were examined by the board that sat in the city. Major General Silas Casey, a hero of the Mexican War and professional soldier, headed the board, which sometimes sat at 212 F Street, N.W.[31]

Colonel John H. Holman, now to be the new commanding officer, was born on October 27, 1824 in North Livermore, Maine. An architect before the war, he was also a veteran of service with the 4th Missouri Reserve Corps, which he had joined in May 1861. Holman was a second lieutenant in the regiment; it was one of the units whose men enlisted for three months service. This was a popular practice at the beginning of the war. Holman's unit saw action in eastern Missouri. When the unit mustered out, he rose to the rank of lieutenant colonel in the 26th Missouri

Infantry Regiment. The unit saw bitter fighting during General Grant's central Mississippi campaign. He resigned from his unit on January 25, 1863.

He was 38 years-old when he received his appointment from the examining board and had been assigned to duty with the board until August when opportunity to command the District's black volunteers presented itself. He was assigned to the unit on May 22 and reported the following month. In the meantime, Holman penned a rallying song for his new unit. A taciturn soldier and Unionist, he believed that slavery was a "...curse..." that... "hung like a pall over their southern country," and the use of black troops was a practical and sensible weapon to defeat the rebellion. His fairness, courage, and insistence on high levels of discipline, training, and leadership would, in time, endear him to his men.

On June 26, Colonel Birney received orders to proceed with two of the commissioned officers to Fortress Monroe and Norfolk, Virginia to perform additional recruiting for the District's African American volunteers. Less than two weeks later, the Secretary of War ordered Birney to Baltimore for similar duty with Major General Robert Schenck. Writing to the Secretary of War, Birney assured him: "I leave good officers here in charge. Have now over (90) recruits. If you will send me to Baltimore two officers, drummer and fifer and twenty (20) picked men, uniformed and armed from the First U.S. Colored Troops, I can raise a regiment in less than ten (10) days."[32]

Birney knew these men and his expression of confidence in their soldierly appearance paid dividends in helping to recruit for other black regiments. He retained his interest in the regiment. By the time of Birney's letter, the First District Colored Volunteers had become - on June 30, 1863 - the First Regiment United States Colored Troops; it was the first unit of black troops formally mustered into the federal service. The other units in South Carolina, Kansas, Massachusetts, and Louisiana were mustered in later.

The United States *In Account with* John R. Ross *of [ ] Company.*

First *Regiment of* U.S. Colored Troops *on Account of Clothing during his enlistment; the money value of each issue being hereby acknowledged.* Enlisted at Washington *on the* Nineteenth *day of* July 1863

Date of Issue.	Money Value.		Rank.	SIGNATURE.	WITNESS.
	Dolls.	Cts.			
1863					
May 22	1 Gt. Coat		Corpl		
	1 F. Cap				
	1 Short F				
	1 Blanket				
	1 Pr Pants				
	1 . Shirts				
	1 . Stocking				
	1 F. Coat				
	2 . . Shoe				William Ross
	1 F. Stock				
	1 Pr Drawers				
Oct 16. 1863	8	52			
Nov 26 "	8	80			Charles H Hill 1st Lt. Co. ...
Dec "	5	48	(Corpl.)	John his X Ross	R Marker 20 Lt
Jan 24th 1864	4	94	"	John his mark X Ross	R Marker 20 Lt ...
March 16. 1864	2	17		John his X Ross	... 1st Sergt
April 10. 1864	3	12		John his X Ross	... Sergt
May May 1864	2	05		John his X Ross	Henry Word Capt.
	34	33	First Issue/63		
1st Year	69	06			
	8	32	Sergt	John his X Ross	...
July 1864	5	40	Sergt	John X Ross	Wallace M Sterling 2d Lieut
July 23 1864	1	85	"	John X Ross	Wallace M Sterling " "
September 1864	6	02	"	John X Ross	Henry Green 1st Sergt
October 20th/64	2	20	"	John his X Ross	Henry Green 1st Sergt
January 1865	7	32	"	John his X Ross	...
April 10th 1865	16	71	"	John his X Ross	E. F. Weidner 2d Lieut
May 14th 1865	11	64	"	John his X Ross	E. F. Weidner 2d Lieut
	59	46			
July 10th Nov 1865	26	43	"	John his X Ross	... M Williams
Sept 1865	0	96	"	John his X Ross	... M Williams
	27	39			
	86	85			

Henry M Van Husse
Capt. Commanding Company.

Clothing account record of Corporal John Ross.

In the meantime, trouble still roiled between the regiment and enemies of black enlistment. In June, the *Christian Recorder* reported this statement by one of its soldiers:

> We have had several fights this week between colored soldiers and white rowdies, or pretended citizens. But Mr. Colored Soldier has come out triumphant every time. ...The soldiers all ride in the street cars or any other cars they want to ride in; and you might just as well declare war against them, as to declare that they can't ride there because they are colored.

The same edition described an eyewitness account of another fight:

> Passing along 7th Street, a few evenings ago, I saw an excited rabble pursuing a corporal belonging to the 1st Colored Regiment, District vols., named John Ross. Among the pursuers, was a United States police officer. Ross protested against being dragged away by these ruffians, at the same time expressing his willingness to accompany the police officer to whatever place he might designate; claiming at the same time his (the police officer's) protection from his assailants. But, shameful to say, that officer, after he had arrested Ross, permitted a cowardly villain to violently choke and otherwise maltreat him. After the melee, the corporal received some pretty severe bruises, whether from the policeman's club or from the stones that were thrown by the mob, I will not say. He quietly walked to the central guard house with this conservator of the peace, amidst the clamoring of the mob, their yells and shouts of "Kill the black _____ _____ _____," &c.,&c., "strip him, we'll stop this negro enlistment," &c.,&c."[33]

Ross, ordinarily a model soldier, was a 36 year-old plasterer with a wife in Chicago, Illinois. He found himself arrested for disorderly conduct. He had come into the city to have a few drinks. Well aware that members of his regiment were quarry for ruffians, and since he was traveling alone,

Ross carried a loaded pistol in his pocket. Showing remarkable restraint, he never used it. Military authorities accused Ross of violating standing orders and "...provoking the violence he suffered at the hands of a police officer." Ross was ordered to Analostan where he received a dressing down from Colonel Holman, who reminded him of the need to always observe military discipline and good order.

A few days later Ross made sergeant.

Although outside the city and appearing in the news with less frequency, the bustle on Analostan continued to attract notice.

Walt Whitman, poet and self-described "Army Hospital Visitor," whose writings revealed much of the agony and sacrifice in the military hospitals in Washington mentions the regiment:

> June 1863 - There are getting to be **many black troops**: There
> is one very good regt. here black as tar; they go around, have
> the regular uniform - they submit to no nonsense. Others are
> constantly forming. It is getting to be a common sight.

Whenever the regiment marched in the city, the men stepped strong and gallant under their flags. Horatio Nelson Taft, a patent office examiner, saw them in late June and wrote "a Negro regt. (one thousand strong) passed through the Ave. yesterday. I never saw a new regt march better."[34]

In July, Whitman visited Camp Greene:

> The tents look clean and good; indeed, altogether, in locality
> especially, the pleasantest camp I have yet seen. The spot is
> umbrageous, high and dry, with distant sounds of the city, and
> the puffing steamers of the Potomac, up to Georgetown and
> back again....
>
> Now the paying is to begin. The Major (paymaster) with his
> clerk seat themselves at a table - the rolls are before them - the

money box is open'd - there are packages of five, ten, twenty-five cent pieces. Here comes the first Company (B), some 82 men, all blacks, Certes, we cannot find fault with the appearance of this crowd - negroes though they be. They are manly enough, bright enough, look as if they had the soldier-stuff in them, look hardy, patient, many of them real handsome young fellows. The paying, I say, has begun. The men are march'd up in close proximity. The clerk calls off name after name, and each walks up, receives his money, and passes along out of the way. It is a real study, both to see them come close, and to see them pass away, stand counting their cash - (nearly all of this company get ten dollars and three cents each.) The clerk calls George Washington. That distinguish'd personage steps from the ranks, in the shape of a very black man, good sized and shaped, and aged about 30, with a military moustache; he takes his "ten three," and goes off evidently well pleas'd. (There are about a dozen Washingtons in the company. Let us hope they will do honor to the name.) At the table, how quickly the Major handles the bills, counts without trouble, everything going on smoothly and quickly. The regiment numbers to-day about 1,000 men (including 20 officers, the only whites.)

Now another company. These get $5.36 each. The men look well. They, too, have great names; besides the Washingtons aforesaid, John Quincy Adams, Daniel Webster, Calhoun, James Madison, Alfred Tennyson, John Brown, Benjamin G. Tucker, Horace Greeley, etc. The men step off aside, count their money with a pleas'd, half-puzzled look. Occasionally, but not often, there are some thoroughly African physiognomies, very black in color, large, protruding lips, low forehead, etc. But I have to say that I do not see one utterly revolting face.

Then another company, each man of this getting $10.03 also. The pay proceeds very rapidly (the calculation, roll-signing, etc., having been arranged before hand.) Then some trouble. One company, by the rigid rules of official computation, gets only 23 cents each man. The company (K) is indignant, and after two or three are paid, the refusal to take the paltry sum is universal, and the company marches off to quarters unpaid.

Another company (I) gets only 70 cents. The sullen, lowering, disappointed look is general. Half refuse it in this case. Company G, in full dress, with brass scales on shoulders, look'd, perhaps, as well as any of the companies - the men had an unusually alert look.

These, then, are the black troops, - or the beginning of them. Well, no one can see them, even under these circumstances - their military career in its novitiate - without feeling well pleas'd with them.

The noted abolitionist and journalist Jane Grey Swisshelm came to Washington in February 1863 to help nurse Union soldiers. Her dispatches back home to the *St. Cloud Democrat* in Minnesota covered the war, fashion, politics, society, and from time to time the First Regiment United States Colored Troops:

July 21, 1863 - ...A regiment of colored troops are camped on the opposite side of the Potomac near Georgetown. Their officers appear to have been very carefully chosen and are men who are anxious they should succeed. In addition to military tactics they are learning to read and may be seen in the intervals between their drills, in little groups with primers and spelling books conning over their lessons. People here are becoming accustomed to see them in United States uniform, and they are more frequently hailed with signs of approbation than with sneers of scorn.[35]

u.S. War dept

U.S. INFANTRY TACTICS,

FOR THE

INSTRUCTION, EXERCISE, AND MANŒUVRES,

OF

THE SOLDIER, A COMPANY, LINE OF SKIR-
MISHERS, AND BATTALION;

FOR THE USE OF

THE COLORED TROOPS

OF THE

UNITED STATES INFANTRY.

PREPARED UNDER DIRECTION OF THE WAR DEPARTMENT.

NEW YORK:
D. VAN NOSTRAND, 192 BROADWAY.
1863.

26/e
Aug. 13. 1863
445 - 34

Manual of tactics for black troops in the Union Army.

In September, Whitman scribbled this passage:

> Sometimes I go up to Georgetown about two and a half miles
> up the Potomac, an old town - just opposite it in the river is an
> island. Where the niggers have their first Washington regt
> encamped. They make a good show, and are often seen in the
> streets of Washington in squads. Since they have begun to
> carry arms, the Secesh here in Georgetown (about three fifths)
> are not insulting to them as formerly.[36]

The following year Whitman recorded that opposition to black soldiers
was melting because of the "determin'd bravery" of these soldiers on
southern battlefields. In February 1866, at Harewood Hospital, Whitman
visited a segregated ward of sick and wounded black soldiers. He wrote
letters for several illiterate men, handed out some tobacco, and mailed a
few letters. He saw a priest give last rites to Thomas King, a discharged
soldier of the 2nd Regiment, USCT. The regiment was raised in
Arlington, Virginia between June and November 1863 and fought in
several battles in Florida before being mustered out in January 1866.[37]

There was also another connection between the First Regiment, USCT
and the Second Regiment, USCT. That connection was the Edmonson
cousins Richard Edmonson of Company B of the First Regiment, USCT
and Ephraim Edmonson of Company D, Second Regiment, USCT were
relatives and descendants of survivors of the Pearl Affair. In 1848, the
Pearl Affair was one of the largest mass escape attempts in the history of
the District of Columbia. Over seventy slaves hired a boat to sail from the
District to freedom. The two soldiers were descendants from two of the
primary participants.

In late July, the First Regiment USCT quietly left Analostan Island. July
was the same month, the President signed (July 30) General Order No. 233
which set forth the government's policy on the "protection of colored
troops." The order promised equal protection for black and white Union
soldiers; it ended with the words: "...for every soldier of the United States,
killed in violation of the laws of war, a rebel soldier shall be executed; and

for every one enslaved by the enemy, or sold into slavery, a rebel soldier shall be placed at hard labor on the public works, and continued at such labor until the other shall be released and receive the treatment due prisoners of war." Such a statement had been a long time in coming. Despite the lives already lost to this horrible rebel practice, the order finally gave local commanders a standard to go by. One of the lives already lost was that of Second Lieutenant Anson Sanborn who had been with the regiment from the beginning. While on detached service recruiting more troops for the regiment he was murdered in Norfolk, Virginia on July 11, 1863 by a Dr. D.M. Wright "a prominent secessionist" who said he would kill the first white officer he saw drilling black troops. After an unsuccessful escape attempt in which he tried to switch clothing with his daughter, Wright was hanged in October by the Northern forces occupying the city. As he stood on the gallows, Wright said coldly, "Gentlemen, the act which I have committed was done without the slightest malice."[38]

As the regiment marched onboard a transport waiting in the Potomac River, rumors were rife about its destination. But such information was given out only on a need-to-know basis. As the half-finished dome of the Capitol and naked granite stub of the Washington Monument slipped from their view, the officers and enlisted men faced south toward the bay and beyond.

CHAPTER II

TURN BACK PHARAOH'S ARMY

"They have never been known to falter."

Thomas M. Chester
Philadelphia *Press*

In early August 1863, the regiment landed at Elizabeth City, a flourishing town on the Pasquotank River in eastern North Carolina. The only town on the 40-mile river, Elizabeth City had a landlocked harbor that lay directly 30 miles from the ocean across nearby Albermarle Sound. The March 15, 1862, *Harper's Weekly* described the town: "It is 225 miles from Raleigh, and 50 south of Norfolk, Virginia. It is one of the most considerable towns in the northeastern part of the State. The population was about 3000, and it contained two banks, two or three printing offices, and several churches."[1]

Since its founding in 1793, Elizabeth City had become a regional water transportation center because of its proximity to the sound, excellent wharfage, and rich local fishing and timber. The town also served as the eastern terminus of the Dismal Swamp Canal. Dug by slave labor at a heavy cost in lives, the canal was a 30-mile channel that carried "a very extensive trade in grain, fruits, and lumber...." through the vastness of the Dismal Swamp. The canal extended to Norfolk, Virginia and the Chesapeake Bay providing access to Washington, Baltimore, Philadelphia, and New York.[2]

Federal forces occupied Elizabeth City in February 1862 and blocked the canal (the Norfolk end was corked in May). As the Union flotilla had approached the town, a number of the residents defiantly set fire to their homes, the courthouse, and the local hotel. Even with the presence of the troops, the region swarmed with Confederate smugglers, guerillas, and collaborators. Local blacks, long the backbone of the workforce, were becoming restive. Whites viewed with particular alarm, the organizing of a black Union regiment a hundred miles away in New Bern beginning in the spring of 1863.[3] Onto this volatile landscape came the First Regiment. Holman set up headquarters in the city and placed his men on guard duty at strategic locations in the area. Companies D and K were deployed at the Coinjock (or Currituck Bridge) 20 miles distant.

At this, its first posting, the regiment tried to maintain a low presence. Holman insisted on lots of fatigue duty and strict military discipline.

On August 28, 1863, Private Henry Burnet, a 21 year-old oyster catcher born in Philadelphia, was sentenced to 10 days in the guardhouse and hard labor in the trenches each day from 8 a.m. until 6 p.m. for "pillaging" peaches.

Far more important was continuing to ensure the high quality of authority and command in the regiment. Unfit officers had to be weeded out. First Lieutenant John A. David of Company F had turned into a brutal martinet. Appointed to the regiment in June, David exploded in a spree of violence throughout August 1863. Holman's investigation found that beginning early in the month, David tied several men by their hands, struck men in the ranks without provocation, beat several men with his clenched fists, pistol-whipped others and punished several of his men by making them carry heavy logs of wood upon their backs for several hours in direct violation of regimental orders. In December, David was dismissed from the service for "cruelty to the men of his command" and "disobedience of orders."

A problem of a different sort and one that would plague the regiment until the end of the war was obtaining suitable medical care. On August 16, 1863, Holman reported that Acting Assistant Surgeon J.B. Pettyjohn, who had been assigned to the regiment by the Medical Director in Washington City, had been AWOL (absent without official leave) since August 2. Holman requested that a "surgeon be ordered to duty with the regiment without delay. On August 20, 1863, Holman was informed that "no medical officer can now be spared." He was further informed that he might receive the services of "hospital stewards who have some knowledge of medicine." Two had been assigned to his local commanding officer, General Henry Wessells based at Plymouth, North Carolina over 50 miles away.

On December 8, 1863, "the subject of obtaining suitable Medical Officers has given me much uneasiness," wrote Adjutant General Thomas to E.D. Townsend, his assistant. On June 14, 1864, Thomas informed the

Secretary of War that Colonel R.C. Wood, the Assistant Surgeon General, headquartered in St. Louis, "...cannot find any Assistant Surgeons for colored regiments."

It was unusually difficult to obtain qualified surgeons for African American regiments. The problem was widespread and persistent. A year later, General Nathaniel P. Banks, commanding officer of the Department of the Gulf (covering a large area of the deep South) could still write:

> ...In the organization of the colored regiments there was a serious want of Surgeons. Competent men declined to enter the service. It was impossible to get good officers to accept such commissions. In very many cases Hospital Stewards of low order of qualification were appointed to the office of Assistant Surgeon and Surgeon. Well grounded objections were made from every quarter against the inhumanity of subjecting the colored soldiers to medical treatment and surgical operations from such men. It was an objection that could not be disregarded without bringing discredit upon the Army and the Government.[4]

As has been noted, there were black physicians who were eager to serve in African American regiments. Major (later lieutenant colonel) Alexander Augusta, a black surgeon, had given enlistment physicals to many of Holman's men. The army reluctantly commissioned only eight black physicians, keeping most of them assigned to hospitals in Washington City. Two saw brief service with black regiments but the disrespectful treatment accorded to one of them, Augusta, when he was with the 7th USCT, demonstrates there was great unwillingness by many whites to serve with or under blacks regardless of their qualifications. In view of such attitudes, the War Department made every effort to keep the number of blacks holding commissions low.[5]

Men not engaged in guard duty drilled or built defensive fortifications. After the regiment's experiences in the District, the men marched together with loaded weapons whenever they were outside camp. While local

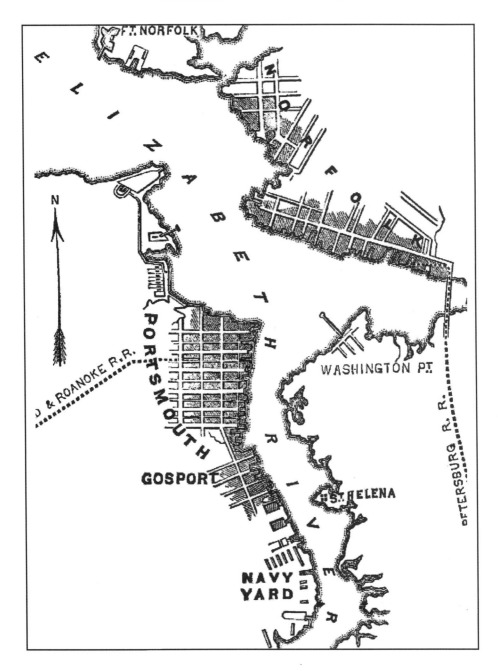

Map of Norfolk and Portsmouth, Virginia.

blacks were inspired by their presence, the regiment received looks and words of disgust and defiance from most whites. The handful of white North Carolinians who supported the Union and were known as "buffaloes" were often furtive in their public dealings with Union soldiers. Many of the citizens of the nearby hamlet of Old Trap were nonslaveholders and had endured great rage and danger for first refusing to support the Confederacy in 1861 and then resisting rebel conscription in April 1862.

In September 1863, the regiment was ordered to Portsmouth, Virginia. Hard by the south bank of the Elizabeth River, which separates it from Norfolk, Portsmouth was founded in 1752. During the next century, its magnificent natural harbor saw its banks fill with docks and freight piers and its waters lapped at the heels of vessels from a thousand ports. Also an important naval depot, Portsmouth, like Norfolk, was lost and reoccupied by Union forces early in the war. Portsmouth was the capital of Norfolk County, only eight miles from Hampton Roads and 160 miles by water from Richmond, the capital of the Confederacy. By the fall of 1863, the city was a beehive of military activity; its geometric tree-lined blocks resounding with the tramp of marching feet and the harbor bulging with schooners, frigates, and transports flying the Stars and Stripes. Portsmouth also served as the embarkation point for a number of expeditions into rebel-held territory.[6]

To the men of the regiment, Portsmouth, with three times the total population and a higher number of blacks overall, was cosmopolitan compared to Elizabeth City. Secessionists abounded. William Lamb, the mayor of Norfolk had to be imprisoned in 1863 for his activities. The officers and men endured their hateful gestures and sullen faces but were happy to be encamped near the city. The somber shadow in their early reverie was the knowledge that a ferry boat ride across the river lay Norfolk where Lieutenant Sanborn had been murdered. Holman made sure there would be scant chance for reflection. He set up around-the-clock guard and work details alternating with constant inspections and drills; all underscored with strict discipline. His design, as always, to establish and then heighten an esprit de corps among his men. He knew all too well that it was an essential, if often overlooked, ingredient of success in the shock and flame of war. In October, he reported the regiment at full strength with 990 men.[7]

In November, the regiment received one of its most prestigious visitors. The famed AME cleric and scholar Bishop Daniel Alexander Payne was traveling through the area. In his autobiography, *Recollections of Seventy Years,* Payne recorded his impressions:

> I visited South-eastern Virginia, in company with Revs. A.W. Wayman and J.M. Brown. At Norfolk we visited the Sunday-school of about five hundred colored children, under the tuition and management of education, pious men and women from the free North; who, leaving all the refinements of home, had descended to one of the darkest corners of the South to educate black children. It was such a sight as I had never witnessed before, and never expected to see. The contrast which this scene made with the previous state of things made me feel that the reign of slavery, darkness, and cruelty was passing away, and that of freedom, light, mercy, and love was dawning upon an outcast, outlawed, enslaved race! We visited and addressed the schools under the American Missionary Association in both Norfolk and Portsmouth, and visited the encampment of the First Regiment of United States colored troops at the latter place. Schools and United States colored troops in Old Virginia in 1863! Just think of that, and the hanging of John Brown for an attempt upon slavery!*

*To me one of the most wonderful things was the sight of United States troops, and freedmen under their protection, felling the tall pines on the plantation of Governor Wise, and sawing them up into timber. Another sight equally interesting and confounding was a "stack of arms" for the use of the freedmen in what was said to be the parlor of Governor Wise, who had threatened, in the event of another John Brown raid, that he would not wait for the aid of United States troops, but he would organize an army in Virginia and drive out of the North all the abolitionists into Canada.

In late November, Holman learned that W. Pryor, the latest appointee for regimental surgeon had refused his September 21, 1863 assignment to the regiment. Foster, head of the Bureau of Colored Troops, revoked Pryor's appointment on November 28, 1863. Pryor's replacement, Assistant Surgeon William H. Crawford, was no better. Claiming "failing health and inability to support my family decently," Crawford began to frequently offer his resignation, first doing so within two months of his enlistment. When those attempts failed, he waited until April, 1864, when the regiment was in the field and attempted to resign again. He was then released from duty and dishonorably discharged for having "...tendered his resignation in the face of the enemy," for attempting to resign "...for insufficient reasons," and "for failure to acquit himself as becomes an officer." While Crawford's fate was being decided, Assistant Surgeon Henry Willougby was assigned to the regiment. He was found to be addicted to whiskey and opium and was quickly cashiered.

Holman was also proceeding to cashier Second Lieutenant Henry M. Day. Appointed to the regiment on June 23, 1863, Day, despite repeated warnings, had continued "...indulging in the overuse of strong drink." On one such occasion, he pulled out his pistol and pointed it at an enlisted man without provocation. His men saw him drunk in his uniform in Portsmouth.

Some of the enlisted men, who had not yet fully adjusted to military life or who would later claim a deficient knowledge of Army regulations, wanted to see more of the Portsmouth they had marched through. A few went off at different times to visit without permission. They were severely punished. Corporal Samuel Chase of Company H had been a sailor in civilian life. For his unauthorized voyage into town, he was court-martialed, reduced to private, and put at hard labor in the trenches for 10 days. Privates Ewell Conway, Buck Hedgeman, and Sergeant (later corporal) Richard Jones of Company E, privates Henry Grinfer of Company B, and John Magruder and Edward Nelson of Company G, received court-martials, various terms of confinement in the guardhouse and/or hard labor in the trenches or public works, or forced to drill all day with weighted knapsacks. And then there was Private James Greyson of

Company C who was sentenced to 30 days hard labor and confinement in the guardhouse. He was still required to attend all company and battalion drills. He had not helped his situation by resisting arrest when he "...ran across a field when pursued by 2 guards" and "...hit one of them in the stomach with a turnip." While the number of men running afoul of the code of military justice was small, it was nevertheless a sign of larger restlessness and discouragement. Being restricted almost exclusively to constructing entrenchments and performing other labor and menial duties, the men were growing restless. This problem afflicted most African American units until Lee's surrender. In spite of this treatment, many enlisted men showed definite promise. John Cumbash, a 23 year-old farmer and Frederick County, Maryland native was promoted to sergeant on November 11, 1863. Orderly, decent, and determined officers and men capable of handling the drudgery and suffering of the soldier's life was Holman's goal. He was closer to it now than on Analostan Island. That was a good thing. The regiment was headed into its first battle.

THE SOUTH MILLS EXPEDITION

On December 5, 1863, 700 men from the First USCT joined men from the First and Second North Carolina Colored Volunteers, 5th USCT, and 55th Massachusetts Volunteers under the command of Brigadier General Edward A. Wild. They became part of his "African Brigade." An ardent abolitionist and supporter of black troops, Wild had seriously injured his right hand at the Battle of Seven Pines and lost his left arm at the Battle of South Mountain. Brave, hot-tempered and an implacable enemy of the Confederacy, Wild was ordered to locate and engage rebel guerillas and recruit local blacks for army service. The distance from Portsmouth to South Mills, North Carolina, the site of the locks for the Dismal Swamp Canal, is a little over 30 miles. When barges carrying food and supplies failed to catch up with his forces, Wild ordered his forces "...to live on the country for a few days, which we did judiciously discriminating in favor of the worst rebels."

At South Mills, Wild's men were joined by white troops from the 5th and 11th Pennsylvania and a section of the 7th New York Artillery. Wild had Holman's men build a bridge over the Pasquotank with materials taken from the house and barn of a Confederate officer living nearby. Wild's forces, now totaling about 1,800 men, crossed the bridge and occupied Elizabeth City for several days. In the meantime, he sent out foraging parties, combat patrols, and escorts for contraband men and their families.

Wild described the enemy's response:

> The guerrillas pestered us. They crept upon our pickets at night, waylaid our expeditions and our cavalry scouts, firing upon us whenever they could. But in marching, our flankers breaking up the woods, generally drove them. We ambuscaded them twice without success; pursuit was useless. Colonel Holman burned two of their camps between Elizabeth and Hertford, taking some of their property, such as guns, horses, provisions, and clothing; catching some of their abettors, but only one of their number, Daniel Bright, of Pasquotank County, whom I afterward hanged, duly placarding thus:

> This guerrilla hanged by order of Brigadier-General Wild.

> All our prisoners had the benefit of a drumhead court-martial. Finding ordinary measures of little avail, I adopted a more rigorous style of warfare; burned their houses and barns, ate up their livestock, and took hostages from their families. This course we followed throughout the trip, and we learned that they were disgusted with such unexpected treatment; it bred disaffection, some wishing to quit the business, others going over the lines to join the Confederate Army. I exchanged communications with two of the captains concerning these hostages, which was satisfactory as far as it went.

On quitting Elizabeth City, I sent 250 to land on Powell's Point and march up, ferried 400 across to Camden Court-House, and returned with the rest to South Mills. There I dismissed the cavalry and artillery and sent home Colonel Holman's regiment with our trains; marched with the remainder to Indiatown, met Colonel Draper, who had gone southward with his party to Shiloh, then northward again.[8]

After nearly three weeks, Wild returned to Norfolk. His forces had, in addition to the actions mentioned previously, captured four large smuggling vessels and many horses, freed 2,500 blacks, and recruited nearly 100 men into his black troops which he dubbed the "African Brigade." At the end of the expedition Wild said his "...men marched wonderfully, never grumbled, were watchful on picket, and always ready for fight. They are most reliable soldiers." Union battle losses were seven killed, nine wounded, and two men taken prisoners. Private George Dunmore, a regimental drummer and District native, was accidentally wounded on the third day of the expedition. His left arm was paralyzed.

Wild's tactics were criticized by the rebels. They later hanged one of the black soldiers captured during the expedition in repayment for the execution of Bright, the guerilla. Wild's commanding officer, Major General Benjamin F. Butler responded that Wild had accomplished his mission with "great thoroughness, but perhaps too much stringency."[9]

For the men of the First USCT, the South Mills expedition was a watershed event. They had surmounted fear and physical hardship to meet the enemy, stand their ground, and do their duty. They knew they would pass the judgment of history.

On January 3, 1864, Colonel Holman issued Regimental Order No. 69 which informed the officers and men that the regiment had been detailed as the provost guard of Portsmouth (see the Documents section). The provost guard was a police detail of soldiers under the provost marshal whose duties included the preservation of order and the arrest and incarceration of soldiers who had committed offenses of a general nature.

The detail came as recognition of the long hours the men had put in perfecting their soldierly appearance and manners. Enjoyment of this tiny victory was fleeting. Late in April, General Butler transferred the regiment to the 1st Brigade, Hincks' Colored Division, 18th Corps, Army of the James. Holman gave his men a week and a half to prepare their weapons and equipment and lay in extra loads of ammunition.

Also in April, Sergeant Major Christian A. Fleetwood was detailed briefly to the First USCT. Born free in Baltimore, Maryland in 1840, and well-educated, Fleetwood had enlisted as a sergeant in the 4th USCT, raised in Maryland. For gallantry in action with his regiment during the Battle of Chaffins' Farm on September 29, 1864, Fleetwood was awarded the Congressional Medal of Honor. After the war, he later settled in LeDroit Park in the District and played significant roles in the colored high school cadet corps and the Washington Colored National Guard. In April 1864, as sergeant major, Fleetwood would have assisted the regimental adjutant in publishing orders in writing, making up written instructions, and receiving and recording reports, returns, and other records.[10]

On May 4, 1864, the First USCT embarked from Fortress Monroe. The regiment was part of General Wild's Brigade, General Hincks' Division, General Gilmore's 10th Army Corps, part of the Army of the James commanded by General Butler. Early the next morning, the First USCT landed, along with other elements of Wild's brigade, including the 22nd USCT organized at Philadelphia, at Wilson's Wharf in Charles City County Virginia, on the north bank of the James River. About 30 miles southeast of Richmond and variously called Kennon's Landing, Wilson's Landing, or Wilson's Wharf, the landing was used to transport tobacco from plantations along the James River to England. At the base of strategic bluffs overlooking the river, the landing had been used during the Revolutionary War by the British in a futile attempt to capture the Virginia Legislature. The rest of the brigade landed at Fort Powhatan a few miles up the river on the opposite bank.

Back at Wilson's Wharf, the First USCT deployed a strong force of pickets and began constructing entrenchments surrounding the landing. On May 6, Second Lieutenant Julius M. Swain, the signal officer at Wilson's Wharf accompanied a detachment of the First USCT, which captured the rebel signal station party and equipment at Sandy Point, on the James River. The enemy's signalists made an armed defense and the sergeant in charge, with three of his men, were killed. The record of all the dispatches and reports sent and received through that rebel station were captured and forwarded to General Wild.

The presence of so many black Union troops in the area drew large numbers of slaves from neighboring plantations. A number of these men took the opportunity to join the black regiments, Lincoln's "broken shackle" army. Robert Brown, Jesse Braxton, and Samuel Harrison were among those who enlisted in the First USCT while it was at the wharf.

On May 10, Sergeant George Hatton recorded an unforgettable event at the regiment's camp at Wilson's Wharf:

> Mr. Editor: -- You are aware that Wilson's Landing is on the James River, a few miles above Jamestown, the very spot where the first sons of Africa were landed, in the year 1620, if my memory serves me right, and from that day up to the breaking out of the rebellion, was looked upon as an inferior race by all civilized nations. But behold what has been revealed in the past three or four years; why the colored men have ascended upon a platform of equality, and the slave can now apply the lash to the tender flesh of his master, for this day I am now an eye witness of the fact. The country being principally inhabited by wealthy farmers, there are a great many men in the regiment who are refugees from this place. While out on a foraging expedition we captured Mr. Clayton, a noted reb in this part of the country, and from his appearance, one of the F.P.V's; on the day before we captured several colored women that belonged to Mr. C., who had given them a most unmerciful whipping previous to their departure.

On the arrival of Mr. C. in camp, the commanding officer determined to let the women have their revenge, and ordered Mr. C. to be tied to a tree in front of headquarters, and William Harris, a soldier in our regiment, and a member of Co. E, who was acquainted with the gentleman, and who used to belong to him, was called upon to undress him, and introduce him to the ladies I mentioned before. Mr. Harris played his part conspicuously, bringing the blood from his loins at every stroke, and not forgetting to remind the gentleman of days gone by. After giving him some fifteen or twenty well-directed strokes, the ladies, one after another, came up and gave him a like number, to remind him that they were no longer his, but safely housed in Abraham's bosom, and under the protection of the Star Spangled Banner, and guarded by their own patriotic, though once down-trodden race. Oh, that I had the tongue to express my feelings while standing upon the banks of the James River, on the soil of Virginia, the mother state of slavery, as a witness of such a sudden reverse!

The day is clear, the fields of grain are beautiful and the birds are singing sweet melodious songs, while poor Mr. C. is crying to his servants for mercy. Let all who sympathize for the South take this narrative for a mirror.[11]

BATTLE OF WILSON'S WHARF

On May 24, Wilson's Wharf was attacked. The black soldiers heard that the Confederates, sure of certain victory, had even brought several wagon loads of shackles as "bracelets for the nigger soldiers" whom they planned to parade in front of Jefferson Davis. The battle was described by an officer from the First USCT, Captain Edward Simonton, in a paper he delivered in 1902 before a Civil War veterans' group. Simonton, like Holman, had been born in Maine. He came up through the ranks from First Sergeant in the 20th Maine Infantry to a second lieutenancy at the time of the battle:

General Fitzhugh Lee's cavalry, about 2,000 strong, came down on us quite suddenly; but he did not find us unprepared. Our force quickly formed in line behind the earthworks. We had at that time about 1,100 men all told, consisting of the First U.S. Colored troops, four companies of the 10th U.S. Colored troops, and a section of the 3rd New York battery of artillery; this force being under the command of General Wild, Brigadier Commander. After driving in our pickets, General Lee sent to General Wild, under a flag of truce, a message stating that he had force strong enough to take the place, and demanded its surrender, promising that in case the garrison surrendered, the troops should be turned over to the authorities at Richmond as prisoners of war, then adding the comforting assurance that if this demand was rejected, he would not be answerable for the conduct of his men. General Wild replied, "We will try that...."

On the receipt of General Wild's answer to his demand for surrender, the enemy began the attack on our position. Dismounting their men, they first made a feint attack on the left and center of our line and then made a direct charge on our right. The surrounding woods favored the enemy so that they were able to advance quite near our works before the fire from our line could have much effect on them. But as some of the "Johnnies" showed themselves to our view, they received a destructive fire from our line. Still the enemy charged on with a yell, firing all the time as they advanced, and seemed confident of their ability to drive all our force into the river. Then it was that our sable warriors showed their fighting qualities. They stood their ground firmly, firing volley after volley into the ranks of the advancing foe. Many of the "Johnnies" had succeeded in approaching quite near our line. The artillery stationed in our works then threw grape and canister into their ranks. Again, the brave and determined foe rallied under the frantic efforts of their officers; again their

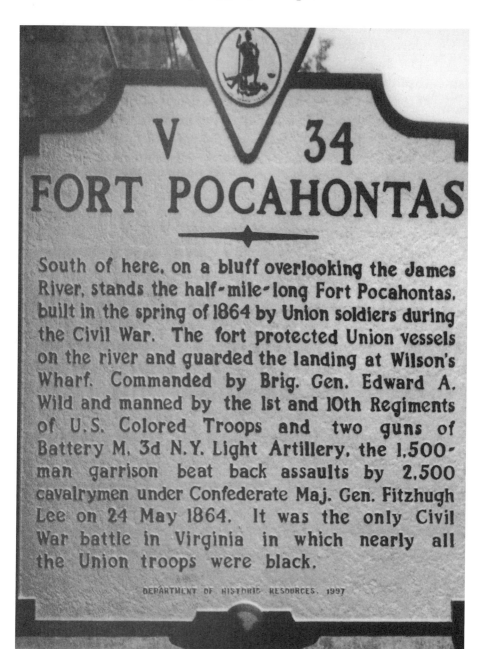

V V 34

FORT POCAHONTAS

South of here, on a bluff overlooking the James River, stands the half-mile-long Fort Pocahontas, built in the spring of 1864 by Union soldiers during the Civil War. The fort protected Union vessels on the river and guarded the landing at Wilson's Wharf. Commanded by Brig. Gen. Edward A. Wild and manned by the 1st and 10th Regiments of U.S. Colored Troops and two guns of Battery M, 3d N.Y. Light Artillery, the 1,500-man garrison beat back assaults by 2,500 cavalrymen under Confederate Maj. Gen. Fitzhugh Lee on 24 May 1864. It was the only Civil War battle in Virginia in which nearly all the Union troops were black.

DEPARTMENT OF HISTORIC RESOURCES, 1997

Commemorative battle plaque unveiled in 1997.

ranks were scattered and torn by our deadly fire. Next, the gunboat in the river began to throw shells into their already demoralized ranks, when they broke and fled in disorder to the rear; then our soldiers poured into their ranks a final volley, and this was the last of the fight. They left on the field a portion of their dead and wounded. It was reported that the enemy's loss was over 100 dead and wounded. We took several prisoners, including one Major. Our total loss was two killed and 14 wounded, including one officer....

The only account that I noticed at that time was in the Richmond Examiner, which was a gross exaggeration of the actual facts and which amused us not a little at that time. Of course, General Fitzhugh Lee and his command desired to make as good a showing as possible from a Confederate standpoint, for their defeat and loss of men, without results. ...No mention was made in the newspaper article that General Lee was defeated and driven back by Union forces consisting nearly all of colored troops. The battle lasted six hours.[12]

At the battle of Wilson's Wharf, 1,100 black Union troops defeated a rebel cavalry force of 2,500, more than twice their number under the command of the nephew of General Robert E. Lee. Military historians consider this battle "possibly the largest single victory" during the entire Civil War won by a force comprised almost exclusively of African American soldiers.

First Lieutenant Myron W. Smith, the regimental adjutant, also published an account of the battle of Wilson's Wharf. He concluded with the words:

That the black men will fight is an established fact. We had a section of the 3rd New York Volunteer Artillery here, and the lieutenant in charge told me, after the fight, that no men in the world could do better than those who supported his gun....

We have taken a number of prisoners, some wounded and some not. We have treated them well, but woe to them if we find that our missing man has been unfairly dealt with.[13]

Before the black troops were transferred, they completed work on a rectangular arrangement of gun ramps, bastions, and breastworks, extending for half a mile along the river. The fortifications were named Fort Pocahontas.

THE OVERLAND CAMPAIGN

On May 26, General Hincks ordered the regiment to proceed at once seven miles up river to Fort Powhatan to relieve the 22nd USCT which had been relocated only a few days earlier and was now being sent to City Point, Virginia, an important logistical and command center.

On June 2, the regiment marched to Cold Harbor, Virginia where it supported Major General Horatio G. Wright's 6th Army Corps as it attacked a rebel force commanded by Confederate General George Pickett. Despite heavy fire, the First USCT pushed back a rebel advance party and captured 50 prisoners.

The First USCT was part of what has become known as the Overland Campaign; the armies of Generals Ulysses Grant and Robert E. Lee grappled with each other throughout central and eastern Virginia. Grant sought to topple slavocracy and end all southern military offensive capability. Butler's mission was to threaten Richmond, the rebel capital and Petersburg, a vital rail and supply hub.

Black soldiers were an indispensable part of the Union effort. Writing in 1913, the Reverend W. Spencer Carpenter, an African American officer who served during the Spanish American War, chronicled the services of blacks in the Nation's wars:

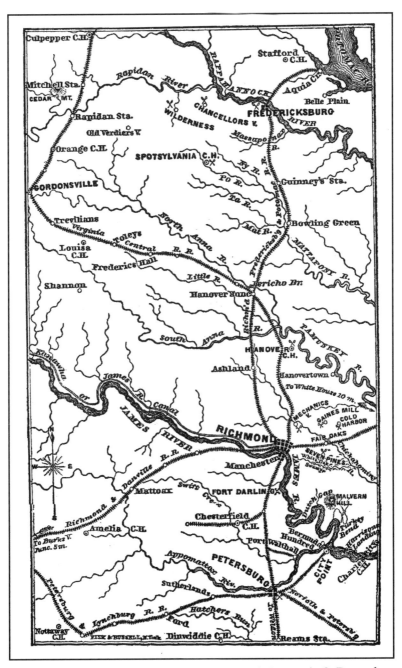

Map of Virginia showing Fredericksburg, Richmond, & Petersburg.

The Virginian Campaign under General U.S. Grant opened in 1864, and of the Union troops engaged, twenty thousand were Negroes. Nobly and fearlessly our troops performed their duties, and long before the campaign ended, the white soldiers declared that the support of their Negro comrades was well worth having. When General Grant wanted Petersburg, of the troops assigned to take that city was a Negro brigade; and to that brigade belongs the honor of capturing a Confederate battery six miles from Petersburg, a capture which resulted in leaving almost uncontested the route to the city.[14]

On the morning of June 15, a few miles outside Petersburg near a place called Baylor's Farm, the First USCT, part of a provisional brigade of 1,300 men commanded by Holman, poised itself for an attack. Since Holman was acting as brigade commander, regimental direction fell to his second in command Major Elias Wright. (Holman's official report to the commanding general dated June 20, 1864, is in the Documents Section). Simonton also wrote about this battle.

Simonton called June 15 "...a memorable date to me...." Here are his recollections of that fateful engagement:

While my regiment was deployed in line and charging upon the enemy's first line of works, I remember that I was charging with my company and running with all speed towards the enemy's line of works; shot and shell fell from the enemy's artillery and now there was heard the zip-zip of the minie balls, causing a number of our men to fall dead and wounded; still we ran charging on, when suddenly a sharp blow struck my leg, causing a benumbed feeling in this limb, though not then accompanied by an acute pain. I thought at first that I was struck by a piece of shell. I was not knocked down by the blow but was made severely lame. Some of my men stopped to offer assistance, but I refused assistance and urged them to go on and help carry the enemy's works which they did. Besides, I saw a few other soldiers of the regiment wounded more seriously and needing more attention than myself. In my desire to see my company help to win a victory over the enemy, no doubt my action in this regard was somewhat influenced by the thought of a possible repulse of our troops, followed by a counter charge of the enemy, and in that event my capture as a prisoner, which event in my wounded condition would be likely to result fatally to myself in the end. Soon afterwards, I was gratified to hear the cheering from our men; the firing from the enemy's line suddenly ceased, indicating that our troops had successfully carried the enemy's line of works in their front. I then began to feel considerable pain in my leg and faint from the loss of blood, when the ambulance corps in search of the wounded picked me up with the other wounded men and took us to the field hospital, where we were examined by the field surgeon. The examination of the surgeon showed that a minie ball had entered my thigh, but fortunately had passed clear through and out without breaking any bones. I was then moved by the ambulance to City Point and placed on a river transport made into a temporary hospital where the wounded had proper care and treatment. We were then taken down the James River to Chesapeake hospital near Fort Monroe, where I found a large number of wounded in the different wards. My wound began to get worse and gave me much pain. After a while gangrene and sloughing set in, making it very painful. My suffering from these causes during the months of July and August was so intense that I remember on one occasion praying for death to relieve the pain. But there were other patients in that hospital whose sufferings were still greater. While lying on my hospital cot, I would see, day after day, the remains of officers, dead heroes, removed from the ward, one by one, who had suffered and died for their country, martyrs in freedom's cause. Then the reflection came upon me, "their souls are marching on."[15]

After several weeks, Simonton was released from the hospital. On crutches he traveled home to Maine for further recuperation. In October,

"...although yet somewhat lame...," Simonton returned to the First USCT and served with it until the end of the war.

June 15 was a hot, long, and murderous day. There was a second battle at Petersburg. The morning attack had ended a little after 8 a.m. About 9 a.m., General E.W. Hincks, the division commander, ordered Holman's brigade to advance by the road from the City Point road to the Jordan Point road. About two hours later having reached the Jordan Point Road, the brigade met the enemy's pickets on Bailey's Creek, near Bryant's house, and drove them in beyond the woods. Holman advanced his command into position in front and to the left of the enemy's works, his movements covered by a line of skirmishers from across the junction of the Jordan Point Road and Suffolk Stage Road on the left, and extending to the right beyond the Peebles' house. The skirmishing line kept up a constant fire upon the gunners in the enemy's works. Rebel cannon continued to shell Union positions, harassing the troops of both Duncan's and Holman's brigades. It was early in the afternoon when a section of Union artillery was pushed into position to the right of Peebles's house and another section to the left of the house. At about 2 p.m., the Union line was extended in preparation for the final charge. Confederate cannons "...kept up an unremitting and very accurate and severe fire" from the batteries now known as Batteries Nos. 6, 7, 8, 9, and 10. At about 5 o'clock, the skirmish line was strengthened and sufficiently advanced to gain the most favorable tactical position, and to drive in all of the enemy's sharpshooters. At about 7 p.m., the command to charge was given. The advance was "executed with great gallantry and promptness, resulting in the carrying of all the works from No. 7 to No. 11 (five in number), and the capture of six guns, with caissons, prisoners, &c."

The African American troops vaulted the breastworks, ran through trenches, and jumped over rifle pits. Soldiers from three different black regiments mingled in the capture of Battery No. 7.[16]

Thirty years later in his mind's eye, a black veteran of the combat that day still recalled seeing his comrades "...advancing, a few yards at a time. Then lying down to escape the fire from the works, but still gradually creeping nearer and nearer, until just as the sun went down, they swept over the works like a tornado and started a race for the city, close at the heels of the flying foe until mistakenly ordered back."

Senior Union generals were unable to follow up the tactical success at Baylor's Farm. Despite thin rebel defenses, poor communication, confusion, and delays led to a missed opportunity to shorten the war. In an after action report dated June 20, 1864 General E.W. Hincks commended his African American infantry:

> In the gallant and soldierly deportment of the troops engaged on the 15th instant under varying circumstances; the celerity with which they moved to the charge; the steadiness and coolness exhibited by them under heavy and long-continued fire; the impetuosity with which they sprang to the assault; the patient endurance of wounds, we have a sufficient proof that colored men, when properly officered, instructed, and drilled, will make most excellent infantry of the line, and may be used as such soldiers to great advantage.

Casualties in the First USCT were heavy: 17 men were killed, 114 were wounded, 25 were listed as missing in action.[17] One of the wounded that day was Private Rufus Wright. He died on June 21, 1864 at the Hampton, Virginia General Hospital of a gunshot wound to the abdomen. (A letter that he wrote to his wife a few weeks before the battle and her affidavit for a widow's pension are in the Documents Section). See Chapter Three for a copy of the couple's marriage certificate.

Captain Giles Rich, of the First USCT, was promoted to lieutenant colonel in his regiment for gallant conduct although wounded in front of Petersburg on June 15. That he had won the respect and goodwill of his men was shown when his promotion came on October 13, 1864. Each man in the regiment chipped in for the purchase of "a sword and riding equipments" which were formally presented to him.

On June 22, 1864, the regiment was ordered to move several miles and deploy in support of a battery of cannon. Holman was also given command of the picket guard along a stretch of the Appomatox, the river that flowed through Petersburg.

There were always reminders of racism and injustice. On July 1, 1864, Hatton wrote the following to the *Recorder:*

> I have been silent for a long time, but today I must speak, for it is a day long to be remembered by me, a wounded soldier of the U.S. Army.
>
> I was wounded at the battle of Petersburg on the 15th of June last, and arrived at the Hampton Hospital on the 20th. On my arrival there, I wrote to my father, stating that I was wounded and would like him to come and see me, and if possible, take me home, where I should have the attendance of my kind and loving mother. My father complied with my request, and arrived at Fortress Monroe on the 30th. I was overjoyed to see him.
>
> Today, he departed with a hung-down head, leaving me with an aching heart. I must here state the cause of my trouble. It is as follows:
>
> On my father's arrival at the hospital, he stated the object of his visit to the doctor in charge, who, very short and snappish, referred him to Dr. White, one of the head surgeons. Father immediately proceeded to Dr. White's office, where he expected to receive a little satisfaction but to his heart-rending surprise, received none. After making every exertion in his power to get a furlough, he failed in so doing, without receiving the slightest shadow of satisfaction.
>
> All of this I was willing to stand, as I had discharged my duty as a soldier from the first of May 1863, up to the time I was

wounded, for the low United States' degrading sum of $7 per month that no man but the poor, down-trodden, uneducated, patriotic black man would be willing to fight for. Yes, I stand all this; but the great wound I received at the hospital was this: A white man, whose name I did not learn, came from Washington with my father for the same purpose to see his son and carry him home. His success needs no comment; let it suffice to say that he was white, and he carried his son home.

Such deception as that I thought was crucified at the Battle of Fort Wagner; buried at Millikens Bend; rose the third day, and descended into everlasting forgetfulness in the Appomattox River at the Battle of Petersburg.

[When] can one of my color, and in my position, at this time, find a comforter? When will my people be a nation? I fear, never on the American soil; though we may crush this cursed rebellion.[18]

George Hatton called the seven dollars a month pay he received "degrading" (white soldiers received $13 monthly). It is evident that many black soldiers strongly felt this way. On September 28, 1863, Private James Henry Gooding, 54th Massachusetts Volunteers, wrote to President Lincoln:

Now the main question is, are we Soldiers, or are we Laborers? We are fully armed, and equipped, have done all the various duties pertaining to a Soldier's life, have conducted ourselves to the complete satisfaction of General Officers, who were, if anything, prejudiced against us, but who now accord us all the encouragement and honors due us; have shared the perils and labor of reducing the first strong-hold that flaunted a Traitor Flag; and more, Mr. President, to-day the Anglo-Saxon Mother, Wife, or Sister are not alone in tears for departed Sons, Husbands, and Brothers. The patient, trusting descendent of Afric's Clime have dyed the ground with blood, in defense of the Union, and Democracy. Men, too, your Excellency, who know in a measure the cruelties of the iron heel of oppression, which in years gone by, the very power their blood is now being spilled to maintain, ever ground them in the dust....

Now your Excellency, we have done a Soldier's duty. Why can't we have a Soldier's pay? You caution the Rebel chieftain, that the United States knows no distinction in her soldiers. She insists on having all her soldiers of whatever creed or color, to be treated according to the usages of War. Now if the United States exacts uniformity of treatment of her soldiers from the insurgents, would it not be well and consistent to set the example herself by paying all her soldiers alike?[19]

In November 1863, Sergeant William Walker of the 3rd South Carolina Infantry ordered a group of men from his company to march to their regimental commander's tent, stack their arms and hang their accouterments on the stacks. Walker made it clear that the men "would not do duty any longer for seven dollars a month." He was arrested, court-martialed, and executed despite a number of mitigating circumstances including the fact that he had been promised full pay when he enlisted.

The February 13, 1864, *Harper's Weekly* labeled the pay inequity a "sheer breach of faith and wanton injustice...." During the first week of June 1864, Private Sylvester Ray of the 2nd U.S. Colored Cavalry was brought up on charges and recommended for trial for saying: "...none of us will sign again for seven dollars a month...." Ray's unit was then serving in the trenches at Bermuda Hundred after having fought at Drewry's Bluff.

The pay difference created great hardships among the soldiers' families making it nearly impossible for them to obtain food, shelter, and clothing for their wives and children. The men of the First USCT watched the debate on fair pay for black troops drag on. Even after Congress granted equal pay in June 1864, the legal technicality that stood until after the end of war limited pay equality to those black soldiers who were "free on or before April 19, 1861." Those who were former slaves, a significant percentage of the men of the First USCT, were excluded. On August 1, 1864, the War Department issued Circular No. 60 which set forth provisions requiring senior officers commanding black units to investigate and determine which soldiers were free on or before April 19, 1861. Each soldier was required to give a statement under oath. The statement was corroborated as best it could be. And then a statement was entered on the muster roll next to each soldier's name: "Free on or before April 19, 1861."

Qualified soldiers were to receive full and equal pay from their enlistment to January 1, 1864. But in order to get every man full pay, several Union commanders employed the so-called "Quaker Oath." Each enlisted man swore that he owed no man unrequited labor on or before April 19, 1861. While many of the men had, in fact, been slaves legally on that day, they took the oath because they considered themselves free under God's law. An examination of a representative sample of compiled service records of the First USCT indicates that men who appear to have been slaves upon enlistment nevertheless had been free on or before April 19, 1861, noted in their records raising the question of whether the Quaker Oath was used in the regiment. Whatever the case, the glacial pace of the Army bureaucracy and belated and sporadic paydays meant that as late as October 1864, the regiment was still paid at the old rate.

Better documented is Holman's own ingenuous attempt at better compensation for his troops. On September 17, 1864, he wrote to the Provost Marshal's Office of the State of Massachusetts to claim the state bounty of $325.00 for each of his men. The state's reply was positive on the condition War Department approval could be obtained. Holman's idea was that the state would pay the bounty if the regiment could be credited to the state's enlistment quota. Holman drew upon a meager technicality: "My regiment was recruited in Virginia.... In view of the recent Act of

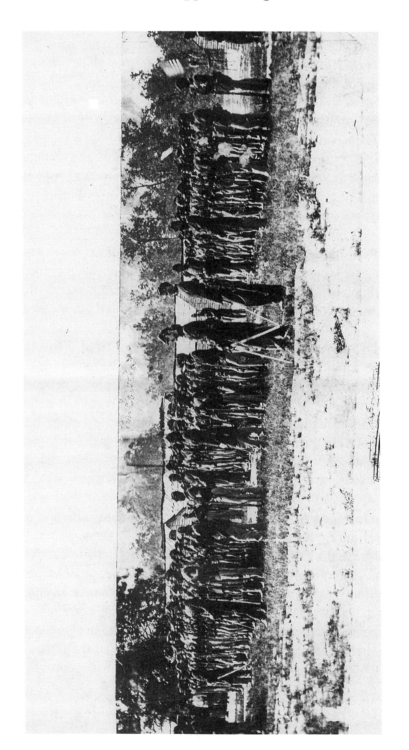

The Regiment in Formation in Virginia in 1864.

Congress authorizing states to fill their quotas by recruiting in those parts of the Enemy's county held by our forces, I wrote the Governor of Massachusetts to know if he would pay my regiment the State bounty; provided I could succeed in having it accredited to the state quota in some future call.... My men have served as faithfully and as well as other troops that have been paid large bounties. They have endured the same privations and suffered the same hardships, and have [illegible] as the field of battle, that they are entitled to every consideration that the brave soldier receives at the hands of the Government he is defending."

He requested permission through military channels from the head of the Bureau of Colored Troops on October 4. The proposal was returned by Butler's staff two days later with the notation: "Respectfully returned Disapproved. The actions proposed would work a palpable fraud upon the U.S. Services and also upon the people of Massachusetts."[20]

Another seldom discussed aspect of the pay issue concerned the right of loyal slaveowners to receive financial payments or bounties when their slaves joined the service. The law providing for these payments was introduced by the indefatigable Congressman Stevens and aimed primarily at slaveowners in the border states. Bounties, however, were normally received by the men who actually enrolled in the military. They were offered as inducements to join. The government believed that instead of paying the slaves who served, the slavemasters should be compensated for the loss of their property in service to the Union. They were offered up to a maximum of $300. The slave's compensation was considered to be his freedom through military service.

Stevens hoped that the prospect of compensation would entice loyal slaveholders to release their male slaves between 20 and 45 years of age. The practice worked well, particularly in Maryland. In retrospect, many historians believe this law assisted in the overall emancipation effort. In the case of Private James Brown of the First USCT, the practice had an ironically tragic result. Private Brown, who was born in Harford County, Maryland, enlisted at Wilmington, Delaware on September 26, 1864. He had been one of "two colored boys" ages five and seven sold in 1849 by

William Dinney to John C. Raymond for $250 until both boys were 25 years-old. Raymond and Brown arrived together at the recruiting station. Raymond presented Brown a deed of manumission and release of service granting Brown his freedom upon his enlistment as a substitute, and he showed military authorities his title to Brown. Raymond signed an oath of allegiance and claimed compensation for freeing his slave. While Raymond's claim was being reviewed, Brown joined the regiment. He was wounded during the battle of Fair Oaks on October 27, 1864. He died at the general hospital at Fortress Monroe on November 11, 1864. He had tasted freedom for less than 50 days. On January 2, 1865, Raymond's claim was approved. Two weeks later and more than 60 days after Brown's death Raymond received $100.

*   *   *   *   *

During July and August 1864, the regiment remained on picket and fatigue duty in the Petersburg area. One man was wounded on August 6. When not at work or on duty, the officers and men reviewed small unit tactics, repaired equipment, and received and trained replacements. Many of these men were draftees and substitutes enlisted outside Baltimore at Ellicott's Mills, Maryland. Also at this time a detachment of volunteers from the regiment was sent to Dutch Gap in Virginia to assist in the construction of a canal begun on August 15, 1864, to shorten the navigation of the James River by about seven miles and avoid rebel cannons dug in at a bend in the river. An attempt to remove a clay bulkhead impeding river traffic by blowing it up failed in January 1865. Work ended that same month. The canal did not see use until after the war.

On September 1, the regiment was ordered to Harrison's Landing on the James River. On September 28, joined by the 37th USCT, the First USCT sailed to Deep Bottom where it was joined by the 22nd USCT. On September 29, after a 10-mile march, the three black regiments advanced against the enemy's works at dawn forming one of three brigades of black

Dutch Gap Canal.

troops along with 20,000 other Union troops at New Market Heights. In that part of the line, however, the brunt of the first assault was born by the 5th, 36th, and 38th USCT. All night, the First USCT and the other regiments in the brigade threw up earthern breastworks. The next day they beat back a rebel counterattack.

The First USCT suffered 3 men killed and one officer and 17 men wounded. The dead men were: Corporal James Chaney, a 17 year-old born in Baltimore, Corporal Charles Smith, and Private John Parker, who was shot in the heart and died on the battlefield. The wounded included Private Edward Dorsey, a married man with a family in Baltimore. He never fully recovered from his injuries and resigned with a disability discharge in April 1865. Private Edward Harris, married, his family in Alexandria, Virginia, was wounded on September 29. He was discharged due to disability because a gunshot wound to his arm caused a permanent contraction of the fingers of his left hand.

The First USCT remained in the trenches in their old positions on the left of the line until the morning of October 26. Along with the rest of the brigade, the regiment marched back some two miles to the rear to get rations and extra ammunition. That night the men sang songs of freedom around their campfires. Private Daniel Brooks, who had just joined the regiment, wrote to his wife. (A copy of the letter is in the Documents Section).

On October 27, starting at 5 a.m., the brigade, under Colonel Holman, marched toward the enemy's works in front of Richmond. Arriving at the Williamsburg road, the unit found the head of the column already engaged. The brigade was soon ordered to proceed to the right across the York River Railroad, and advance up the Nine-Mile Road until within sight of the enemy's fortifications, which were about one mile above Fair Oaks Station. Holman then halted and reported to corps headquarters. The brigade moved to the right and across the York River Railroad, then advanced to the front up the New Bridge Road. Moving up this road about a mile it came in sight of the enemy's cavalry and immediately formed line, the First and 22nd USCT on the left of the road, and the 37th

USCT on the right of the road in reserve. The brigade advanced a little farther, when a column of rebel cavalry was discovered, estimated to be about 1,500 or 2,000 strong.

Holman then ordered the 37th to form a square, as he believed that the cavalry were about to charge. When the rebels did not attack, the regiments of the brigade were deployed as follows: The 37th USCT in a hollow on the right of the road, in reserve; the First USCT with its right resting on the road, and the 22nd on the left of the First. By this time, the enemy had hauled two cannons into position in front and began firing on the Union position. Holman then ordered the charge. The First USCT had open ground for their charge; the 22nd USCT had to charge through the woods. The First was exposed to "severe" musket and artillery fire but advanced across the open field and carried a part of the enemy's line, getting possession of the two guns.

The 22nd USCT, charging through a wood at double-quick in great confusion, arrived within about 100 yards of the enemy's works when Colonel Kiddoo, of the 22nd, fell dangerously wounded, whereupon the regiment, with a large number of green recruits "broke and commenced fleeing" to the rear. Lieutenant Colonel I.C. Terry, of the 22nd, assisted by Major Weinmann, of the sharpshooters, made every effort to rally them, but with only partial success. Lieutenant Colonel Giles H. Rich, the acting commanding officer of the First USCT, had begun making preparations to charge down the enemy's line to the left, which was still held, but finding himself unsupported and exposed to a fire in his flank from the woods, and learning that a strong force of rebel cavalry was forming in the open field to the left and front of the enemy's lines in such a position as to cut off his retreat, he was forced to give up the advantage which he had gained and to retire from the enemy's works, abandoning the captured guns.

Despite the general confusion in the 22nd USCT, the right company, under the command of Captain Albert James, advanced in the charge in good order, arriving within five yards of the enemy's line and retired in good order, covering the retreat, and adding materially to the safety of the regiment. The confusion in the 22nd was caused, at the beginning of the charge, when the order was given by Holman to march by the left flank, which movement was promptly executed by the First USCT, but at this time the 22nd USCT was thrown into disorder, either because Holman's command was not properly repeated, or because it was not fully heard, or the movement was not seen by the regiment because of the noise and smoke. Instead of being halted for the formation of the line, the regiment was allowed to charge as it was, and therefore accomplished little. The First USCT remained in the enemy's works from ten to fifteen minutes before retiring, and succeeded in spiking the two captured guns. After the order to retire had been given, Captain Henry Ward, of the First remained behind with a few of his men, and attempted to bring off the captured guns, but they were taken by the rebels as they struggled to unhitch the cannon from the dead and wounded horses.

As the two regiments were falling back, Lieutenant Colonel Abial G. Chamberlain received notice that both Holman and Kiddoo were wounded, he then assumed command as senior officer. At about the same moment he received an order from Major General Godfrey Weitzel to fall back, which he immediately did, bringing off such wounded as could be found, and covering his retreat with a strong line of skirmishers.

Holman received a gunshot wound in the thigh and fell seriously wounded within 200 yards of the rebel entrenchments. He was declared temporarily unfit for duty and later joined his wife in Chelsea, Massachusetts for extended recuperation. He rejoined the First USCT in May 1865.

Casualties in the First USCT were two officers and 10 enlisted men killed, four officers and 92 men wounded, and 16 men captured or missing in action. A total of 124 men; a staggering loss.[21]

Ward, the commanding officer of D Company and 10 of his men who had been captured while taking the Confederate cannon were praised in official reports. Ward's African American companions were: Corporal Thomas Gant, and Privates William Abrams, Daniel Addison, William

Britt(en), David Brooks, James Brown, Samuel Freeman, John H. Quaintance, Thomas Quaintance, and John Williams. Gant had shown heartening signs of soldierly promise even helping to recruit soldiers for the 10th USCT, a Virginia regiment. Brooks and John Quaintance, once a Maryland slave, were wounded during the charge.

Thomas M. Chester, the only black war correspondent for a major daily during the War reported on the conduct of the black troops during the battle of Fair Oaks in an October 31, 1864 dispatch. His report to the readers of the Philadelphia *Press* included an account of the First USCT:

> The troops immediately rushed over an uneven ground for about half a mile; then passing over two unfinished lines of the enemy's works, and when within a few yards of his entrenchments, not liking to meet colored troops on anything like equal terms, he fled from the works, leaving two guns in our possession. Being inside of the enemy's entrenchments, this gallant regiment was preparing to charge down the interior of his line, when it discovered that it was being rapidly flanked by a large force, which obliged it to retreat, after having spiked the guns and brought off some prisoners. All of their wounded, with the exception of thirty, were carried from the field as the movement was made to the rear.
>
> The colored troops are the only ones that entered the enemy's works and made any captures on that day, and if it had been intended that they should have done more than make a demonstration they would have been sufficiently supported to have enabled them to hold them. The 1st USCT is a fighting regiment, and when Colonel Holman urges them forward they have never been known to fail or falter.

Chester, reporting on the battles around Richmond and Petersburg, specialized in the stories of the officers and men of the USCT. To Chester, Holman combined "...the affability of a gentleman with the devotion of a patriot..." and he had no doubt that his men "...will cheerfully follow wherever this brave officer may lead." Chester's admiration for Holman stemmed from his efforts on behalf of his men.

Chester recounted for his soldiers the case of Lieutenant J.B. McMurdy, a staff officer, Holman had sent him off "in disgrace" to report to General Butler, for "unwarrantable treatment to a colored sergeant," detailed at headquarters, and "disrespectful conduct to his superiors." Chester wrote that the "...undignified character and swaggering bearing of the lieutenant, with other traits which need not be mentioned, wholly disqualify him to command colored troops or to be brought into association with the gentlemanly officers upon Colonel Holman's staff. General Butler I commit him, with the remark that he will give him the full measure of justice. To the high credit of Colonel Holman, it must be said that no one in this division, so long as he commands it, will be permitted to abuse any man, whether he be white or black. His impartiality is well known and highly appreciated, and has made him the idol of his command."[22]

In the wake of the battle of Fair Oaks, the First USCT, traveled back across the James at Aikens' Landing and went into camp near Varina, Virginia. There, regular camp life began again: reveille at 6 a.m., drill, picket duty, cleaning and repairing of weapons and equipment, reviewing of small unit tactics, and, where possible, time was set aside for the study of spelling, penmanship, reading, and arithmetic; learning dutifully presided over by Reverend Turner, the chaplain.

RETURN TO NORTH CAROLINA

Due to the wounding of Kiddoo and Holman, in early November Colonel Elias Wright, 10th USCT, was made brigade commander. He had formerly served with the First USCT. In December, the Army of the James which had consisted of black and white units of the Tenth and Eighteenth Army Corps was discontinued. The white troops were formed into the 24th Army Corps. The African American troops were organized into the 25th Army Corps commanded by Major General Weitzel.

Bombardment and landing at Fort Fisher.

On December 8, 1864, the First USCT embarked on the transport "Herman Livingston" which formed part of the Union amphibious expedition of almost 60 warships sailing against Fort Fisher, which protected Wilmington, North Carolina, the South's only remaining major Atlantic seaport. The fort, the largest of three protecting the city, was known as the "Gibraltar of the South." Fort Fisher was a sprawling earthen bastion with walls 20 to 30 feet high with a length of over 1,300 yards along its ocean side. Timely Confederate reinforcements blunted the initial phase of the assault and the few troops that landed were taken off. The regiment did not see action. The First USCT returned and disembarked at Jones Landing, Virginia on December 28, 1864, and went back into camp at Varina.

General Grant relieved General Butler of command after the failure of the attack on Fort Fisher. Major General Alfred Terry was placed in command of a "provisional corps" consisting of 8,000 black and white soldiers culled mostly from the 24th and 25th Army Corps. On January 4, 1865, the First USCT sailed from Bermuda Landing onboard the steamer "Champion" with the rest of Terry's fleet of about 60 vessels and over 600 guns. Each man carried 40 rounds in his cartridge box and three days cooked rations in his haversack. Stormy weather delayed the fleets' arrival until January 12. On the morning of the next day, the First along with the 5th, 10th, 27th, and 37th USCT, shaking off a bout of overnight sea-sickness and dodging a strong undertow, landed in high surf on the sandy beach. The brigade, one of two brigades of black infantry in the landing, lined up and moved out across Federal Point, the narrow peninsula separating Fort Fisher from the Cape Fear River behind it. About two and a half miles from the fort, the brigade constructed two lines of breastworks in anticipation of a rebel counterattack, "which ended in a mere demonstration.

On January 14 and 15, the First USCT assisted in the landing of large and small pieces of artillery and digging gun emplacements. The regiment camped in those breastworks for the rest of the month. Chaplain Turner, meanwhile, was on detached assignment as an aide to the medical director. He landed with the attacking party and saw the bloody story of the fort.

"The fort had been ploughed by our shells until everything looked like a heap of destruction," he wrote. "All the barracks had been burned to the ground and dead bodies were lying in desperate confusion in every direction.... Guns of the largest caliber had been broken to pieces and their carriages swept from under them. The wounded were groaning and begging for assistance."

The care of the regiments' wounded and sick finally appeared stable with the return of regimental surgeon Jacob R. Weist in January 1865. He had initially been assigned in November 1864 but was ordered to the 18th Army Corps Base Hospital at Point of Rocks, Virginia. In December, again due to the shortage of physicians, he was made medical director of the 25th Army Corps.

Sickness and injuries from frequent spells of prolonged fatigue duty, battle-related casualties, and a series of unfit surgeons had made quality medical care a near impossibility. As surgeons had come and gone, Charles V. Sands, a Hospital Steward, was the only consistent provider of care. Assigned to the regiment on April 16, 1864, he had assisted the parade of physicians as best he could but he was not a trained doctor. Little more than medics, hospital stewards were supposed to be temperate, honest, reliable, "sufficiently intelligent and skilled in pharmacy." Army regulations provided for the appointment of ordinary soldiers as temporary stewards. This was, of course, only a stopgap measure. Several enlisted men were, at various times, appointed as nurses or stewards. Private Philip Brookins served as a nurse from July 20, 1863 to May 11, 1864.

For the rest of January, the First USCT fended off rebel probes. Private Sandy Gordon, a resident of Alexandria, Virginia, was killed in a skirmish on January 17. On January 19 Private Charles Brown, a sharpshooter, was wounded in the chest at Half Moon Battery. Private Horace Greely died on January 31 from wounds he had received on January 15. (A letter from his grief-stricken mother located in his compiled service record is in the Documents Section) .

THE UNITED STATES, In account with _William Douglass_, of [ ] Company,
First Regiment of _U. S. Col. Troops_, on account of Clothing during his enlistment; the money value of each issue being acknowledged.   ENLISTED at _____ on the ___ day of _____ 1864.

DATE OF ISSUE	MONEY VALUE Dolls.	Cts.	RANK	SIGNATURE	WITNESS
July 4th 1863	31	60		William Douglass	Edward Simonton 2d Lieut
July 25th "	1	96		William X Douglass	Edward Simonton
Aug. 15 "	2	55		William X Douglass	Edward Simonton
Sep. 7 "	7	37		William X Douglass	Edward Simonton
November 1863	6	71		William X Douglass	Edward Simonton
December 1863	4	67		William X Douglass	Edward Simonton
January 1864	2	40		William X Douglass	Edward Simonton
March 1864	3	44		William x Douglass	Nathan L. Bishop 1st Lieut
April 1864		32		William Douglass	Nathan L. Bishop "
				24 67 Charged on Muster & Pay Roll Apr. 30 /64	
May 1864	5	17		William x Douglass	Nathan L. Bishop 1st Lieut
June 1864		32		William x Douglass	Nathan L. Bishop "
	66 11 -42.35= 23.76			Charged on Rolls Aug 31/64	Settled August 31 1864
July 1864	5	45	Corporal	William Douglass	Nathan L. Bishop
November 1864	9	60	"	William Douglass	A. H. Davis Capt
September 1864	10	90	"	William Douglass	A. H. Davis "
March 1865	2	70	"	William Douglass	A. H. Davis "
April 7 1865		96	"	William Douglass	A. H. Davis "
May 15 1865	12	67	"	William Douglass	Frank Otto Lieut
July 1865	22	12	Sergeant	William Douglass	Frank Otto Lieut

Mustered Out Sept. 29th 1865

A. H. Davis
Capt.   Commanding Company.

Clothing account record of William Douglass (A married, native Washingtonian who rose to the rank of sergeant).

On February 11, 1865, the regiment was part of the federal column that engaged the enemy near Sugar Loaf Mountain, a towering cone-shaped peak of stone dotted with stubby trees about six miles north of Fort Fisher. The Confederates were pushed back to their primary lines. Eight days later orders came down to pursue the rebels as they retired toward Wilmington. On February 20 less than 10 miles outside the city, the regiment slammed into strong rebel positions. Second Lieutenant Charles Barr, who had been a first sergeant in the 98th Regiment, New York Volunteers, died of wounds he received in the battle. Private Peter Lee was killed in action by an artillery shell. Fifty one officers and enlisted men were wounded. One of the wounded was Private Edward Henry whose "left foot was carried away by a solid shot." He received a disability discharge that October.

The regiment, with the rest of the column, passed through Wilmington, North Carolina on February 22. Wilmington had been the main haven for the sleek Confederate blockade runners. The state's principal seaport and largest city, it was also the site of Berry's shipyard also known as the Confederate Navy Yard. In 1862, the ironclad "North Carolina" was built there. The city's strategic importance was amplified because it was linked to three railroads and from its docks the Cape Fear River was navigable for 100 miles. Once known as the "life line of the Confederacy," Wilmington fell without resistance. The black troops striding through the streets were surrounded by the cheers and prayers of the city's black residents. A journalist for the *Philadelphia Inquirer* recounted the scene: "The men danced in jubilation, the women screamed and went into hysterics then and there on the sidewalks. And their sable brothers in arms marched past, proud and erect, singing their John Brown hymn, where it was never known." A number of local blacks gave important information on rebel troop movements and stockpiles to Union forces as they marched through the area.[23]

The First USCT arrived at Northeast Station and camped there until March 15. The next day, the regiment was part of a force marching north toward Goldsboro, a farm town over 80 miles away on the muddy Neuse River in tobacco country. The advance took six days. The regiment

occupied the city on March 21. On March 23 the regiment crossed the
Neuse and threw up breastworks. Two days later the regiment repulsed
a light attack. Regimental headquarters was established at Warsaw Station
on March 29. While guarding freedmen at Warsaw Station, Private
Andrew Gibson was killed by rebel guerillas.

On April 9, 1865, General Lee surrendered his forces at Appomatox. A
Confederate Army under General Joseph E. Johnston was still active. At
that time Johnston's forces were larger than those surrendered by Lee. On
April 10, the regiment, now part of the First Brigade, Third Division, 10th
Army Corps, turned northwest toward Raleigh. The regiment reached the
city on the afternoon of April 14. Union General William T. Sherman had
crossed into North Carolina in early March. His forces joined with those
at Goldsboro and the First USCT was part of a force of some 60,000 that
occupied the city. Sherman's mission was to join with Grant in Virginia.
Raleigh, the capital, sat in a wooded expanse on a hill near the
geographical center of the state. Once a focal point for Confederate troops
and munitions, Raleigh fell without a battle.

The town was also the birthplace of Vice President Andrew Johnson.
Encamped about a mile or two from the city, the regiment learned on April
16 of Lincoln's assassination the previous day. Outraged and
disconsolate, the members of the regiment, like all the Federal troops in
the area, wore badges of mourning in honor of the slain president. The
First USCT, with the rest of the division, marched back to Raleigh and
passed in review in front of General Sherman, a well known critic of black
enlistment.[24]

Medical problems in the First USCT surfaced yet again in April, 1865.
Sands, the hospital steward, was ordered to report to Dr. Mitchell at the
10th Army Corps field hospital. Holman requested his return in a June 8,
1865 letter to Lieutenant Colonel J.A. Campbell, the assistant Adjutant
General of the Department of North Carolina: "for the reason that his
services are much needed at this post. One assistant surgeon is the only
medical officer connected with my command. He will have charge of the
post hospital at this point and in the absence of all other medical aid it is

highly necessary that he have the assistance that could be afforded him by Hospital Steward Sands." Weist had been relieved from regimental duty in May 1865 to take charge of a hospital at Goldsboro. He remained on the regiment's rolls. In June, Assistant Surgeon Samuel Bell, who had just received his commission, joined the regiment.

The regiment was just outside Raleigh when Johnston surrendered to Sherman 30 miles away at Bennett House on April 26, 1865. It was there that the largest troop surrender of the American Civil War took place. The war in the Carolinas was over. April 26 was also the same day John Wilkes Booth, Lincoln's assassin was caught and killed.

The First USCT returned to Goldsboro, having passed through Smithfield, a tobacco town on the Neuse River. The regiment paused there April 29 - May 1 for muster and moved on. Holman rejoined the regiment in May. In early June as part of federal occupation forces, the regiment left Goldsboro and was placed at strategic points at or on the Outer Banks. Companies A & F were sent to Fort Hatteras on Hatteras Inlet, the principal inlet on the North Carolina coast. Company B was dispatched to Plymouth at the mouth of the Roanoke River. Company K guarded the Coinjock Bridge near Currituck. The rest of the regiment sailed to Roanoke Island, a strip of land 12 miles long and about three miles wide in Roanoke Sound. Duty on the Outer Banks was dull, monotonous, and remote compared to units posted near town. With the fighting over, Holman sought to relax pass and duty rules. Soldiers were allowed in town as long as proper military bearing and courtesy toward former Confederates were observed. The few who violated the rules, for example, theft or drunkenness, were punished with court-martials, losses of pay and allowances, and time at hard labor. Holman then limited passes to the best soldiers from each company. Many men spent their off duty time studying and thinking about the profound changes that had occurred in the last two years of their lives. But it was the future that was uppermost in their dreams and expectations.

Company I was posted to Edenton during July and August 1865. Edenton, a picturesque hamlet on a peninsula flanked by creeks that fed

Albermarle Sound, had been occupied by Union troops since February 1862. Company C was ordered back to familiar territory - Elizabeth City - at the same time.

On September 29, 1865, the men were assembled at their respective locations. The clerks hauled out the muster rolls. The men nervously joked and jostled each other. Then they stood to attention. A close roll was called and formal muster was taken with certificates written for those absent. Account books were checked, pay, casualties, and promotions were listed and verified. The men were informed that the government no longer needed their services. Thirty three officers and 768 enlisted men were mustered out of federal service. The regiment was returning to Washington City for a formal ceremony. Shouts, handshakes, prayers, and handclaps rent the air.

Going home was a dream no more.

CHAPTER III

REVEREND HENRY McNEAL TURNER

"First ...let us see him as chaplain of the United States Army, commissioned by the illustrious Lincoln to go in the field amidst the smoke and fire of contending armies and do service for his country, his God, and his race. Did he shrink, and say, I can't go? No. Such words never fell from the lips of Bishop Turner. He regards no sacrifice too great, no peril too dangerous, no enemy too hostile when duty calls."

Rev. Alfred Lee Ridgel,
Africa And African Methodism

In 1862, at the age of 28, Reverend Henry McNeal Turner took the helm of Israel Bethel Church, the first African Methodist Episcopal Church in Washington City. It had been a long way from Newberry Court House, South Carolina to a church in the nation's capital. Turner was born free on February 1, 1834.[1] His parents Hardy and Sarah nurtured his innate spirituality and nascent racial pride by telling him stories of his mother's noble African blood. Her father, David Greer, was the son of a king who was kidnaped, enslaved, and brought to the colony of South Carolina. Before his death around 1819, he obtained his freedom. His commanding presence and scrupulous reputation were recalled with pride and warmth by blacks throughout that portion of the county. Greer's wife, Hannah, was known for a volcanic temper and legendary strength. One historian described Turner's grandmother: "No one in the neighborhood of her dwelling ever dared interfere with her children, animals, fences, or anything that she owned at the risk of being fearfully handled, if she got within reach of them."[2]

Newberry was the county seat of Newberry County which had been established in 1785 as a section of Ninety Six District in the central uplands of the Palmetto State. By the mid-1700's the rich stands of timber and verdant farmlands had been largely settled by English, Scotch-Irish, and Germans many of whom had brought their slaves from the low country. Cotton farming had also begun to make an appearance in the country by the time of Turner's birth.

In the 1830's all throughout the South, state governments, driven by the news of Nat Turner's rebellion and by rumors of plots and revolts within their own borders, passed laws banning any teaching of slaves, restricting black preachers, outlawing the use of whistles, drums, and other musical instruments, and curtailing the manumission of blacks. In South Carolina it also became unlawful to keep a school for the teaching of free blacks. The penalty was a fine up to $100 and imprisonment up to six months for whites and a $50 fine and 50 lashes for free blacks or slaves. The informer was declared a competent witness and given one-half of the fine.[3]

Free blacks, like Turner's family, constantly walked a tightrope of suspicion and fear. Seen always by the authorities as potential leaders of revolts, their very existence vexed those who believed in the utter enslavement and inferiority of blacks. Added to this hardship was the loss of Turner's father about this same time. The absence of a good father is a hard blow to any family even in the best of times. Those were, however, far from the best times and conditions. His father's death also represented a catastrophic blow to his family's already fragile economic condition. Turner was no stranger to long, wearying labor. Often working alongside slaves, he had picked cotton in the merciless sun and pounded an anvil as a blacksmith's apprentice. He had contributed to his family's meager larder from his earliest days. What the loss of his father really represented to him was the theft of a male parent's protective, nurturing care. And, as a fatherless poverty-stricken lad, he could be gravely exploited and abused. But something in his young character gave him the strength to resist his circumstances:

> He generally whipped all the overseers that tried to whip him, knowing that he was free-born and could never be legally reduced to slavery. He was determined that no white man should scar his back with a lash, and from the time he was thirteen years old till he reached manhood he resented every attempt to whip him, though grown men and women were whipped around him in many instances from the rising of the sun until the going down of the same.[4]

Something else was happening to this young man; not simply his battle to keep whole his own mind and body. There were stirrings in his spirit as well. His friend and fellow bishop, Benjamin T. Tanner described an important event:

> It is said that at the tender age of twelve, he had a dream in which he saw multitudes of men coming to him to be taught. That dream made an impression that followed him to the

present time, and no doubt had much influence in shaping the course of his life. He was licensed to preach before he had reached his twenty-first year.[5]

But much would have to happen before he answered the Lord's call. He had always hungered for knowledge. He craved the secrets of books. But how to get them and how to unlock the power of words? Though not legally a slave, Turner knew that state law manacled him as firmly to ignorance as any slave. As he worked, he formed a plan to liberate his dreams:

> He procured a spelling book, and an old white lady and a white boy with whom he played, taught him the alphabet and how to spell as far as two syllables; but one day the boy's father seeing him instructing Turner, told him that he had no right to teach a Negro, and that he was violating the law of the State in doing so, and if he undertook such a task any further he would receive severe punishment. This threat so frightened his boy teacher as to deprive him of the lessons thereafter. Many days did he weep over this, but he was compelled to submit to fate.
>
> Soon he found an old colored man who did not know a letter but was a prodigy in sounds. The ambitious Turner would spell the words as they were syllabified, and the man could pronounce them accurately. Thus his unlettered instructor helped him to spell and pronounce words about half through the old Webster's spelling book. But another misfortune awaited him. This teacher was removed to another plantation and he was again without an instructor. He was doomed to weep more bitterly than at first.[6]

The following Sunday, Turner went to church. At some point in the service, he heard the preacher tell his flock that whatever you ask God for in faith will be granted. Only thirteen years old, he began to fast and pray that God would grant him a way to learn. Somehow, his mother found a white woman willing to teach him what she knew for a few hours every

Sunday. But almost as soon as they began, the lessons were ended when the woman was threatened by her neighbors that her activities on the little boy's behalf would be reported to the authorities.

On his own now but with the barest gleanings of knowledge, Turner worked all day but committed each night to intensive prayer and study until he could hardly keep his eyes open:

> I would kneel down and pray, and ask the Lord to teach me what I was not able to understand myself, and as soon as I would fall asleep an angelic personage would appear with open book in hand and teach me how to pronounce every word that I failed in pronouncing while awake, and on each subsequent day the lessons given me in my dreams would be better understood than any other portions of the lessons. This angelic teacher, or dream teacher, at all events, carried me through the old Webster's spelling book and thus enabled me to read the Bible and hymn book.

> I may note at this point, however, that this angelic teacher would never come to my assistance at night unless I would study the lessons with my greatest effort and kneel down and pray for God's assistance before going to sleep. So familiar did the features of general appearance of my angelic, or dream teacher become to me, that if I should ever meet it in the spirit world I would readily recognize it.

> By the latter end of my fifteenth year I was providentially employed to wait around an office of a number of white lawyers at Abbeville court-house, where I filled the exalted station of fire making, room sweeping, boot blacking, etc. I soon won the favor of every lawyer in the office, especially the younger portion of them. My tenacious memory being such an object of curiosity, I soon attracted special attention. They thought it was marvelous that a common Negro boy could carry any message however, many words it contained or

figures it involved, and repeat them as accurately as if written upon paper. In many cases, too, these messages contained a multiplicity of the highest law terms. The sequel of this and much more night study was, those lawyers taught me, in defiance of State laws forbidding it, to read accurately, history, theology and even works on law. Also taught me arithmetic, geography, astronomy and anything I desired to know except English grammar, which I manifested no desire to study.

I shall always regard my contact with those lawyers, and the assistance given by the young lawyers of the office, as an answer to my prayer.[7]

In 1848, he "joined" the Methodist Episcopal Church South, on a probationary period and as he would laughingly later recall he "must still be on probation" because he was never fully accepted into membership. Not without good reason would Turner refer to South Carolina as that "pestiferous state of my nativity." The Methodist Episcopal Church in the United States had split into southern and northern conferences in 1845 in the wake of Georgia bishop James O. Andrew's refusal to give up his slaves or resign his bishopric.

In 1853, after much inner struggle, he felt the need to proclaim God's message and was licensed to preach by a Rev. Boyd at the Abbeville Court House. For four years Turner preached throughout the South. In 1856 he married Eliza Ann Peacher. He left the M.E. Church South the following year and joined the AME Church. It was here that Turner came under the guidance of Bishop Daniel A. Payne, a fellow South Carolinian who like Turner was born of free parents, joined the Methodist Episcopal Church South, and taught, preached, and pastored in South Carolina - which he was forced to leave for the crime of teaching blacks. Payne had joined African Methodism in 1841 and by the late 1850s, had emerged as one of the denomination's leading intellectuals.

Bantam-sized with a large forehead and thick wire rimmed glasses Payne, had, by various means, including a private tutor, attained a formidable education including the study of the classics and fluency in Latin, Greek, and French. To him, a relentless scholar with lofty, demanding standards, knowledge literally was greater than gold. This was, he believed, the chief reason that slaveholders resisted educating their bondsmen while nevertheless proclaiming them incapable of learning.

Payne guided this pivotal phase of Turner's education. He placed him in the hands of a succession of professors and theologians steadily cultivating his mind and preparing him for greater work. Payne sent him to Baltimore not only to run a small mission but also to acquire a much needed formal education at Trinity College. Turner impressed his professors with the power of his preaching style. It was equally clear to them, however, that in order to be as effective as he could, his grammar - in which he had no interest in Abbeville - would have to be improved. This he accomplished with speed and purpose.

For the next four years, the young preacher received lessons in Latin, Greek, German, and theology. Turner took a special course in elocution from Bishop Cummings of the Protestant Episcopal Church. Rabbi Ginsburg instructed him in Hebrew. Turner discovered he had a prodigious memory and an incandescent love of learning. He also traveled with Payne to AME churches and missions in Washington and Georgetown, Payne ordaining him a deacon there in 1860.

This was familiar territory for the AME church and Payne. In 1818 Richard Allen, a founder of the denomination, dispatched Reverend David Smith to establish a presence in Washington City. In less than six months, they had assembled a handful of worshippers on Capitol Hill, first at Basil Sims' Ropewalk at 3rd and Pennsylvania Avenue, S.E. Later they briefly prayed at Rev. Mr. Wheat's schoolhouse a short walk away near Virginia Avenue. By the 1820's many of these early members were refugees from a nearby white church, Ebenezer Methodist Episcopal. There African American Methodists wanted a greater role in shaping their own religious destiny and to be free of the humiliating restrictions they had to endure when they worshiped with whites. All over the city blacks in white churches had to enter and leave by side doors, were restricted to church balconies which they often had to reach by outside stairs, endured segregated communion services, chafed at the hypocrisy of receiving moral direction from slaveowning pastors, and frequently saw their children refused baptism by white ministers reluctant to place their hands on black skin. Several of Smith's congregants were leaders of the city's black community: William Costin, William Datcher, George Bell and Alethia Tanner.

Payne, also a carpenter, helped build pews for the congregation's next home, a wood frame church near the intersection of New Jersey Avenue and South Capitol Street. City law discouraged the immigration of free blacks like Payne. He had to first obtain a bond of a thousand dollars before he could even continue his ministerial duties. Christened Israel Bethel, this church would become one of the two predecessor churches of Metropolitan AME, a citadel of the denomination whose building at 1518 M Street, N.W., was completed in 1886 and still stands today.

Israel Bethel's size steadily increased in the next few decades as did that of African Methodism in the District of Columbia. And along the way a unique relationship was forged between the new sect and the 15th Street Presbyterian Church.

John F. Cook, Sr. is best known as the founder of the 15th Street Presbyterian Church in 1841. What is less well known is that Cook first began preaching at Israel Bethel around 1838. That same year he led a group of members out of the church to form Union Bethel AME Church (the other predecessor of Metropolitan AME). Minutes of the meeting of the Union Bethel Society are among the Cook Family Papers at the Moorland-Spingarn Research Center at Howard University and indicate that the split was amicable and "volentary." The primary reason seems to have been the distance members "residing in the western of the city" had to travel, usually by foot, to get to church. The members of Union Bethel agreed to make contributions "...to pay for lot No. 5 on K Street between 15th and 16th Streets."[8]

Cook's ties to the AME church were familial and spiritual. He was also related by marriage to Absalom Jones, who with Richard Allen had founded, "The African Church" (later St. Thomas African Episcopal Church) in Philadelphia in 1791. Jones assisted in the consecration of Richard Allen as the first bishop of the AME church in 1816.

Cook's search for spiritual growth and contentment, however, had one more turn to make. In 1840, he left Union Bethel to found what became known the following year as the First Colored Presbyterian Church and subsequently as the 15th Street Presbyterian Church. His reasons for switching are unclear but it is known that a number of black Presbyterians had begun attending church services at his schoolhouse and wanted to establish a separate congregation to allow themselves to practice their faith with greater control and dignity. Cook remained head of the church until his death in 1855.

In 1856, in Georgetown, 13 members left Mt. Zion Methodist Episcopal Church, the oldest black congregation in Washington, D.C. In their desire for culturally fulfilling worship and guidance they chose African Methodism. The congregation became known as Ebenezer AME Church. To the Reverend Alexander Wayman goes the credit of founding and guiding the little church in its infancy. The building at 2727 O Street, N.W., still stands and today houses the Episcopal Heritage Church. Ebenezer relocated to the Maryland suburbs and now has a congregation of over 5,000 members.

In 1860 Payne took the extraordinary step of permitting another young AME minister he was grooming to accept a temporary "supply" pastorship at the 15th Street Presbyterian Church. His name was Benjamin Tucker Tanner. Only a year younger than Turner, with whom he would maintain a life long friendship, Tanner was a free-born, self-taught barber who had briefly attended Avery College and a seminary in his native Pennsylvania before joining the AME church. Like Payne, Tanner was short, barely above five feet. A good preacher, high-spirited, Tanner was in the process

of discovering his own impressive literary gifts which made him in many
ways the inheritor of the intellectual tradition of church leadership begun
by Payne.

In September, 1860, Tanner stepped into the pulpit of the presbyterian
church to speak for the first time and noted in his diaries that "I preached
for them twice today and they were much delighted indeed." His wife and
18 month old son Henry, who would become a renowned painter, joined
him in Washington. Tanner served a year and a half as pastor. Then Payne
chose him to head the Alexander Mission on E Street, N.W., the
denomination's first domestic mission at the time. Payne later sent him
to Georgetown and then Frederick, Maryland.

* * * * * * * *

Turner was married and the father of two sons, David and John, when
he became pastor of Israel Bethel. The family took lodgings near the
Capitol. Literally at the foot of Capitol Hill on B Street (now
Independence Avenue) near South Capitol Street, the church was fast
progressing from its modest beginnings. The former quarters of the First
Presbyterian Church, a white congregation that traced its roots back to
1804, had been purchased (square 636, lot 13) and improved.

Turner presented quite a figure at the lectern. Writing just a few years
later, William Wells Brown depicted him as "a good sized, fine looking,
brown-skinned man ...with a splendid voice, fluent in speech, pleasing in
gestures, and powerful in delivery."[9]

Beginning in 1862, the young minister would have to call on all his
budding skills as he guided his flock through one of the most tumultuous
periods in the history of the city. Slavery reigned. War thundered. And
portents of greater change rode the winds.

Israel Bethel's members were slave and free, laborers and
washerwomen, hackmen, servants, cooks and carpenters, waiters and
mechanics. By at least one estimate, Turner's church had 500 members

making it the second largest church in the city behind Asbury AME at 11th and K Streets, N.W., with 600 souls.[10]

Based on city directions and news accounts (1860-62) this is a list of major Black churches scattered across the city (exclusive of Georgetown):

The Nineteenth Street Baptist Church -- 19th and I Streets, N.W.
Second Colored Baptist Church -- 3rd and I Streets, N.W.
Asbury African Methodist Episcopal -- 11th and K Streets, N.W.
John Wesley Church -- Connecticut Avenue at M Streets, N.W.
Island Baptist Church -- 6th and G Streets, S.W.
Little Ebenezer Methodist Episcopal -- 4th and D Streets, S.E.
Union Bethel African Methodist Episcopal -- 15th and M Streets, N.W.
Union Wesley Chapel -- 23rd and L Streets, N.W.
15th Street Presbyterian Church -- 15th between I and K Streets, N.W.
Zion Wesley Chapel - 2nd and D Streets, S.W.
Israel Bethel African Methodist Episcopal -- South Capitol and B Streets, S.W.

Next door to Israel Bethel stood its Lyceum, named after a place near Athens in whose shaded precincts Aristotle taught; school house, lecture hall, it functioned as a house of knowledge. Art, science, religion, and politics were all assayed and dissected there. During the organization of the regiment, the Lyceum served as recruiting center, training hall, and examination room (see Chapter One). The building's multi-purpose areas were emblematic of an underlying reality about the function of the church in the black community: the church was the religious sun around which secular issues and institutions orbited.

Between 1862 and 1864 the Lyceum hosted such personages as the black abolitionist and recruiter Charles Lenox Remond, Robert Smalls, the pilot of the "Planter," Bishop Payne, and a number of well known Republican Congressmen and Senators including Henry Wilson (later Vice President) of Massachusetts, Ben Wade of Ohio, Owen Lovejoy of Illinois, and Thaddeus Steven of Pennsylvania. Turner was astute enough to nurture these influential contacts through visits, letters, and gifts.

Even before the arrival of thousands of self emancipated blacks in the nation's capital, Israel Bethel's role as a social service provider had been well defined. Few blacks anywhere in the city were financially well off. Wages of a dollar or two a day were the standard for laborers and domestics. The prosperity boomlet just before the war had skipped most of the black residents locked as they were into the least profitable, disproportionately arduous jobs. Racism and segregation cast a corrosive pall over the city and built a legacy of distrust and hostility still evident today. Of the 11,131 blacks in the District in 1860, only 10 percent owned property. The city refused to educate African Americans. There were no public schools for black children. Although blacks paid taxes for public education, the money went to educate white students only. Yet the number of black children of school age (2,585) exceeded the total number of white children (2,326) enrolled in the city's 30 public schools. Six hundred seventy eight black children had received some instruction that year in church run Sabbath schools, seminaries, academies, through tutors, and other privately run schools such as the one operated by Mrs. Charlotte Gordon, a black woman on 8th Street, N.W. Mrs. Gordon, assisted by her daughter, had as many as 150 students at a time. George Bell and Enoch Ambush ran a large school in the basement of Israel Bethel that lasted 32 years.[11]

While no law expressly banned education for District blacks, white opinion and custom were largely against it. Now generally forgotten are the efforts of a local white politician Jesse E. Dow, who in the late 1840s supported the establishment of free schools for white and black children. He had backed Charles Middleton, a black teacher, who had a popular school downtown between 15th and 16th Streets, N.W. When Dow ran for mayor and his opinion on black education was revealed his political career was ruined. Freedman's Bureau records show that black schools and churches in the city were particular targets of thugs and vandals well past the end of the Civil War.

Turner threw himself into the fight against slavery in the city. As pastor he became aware of the personal plight of the slave members of his congregation. He saw suffering that called to mind his boyhood days in

South Carolina: seeing families sold apart, ministering to lash-scarred bodies, and opposing the poisonous toll that slavery's code and custom could exact on the human spirit. He joined with the local ministers council, abolitionists, and friendly politicians, to agitate an end to the "national shame" of human bondage in the seat of liberty. With emancipation a reality in the city, "Elder" Turner led his flock to serve the needs of the freedmen coming to the capital.

They formed the Union Relief Association of Israel Bethel. On November 8, 1862, the organization published an appeal in the denomination's newspaper, The *Christian Recorder*. They enclosed a copy of their constitution and asked that "... in the name of humanity, and the ties that bind us together in the bonds of a common brotherhood, you will give us all the aid in your power by contributing clothing for adults or children...bedding or bed clothing, old or new, money, as any nourishment for the sick will be thoughtfully received by the association. The freedmen were described as "poor, destitute, and suffering...without a covering or place to rest their heads upon at night, except the cold earth."

The association merely formalized Israel Bethel's efforts. Earlier that year on April 30th, $61 had been collected for these refugees from war and slavery who were also called "contrabands." This name applied to any former slave, who escaped to or was brought within Union lines and was therefore considered "contraband of war."

In October, Turner painted the following picture in the *Recorder*:

> The great quantity of contrabands (so-called), who have fled from the oppressor's rod, and are now thronging Old Point Comfort, Hilton Head, Washington City, and many other places, and the unnumbered host who shall soon be freed by the President's proclamation, are to materially change their political and social condition. The day of our inactivity, disinterestedness, and irresponsibility, has given place to a day in which our long cherished abilities, and every intellectual fibre of our being, are to be called in to a sphere of requisition.

The time for boasting of ancestral genius, and prowling through the dusty pages of ancient history to find a specimen of Negro intellectuality is over. Such useless noise should now be lulled, while we turn our attention to an engagement with those means which much, and alone can, mold out and develop those religious, literary, and pecuniary resources, adapted to the grave expediency now about to be encountered.

Thousands of contrabands, now at the places above designated, are in a condition of the extremest suffering. We see them in droves every day perambulating the streets of Washington, homeless, shoeless, dressless, and moneyless. ...Every man of us now, who has a speck of grace or bit of sympathy, for the race that we are inseparably identified with, is called upon by force of surrounding circumstances, to extend a hand of mercy to bone of our bone and flesh of our flesh. ...

The proclamation of President Lincoln has banished the fog, and silenced the doubt. ...We have stood still and seen the salvation of God, while we besought Him with teary eyes and bleeding hearts; but the stand-still day bid us adieu September 22, 1862. A new era, a new dispensation of things, is now upon us - to action, to action, is the cry. We must now begin to think to plan, and to legislate for ourselves.[12]

The proclamation Turner referred to was the preliminary Emancipation Proclamation, issued on September 22, 1862. Now the President's intent was clear. What had begun as a war to reunite the Union was also now a war to end slavery. Freedom would come at the first moment of the first day of the next year. Not a practical freedom, for most, the document was essentially symbolic but few men or women, black or white, doubted its historic impact. "A new dispensation of things is now upon us," Turner wrote.

The New Year's Eve watch night service at Israel Bethel drew an immense throng filled with anticipation. Recalling the events of that long day fifty years later in 1913, on the half century anniversary of the proclamation Turner wrote:

> Long before sunset Israel Church and its yard were crowded with people. The writer was vociferously cheered in every direction he went because in a sermon I tried to deliver I had said that Richmond, the headquarters of the Southern Confederacy, would never fall till black men led the army against this great slave- market nor did it fall and succumb to the general government till black men went in first. This was only a popular prediction, and delivered under a general excitement, but strange to say, it was fully realized.
>
> Seeing such a multitude of people in and around my church, I hurriedly went up to the office of the first paper in which the proclamation of freedom could be printed, known as the *Evening Star,* and squeezed myself through the dense crowd that was waiting for the paper. The first sheet run off with the proclamation in it was grabbed for by three of us, but some active young man got possession of it and fled. The next sheet was grabbed for by several, and was torn into tatters. The third sheet from the press was grabbed for by several, but I succeeded in procuring so much of it as contained the proclamation, and off I went for life and death. Down Pennsylvania I ran as for my life, and when the people saw me coming with the paper in my hand they raised a shouting cheer that was almost deafening. As many as could get around me lifted me to a great platform, and I started to read the proclamation. I had run the best end of a mile, I was out of breath, and could not read. Mr. Hinton, to whom I handed the paper, read it with great force and clearness. While he was reading every kind of demonstration and gesticulation was going on. Men squealed, women fainted, dogs barked, white and colored people shook hands, songs were sung, and by this

time cannons began to fire at the navy-yard, and follow in the
wake of the roar that had for some time been going on behind
the White House. ...Great processions of colored and white
men marched to and fro and passed in front of the White
House and congratulated President Lincoln on his
proclamation. The president came to the window and made
responsive bows, and thousands told him, if he would come
out of that palace, they would hug him to death. Mr. Lincoln,
however, kept at a safe distance from the multitude, who were
frenzied to distraction over his proclamation. ...It was indeed
a time of times, and a half time, nothing like it will ever be
seen again in his life."[13]

On January 4th, Turner opined:

The time has come in the history of this nation when the
downtrodden and abject black man can assert his rights and
feel his manhood. ...The first day of January, 1863 is destined
to form one of the most memorable epochs in the history of the
world. ...The seeds of freedom which are ever rejuvenescent in
themselves, have now been scattered where despotism and
tyranny ranked and ruled, will be watered by the enlivening
laws of God's clemency, till the reapers (abolitionists) shall
shout the harvest home.[14]

The proclamation had shattered Turner's initial skepticism about
Lincoln. Like many in the black community, Turner had become weary
and wary of the President's hesitancy in delivering what they considered
such a bold and obvious stroke against the Confederacy. At one point he
had referred to Lincoln as a "mystic Pharaoh...[who] hardened his heart"
thwarting early efforts by Union generals Fremont and Hunter to
emancipate and enlist blacks in the field.

Rev. H.M. Turner, Chaplain, First United States Colored Troops, (*Harper's Weekly*, December 12, 1863)

In the early days of the war, Turner had watched in horror as the long trains of ambulance wagons filled the streets carrying wounded soldiers to the growing number of hospitals dotting the city's hilltops and boulevards.

He grieved over the loss of life caused by the war. He called secession a "hell-forged schism." As early as August 1862, Turner had supported the use of African American troops as a means to bring both the war and slavery to a definitive end. The emancipation proclamation, Turner understood, was not the end but the means to the end. Beyond its symbolism, the document effectively provided for freedmen "...to be received into the armed service of the United States, to garrison forts, positions, stations, and other places, and to man vessels of all sorts in said service."*

Turner resolved to become chaplain of the regiment from the first days of its organization in May 1863. Already widely known as a leader, some historians believe he had first hoped for an officer's commission but soon realized the War Department's opposition to black men in command positions. But there was no mistaking Turner's pride in being allowed to serve the regiment as chaplain. He did so unofficially for several months before receiving his commission and he opened his church as a recruiting center. The road to his chaplaincy was tedious and difficult.

That Turner met the official qualifications and duties for army chaplain - now that African Americans were formally accepted into Federal service - cannot be doubted. According to initial army regulations a chaplain had only to be "a regularly ordained minister of some Christian denomination." His chief duty was to issue quarterly reports to the colonel of his regiment on "the moral and religious condition of the regiment, and such suggestions as may conduce to the social happiness and moral improvement of the troops."[15]

*Turner's involvement in recruiting men for the 1st Regiment United States Colored Troops is covered in Chapter One.

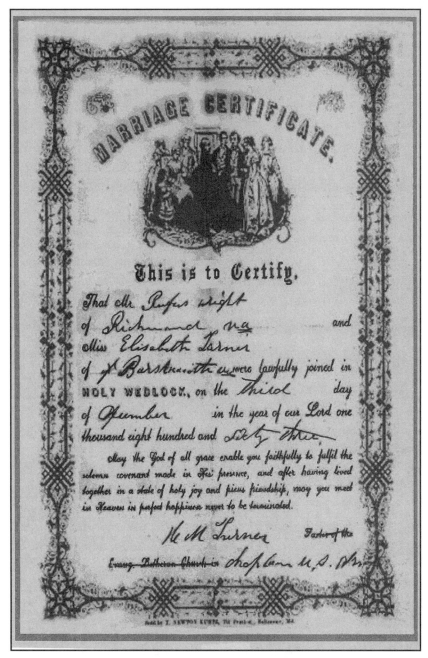

Marriage certificate of Private Rufus Wright and Elisabeth Turner
bearing Chaplain Turner's signature.

Turner submitted his request for the chaplaincy in May of 1863 accompanied by a letter of endorsement signed by five of his colleagues. An undated copy is in his compiled service record (see Documents Section). On August 1, 1863, with the regiment having departed the city for training in North Carolina, Turner wrote to the Secretary of War (see Documents Section). Increasingly impatient and concerned about missing service with the regiment, he wrote to the Secretary of War again on August 24, 1863. Around this time he must have begun to lobby his contacts on Capitol Hill and in the executive branch because the Secretary of Treasury and an Illinois congressman who had spoken at Israel Bethel co-signed a letter of endorsement (see Documents Section).

Exactly when Turner received his commission is in doubt. Despite the repeated claim that he was the first black army chaplain, there is disagreement on the date of his commission. The *Official Army Register of Volunteer Officers* lists the date of Turner's commissioning as November 16, 1863. Berlin, et al., *Black Military Experience*, gives November 6, 1863. The *Colored Chaplain* and Turner's compiled military service record at the National Archives indicate he was appointed by President Lincoln on September 10, 1863. Still other works on black officers have listed Turner's commission as dated December 2, 1863.

A valuable clue toward the confirmation of the September 10th date lies in a signed copy of a letter in Turner's service record. Dated October 9, 1863, the letter is from Major C. W. Foster, Chief of the Bureau of Colored Troops, to Colonel Holman. In addition to requesting a roster of the regiment's first lieutenants, Foster clearly mentions Turner's September 10th appointment as chaplain and indicates that he "...has not yet sent in his acceptance. If he has joined for duty, please direct him to forward acceptance immediately." The September date would make Turner the first African American to receive a federal chaplain's commission. It should also be noted that Reverend Samuel Harrison, chaplain of the famed 54th Massachusetts Volunteer and subject of the film "Glory" received a chaplain's commission before Turner but it was a state commission signed by Governor Andrew of Massachusetts.

Turner first appears as "present" on the regiments' rolls in November, 1863, and would have officially assumed his duties. On December 3, 1863, while in Virginia he married Rufus Wright, a soldier in the regiment to Elizabeth Turner of Portsmouth, Virginia and then issued them a marriage certificate bearing his signature.

It was his pleasure to preside over the uniting of over a dozen couples while chaplain. He was a regimental chaplain, the largest of three categories of chaplains authorized by the Union Army. There were also hospital chaplains and post chaplains. There were 930 regimental chaplains. Of the 133 chaplains in the U.S. Colored Troops only 14 were African American. Several, in addition to Turner, were AME ministers. They included David Stevens, William Hunter, and Garland H. White, among others.[16]

Chaplain's pay was $100 a month plus two rations, equal to a captain's pay. The approved uniform was a "plain black frock coat, with standing collar, and one row of nine brass buttons; plain black pantaloons, black felt hat or army forage, without ornament according to General Order 102 (1861) which remained in effect throughout the war." Black chaplains were discriminated against in pay as were black enlisted men. Both received $10 a month. Chaplains' pay was not equalized until April, 1864.

Civil War chaplains in black regiments had especially difficult jobs. Not only did they provide for the moral and spiritual welfare of the men of their regiments but many of the men were newly freed with a host of bad habits, attitudes, and psychological problems brought with them from the plantation. Such issues as profanity, gambling, fighting, and theft were found in every regiment. Black troops, however, had to face assumptions of inferiority, cowardice, and criminality. Until June, 1864, black men in Union blue also suffered pay inequity with the result that often they could not provide for their wives, children, and parents. In short supply as well were spelling books, religious tracts, bibles and periodicals, anything with which to read or teach reading and writing. Above all, to black soldiers, purchasing their liberty through the force of their own arms and getting an education were the essential accoutrements of their manhood.

Sickness and disease struck black regiments with unusual severity. Turner's regiment often had trouble obtaining competent medical personnel. Without good physicians and surgeons, battle casualties and overall mortality climbed and it was the chaplain's duty to comfort the wounded and the dying and pray for the dead.

On December 19, 1863, Turner writing from the regimental camp near Portsmouth, requested leave, "having received intelligence from home relative to some family affairs the adjustment of which demands my presence a short time." Three days later, he was granted eight days leave. Some historians have speculated that he was ill. He certainly was sick two months later. Regimental records list him "absent, sick in hospital" during February, 1864. In March he applied for a leave of absence. He was examined by the command surgeon who found him "...suffering considerable debility especially of the pulmonary orgains... and that in consequence thereof he is, in my opinion, unfit for duty." What clinched the surgeon's decision was the discovery that Turner was also found to have contracted smallpox, possibly while visiting a sick soldier. Highly contagious, smallpox is a virus disease accompanied by prolonged fever, vomiting, and pustular eruptions that often leave scars or pockmarks when healed.

Long after the war, one of the enlisted men remembered Turner's bout with smallpox: "For many days we thought we lost him, he having been reported several times as dead. But God raised him up." His condition was so serious he was reported as a "loss" and dropped from the regiment's list of commissioned officers by order of General I. N. Palmer. In May, 1864 after a leave of absence to allow him time to rest and recuperate, Turner returned to his regiment and was listed as a "gain" and placed back on the roster of officers. His face was now forever pockmarked displaying the effects of the disease.

Turner continued his dispatches to the *Recorder* when he rejoined the regiment. They and his letters give important insight on the young pastor, his new flock, and army life. On June 25, 1864 the *Recorder* published his account of the battle of Wilson's Landing (wharf) which occurred on May 24, 1864:

...Things, however, moved on quietly until the 24th ult, on which occasion I was retiring from dinner, feeling very jolly over the idea of having eaten quite heartily once more of a fat chicken, &c., which is generally something special in camp, when my attention was called to the front of our works by a mighty rushing to arms, and shouts that the rebels were coming. I immediately joined the proclaiming host and bellowed out, (I reckon in fearful tones) "The rebels! The Rebels! The Rebels are coming!" At this period the long [drum] roll began to tell that doleful tale that she never tells unless the enemy is about to invade our quarters. Then commenced another rush to arms, fearful in its aspect. Notwithstanding many were at dinner, down fell the plates, knives, forks, and cups, and a few moments only were required to find every man, sick or well, drawn into the line of battle to dispute the advance of twice, if not thrice, their number of rebels. Captains Borden and Rich of the 1st U.S. Col'd Troops, with their gallant companies, were at some distance in front, skirmishing with the advance guard of the rebels. And here permit me to say, that this skirmish was the grandest sight I ever beheld. I acknowledge my incapacity to describe it, and thus pass on. By the time our pickets had been driven in, a flag of truce was seen waving in the distance, when General Wild gave orders to cease firing. Lieutenant Colonel Wright was immediately dispatched to meet it, and found it to be a peremptory demand from Gen. Fitz Hugh Lee for the unconditional surrender of the place, with the promise that we should, upon such compliance, be treated as prisoners of war; but upon a refusal, we would have to abide by the consequences, assuring us at the same time, that he intended

to take us, for he could and would do it. Gen. Wild told him
to try it. In fifteen minutes rebel balls were flying like hail all
around our heads; but gallantly was the compliment returned.
It would be contraband to tell you our force on that occasion.
But this much I must tell you, that the 1st Regiment of the
United States Colored Troops, with a very small exception, did
all the fighting. I am also sorry that it is inexpedient to give
you a full description of that terrific battle, which lasted
several hours; but the coolness and cheerfulness of the men,
the precision with which they shot, and the vast number of
rebels they unmercifully slaughtered, won for them the highest
regard of both the General and his staff, and every white
soldier that was on the field. And the universal expression
among the white soldiers was, That it is a burning shame for
the Government to keep these men out of their full pay. ...

Allow me to say that the rebels were handsomely whipped.
They fled before our men, carrying a large number of their
dead, and leaving a great many on the field for us to bury.
They declared our regiment were sharp-shooters. Our loss,
considering the terribleness of this conflict, was incredibly
small.

From that place we went to Fort Powhattan, a few days after
which we came here, and will remain here till we receive
marching orders. A few days ago, we went in front of
Petersburg, our regiment even went under the guns of the
rebels, and laid down while their bombs were flying over our
heads. We would have gone into the city had we been
permitted; but we accomplished all we were sent to do, and
then we returned....

At the end of June, 1864, Turner wrote directly to the Secretary of War
on behalf of himself and the chaplains of three other black regiments:

...to petition your honor to set some mark that will designate the position of Chaplain, we not having any badge or mark by which we are known, subjects us to a thousand inconveniences, especially at hospitals where we are at the most needed, unless the guards know us personally, we are often treated below a private, not allowed to enter where we have important business, and sometimes driven away unless we show our Chaplain's appointment. We most respectfully ask for some special mark, either a strap on the shoulder, or a stripe on the arm, And we will even pray yours most truly.

H.M. Turner[17]

The three chaplains were Hunter of the 4th USCT, and Asher of the 6th USCT who were African American, and Green of the 37th USCT was white.

For several days at the end of July, 1864 Turner visited local army general hospitals in the Norfolk area "...looking after wounded soldiers, giving them good cheer, and pointing them to Christ." Turner's visits to these hospitals made him aware of the toll that rampant disease and opportunistic infections took on the men of the regiment. As was true for most units whether Union or Confederate, disease was far deadlier than bullets or shrapnel. The sick and wounded of the regiment were being dispersed to increasingly more distant locations which made it more difficult for him to see his men. The assaults on Petersburg and Richmond in the summer were brutal, nasty operations that swelled the ranks of the infirm, wounded, and dead.

Turner began a "glorious revival" in October 1864 for the men of the regiment. On these occasions he became the sword of the spirit using prophetic, apocalyptic oratory to win souls. Vivid pictures of hell fire and smoking brimstone were punctuated with calls for prayer and redemption. Hell-bent, hell-bound souls could only be saved, Turner would remind them, through heavens' mandate to win the lost. Such was the power of the religious fervor brought forth at these meetings that many of the men often swayed back and forth and groaned aloud. This was much more than a demonstration of primitive religious fundamentalism, it was an evocation of a black worship tradition with roots stretching back to Africa.

Allied to this was the use of highly charged corporate prayer which still provided for individual displays of piety and reformation through personal testimonials of the influence of God's divine force. And as was standard with nineteenth century protestant evangelicalism, Turner reiterated the importance of sobriety, education, and respectability. Juxtaposed against the euphoria of winning souls for Christ, an incident in the same month reminded Turner of the depressing reality of racial discrimination. The African American war correspondent T. M. Chester reported it to his readers:

> Day before yesterday Chaplain H. M. Turner, of the 1st U. S. C. T., made a serious complaint against Joseph Weir, steward of the steamer Manhattan, for inhuman treatment while coming up from Fortress Monroe on the 12th inst. The conduct of the steward was outrageous, if one-half that is alleged against him be true. It appears that he locked the entrance through which passengers passed to their dinner, and obliged this officer and two soldiers' wives, who were in his charge, to go down between decks, through intense darkness, to reach the table. Everything was pretty well gotten up, yet the chaplain and his charges attempted to dine off the crumbs, for which the steward demanded one dollar cash. This brought a protest from the officer, which was replied to by the steward in the most brutal and insulting manner, flourishing a knife which he happened to have in his hand, and threatening the most fearful consequences if the chaplain did not immediately leave the dining-saloon. The full price was paid, and the officer, as soon as his affairs would permit, preferred charges against the steward, and on the arrival of the boat at City Point, evening before last, he was arrested, and is now detained upon the charges as alleged. He will likely be arraigned before Gen. Butler, and should these facts be substantiated, and that just

man squint at him under the impression that such conduct is the effervescence of concealed disloyalty, an individual about his proportions will be sent to Dutch Gap to assist with others of corresponding sentiments in cutting through the canal amid the showers of shot and shell from rebel batteries. The Manhattan is in the employ of the Government, and carries the mail between Washington and City Point. These Negro-haters do not incur much risk in their ill-treatment of unprotected colored persons; but when they insult, on a Government boat, a chaplain, though he may happen to be a little darker than themselves, they become involved in a difficulty which is rendered worse by the prospect of being summoned before Gen. Butler.[18]

Butler brought the incident to General Grant's attention. His response, a copy of which is in Turner's service records, reads, in part:

The communication of Chaplain Turner 1st U.S. Colored Troops an accompanying statement from yourself has been received and the matter complained of investigated. It appears that immediately after the occurrence referred to, the steward of the boat was arrested and sent beyond the lines of the Army, that being the only punishment which, from the limited information that could be obtained seemed necessary. He having been thus disposed of before the receipt of your communication no further action in the case is now possible.

By command of,

Lieut. Gen. Grant

Harder to handle were social indignities from the men with whom he served. Turner once described how during his preparations to sermonize the regiment's white officers, by their request, separately from the black enlisted men, he observed "...some misconduct, exhibited by men [officers], whose character should be exemplary, I stopped immediately."

Going instead to preach to the enlisted men, he reflected, with evident restraint, that he thought officers' rudeness "very ungrateful to God." Overall, Turner maintained cordial relations with the officers of the regiment. This was due as much to the support of Colonel Holman as it was due to Turner's own abilities. Undoubtedly he impressed some of the officers with his education and oratory. He was, in effect, the most senior black man in the regiment. He too possessed a signed commission and there are numerous references in his writings to the importance that he placed on his own personal bearing, conduct, and the performance of his duties.

Turner was typical of the better civil war chaplains. He led religious services several times a week, if possible, with particular emphasis on Sunday services. He often tried to have three Sabbath services. His schedule of worship was always subordinate to military necessity. So he often was unable to provide services if the regiment was in combat, on bivouac, or on the march. A tent, often called a "tabernacle tent" for services was a rare luxury. He often conducted services, including revivals, outdoors sometimes at night around a campfire, or in local churches. He prayed during dress parades and conducted weddings, baptisms, and funerals. He often helped write letters or carried them and held money for his men when they requested. And we have seen how he visited the sick and wounded of his regiment. In these duties, he proved himself faithful, honest, and conscientious.

There were two things, however, that most endeared him to his regiment: he shared their daily hazards and worked tirelessly in behalf of their educational advancement.

Turner was a fighting parson. He was no stranger to the front lines. In October 1864, he was so far forward on the battlefield near Fair Oaks that he was nearly captured by rebel troops. On other occasions, he claimed to have had the heel of his boot shot off and his frock coat and hat punctured by bullets. He consciously took these risks because he believed in the cause for which they were fighting and wanted to earn their trust and respect.

The *Recorder,* on October 1, 1864, carried a dispatch by a soldier who engaged Turner in another kind of encounter. "Said I, Sir what is your rank? 'He replied: I don't know, but as I have not done much washing lately, I reckon I rank in smell very high now, under my arms.' " When asked to rate his rank and soldierly accomplishments with those of Generals Butler and Grant, Turner reminded his questioner that his pastoral commission came from God where the generals had only received their assignments from the President. Having been defeated in his rhetorical battle with the chaplain, the writer declared him "a very learned and well informed divine."

Turner understood how critical education was to the future of his regiment and his race: "It is not natural that a people who have been held as chattel for two hundred years, should thoroughly comprehend the limits of freedom's empire. The scope is too large for minds so untutored to enter upon at once." That the men were eager to understand their freedom and its attendant responsibilities is shown in their eagerness for learning. "As soon as my return is known, my quarters are surrounded by hundreds of soldiers, shouting over each other's head. 'Chaplain, for pity's sake, if you have a spelling book, let me have one.' No, says another, I am ahead of you and thus rages the spelling book clamor until one or two hundred are eagerly grabbed and carried off."[19]

Chaplain Turner also distributed black newspapers not only with an eye toward literacy but also to acquaint his charges with the words and thoughts of literate black men and women who could serve as role models for these aspiring students. Even when adverse weather conditions or deployment over a wide area made teaching difficult, Turner kept classes going as best he could. Whenever he traveled he would ransack all the benevolent institutions that could spare a book or primer. And there was a great and corresponding need for books, pencils, and paper.

His task was made easier somewhat in December 1864. General Butler consolidated 37 black regiments into the 25th Corps and formally directed the chaplains to conduct a school in each unit. As one historian noted:

Thus with a stroke of his pen, Butler guaranteed that 29,875 Negro soldiers would receive systematic instruction. The commander of the Twenty-Fifty Corps, Brigadier General Godfrey Weitzel made a determined effort to implement Butler's orders. First, he levied a tax on the regimental sutlers to finance the schools. Next he threatened the officers with dishonorable discharges if they did not improve their troops in drill, discipline, and education. Accordingly as military operations permitted, the officers aided the chaplains (many of them college trained) in teaching the men in a two-hour school period every week-day. The officers made a concerted effort to improve sloven habits formed by the troops in slavery. Hence, there was a great deal of emphasis placed on personal pride, appearance and cleanliness. To provide motivation, the cleanest man of each guard detail was excused from the detail and given a three-hour pass. A full day's pass was given to the cleanest man in each company's morning inspection. In addition, the cleanest man in corps reviews received a twenty day furlough and the two cleanest men in each division received fifteen day furloughs.[20]

The impact of Butler's efforts to educate black soldiers can be seen in the letter from the chaplain to the general written in February 1865, after the second Union assault on Ft. Fisher:

Honored Sir: I avail myself of this opportunity to tax your kindness to read a letter from one who, notwithstanding his humble sphere in life, desires nevertheless to correct any false statement which he believes was created and circulated for malicious designs.

I have only had the pleasure of reading two newspapers since we captured this place, one of which is an editorial relative to your removal from your late command, went on to say among many other abominable falsehoods, "that even the colored troops received the intelligence with joy."

And the said editorial went on in a lying train of arguments to use several other phrases in giving vent to its miserable spleen, in which it tried to thread colored soldiers hate, and which to my knowledge were unpardonable misrepresentations.

Sir, permit me to inform you that there never was a man more beloved than you were by the colored troops. They not only regarded you as their invincible friend, but as a benign father, one in whose hands their interests and rights were safe. And, when the news of your removal reached us at the landing near Fort Fisher, it gives rise to more bitter expressions than I ever heard before among these men. To say nothing of the frightful oaths and desecrations, which were uttered without stint or measure. Some even became despondent, and many remarked that everything looked gloomy, -- yes, I could say a great deal more, but prudence forbids me.

But be assured, Sir, that the oppressed and degraded sons of Africa are not blind to their benefactor, they know that Maj. General has done more to raise them to manhood than all the other Generals who have lived since the nation breathed its existence. Your name, like Jesus of Nazareth, will stand chiseled in the principles of justice and righteousness as long as God shall revolve this world. For posterity, a thousand ages to come, will only remember Gen. Butler to worship at his shrine. You need not care whether your historian inks his paper in malice or friendship, for the black men of the South will transmit pure, undefiled, and garland with eternal honors upon the pages of tradition.

I could say a great deal about the prohibities and the impossibilities of you capturing Fort Fisher on Christmas day.

But as I only intended to assure you of our high esteem, and correct those newspaper misrepresentations, I forbear to go any farther. I am, General,

Your obedient Servant,
H. M. Turner, Chaplain 1st U. S. C. Troops

Butler's answer was remarkable for its warmth and in his case, unusual brevity:

From General Butler to H. M. Turner

My Dear Sir: I am much obliged for your kind expressions of regard, and I am very proud of the fact that the Colored Troops look upon me as their friend. Let them go on and fight for the right as ever.

Yours truly, B. F. B.[21]

Turner had a front row seat during the attack on Fort Fisher as he later informed the readers of the *Recorder*: "Notwithstanding my regiment was not engaged on the fort, yet it fell to my lot to accompany the attacking party, as I had been chosen by Surgeon Barnes (medical director) to act as his aide for the occasion, which was no easy job, considering the land was sandy and no horses were to be had."

He noted the losses among the attacking Union forces:

"...the rebels replied to the charge and yells of our boys with the most awful volleys of musketry, grape, and canister. ...

Finally the marines and sailors came off the gunboats and war-ships, and helped to charge the fort. They were cut down in frightful numbers. They fell so thick and with such destruction that the marines at one time broke and fled; but the sailors stood their ground. Thus the sailors actually evinced more courage and bravery than the marines. The land forces on the left, however, in no instance broke nor exhibited any cowardice, yet they were terribly slaughtered. ...At one time I thought they could never stand it; neither do I believe they would have stood, but for the fact that they knew the black troops were in the rear, and if they (the white troops) failed, the colored troops would take the fort and claim the honor. Indeed, the white troops told the rebels that if they did not surrender they would let the negroes loose on them.

Turner was later shot at twice by rebel snipers as he walked around the fort. And there was another task he had to perform:

> It fell to my lot to bury with religious ceremony many of our noble dead, which I did with a sensation not felt in any previous instance since I have been connected with the army. It would be impossible to describe what I witnessed among the wounded. But one thing I must mention as a fact. I found twice the number of rebels calling upon God for mercy to what I found among our own wounded soldiers. One rebel particularly, whom I passed, was saying in a most pathetic tone, "O, Lord God, have mercy on me! Please have tender compassion on one who is a sinner, and comfort me in this my hour of trial! O, Lord, have mercy on me this one time more." When I commenced talking with him, and he discovered I was a chaplain, his countenance seemed to be illuminated with joy. But the prayers that went up from the rebel wounded completely bought off my prejudice, and I rendered them every comfort in my power. ...
>
> I asked several rebel officers if they killed the colored prisoners they took. They told me they did not. They also told me if they were free men from the North, or even from any slave State in our lines, they were treated as other Yankee prisoners are; but if they were slaves, whose

owners were in the Confederate States, and such colored men could be identified, they were treated as house-burners and robbers. And as for you, said they, you would get the same treatment as other Yankee officers.[22]

The next few months passed swiftly. The pace of fighting slackened. The regiment became part of the Union Army of occupation. In Smithfield, North Carolina, Turner recorded a confrontation between a black woman in her yard and several white women over some wood

"...which the colored lady was appropriating to her use. She told them it was Yankee wood, and not theirs, and the tongue battle raged most furiously for some minutes, when one of the white women called her a liar, with another expression too vulgar to mention. To this the colored woman responded, "I am no more a liar than you are." This expression, from a Negro wench, as they called her, was so intolerable, that the white women grabbed up several clubs, and leaped in the door, using the most filthy language in the vocabulary of indecency. They had not yet observed me as being on the premises. But at this juncture, I rose up, met them at the door, and cried out, "Halt!" Said they, "Who are you?" "A United States Officer," was my reply. "Well, are you going to allow that Negro to give us impudence?" "You gave her impudence first," was my reply. "What, we give a Negro impudence! We want you to know we are white and are your superiors. You are our inferior, much less she." "Well," said I, "all of you put together would not make the equal of my wife, and I have yet to hear her claim superiority over me." After that, I don't know what was said, for that remark was received as such an aggravated insult, that I can only compare the noise that followed, to a gang of fice dogs, holding at bay a large cur dog, with a bow-wow-wow-wow. Finally, becoming tired of their annoying music, I told them to leave or I would imprison the whole party. They then went off, and dispatched one of their party to Head Quarters, to Colonel Barney, to induce him to send a file of men, and have me arrested. But the Colonel, I believe, drove her off, and that was the end of it. I afterwards learned that they were some of the Southern aristocracy.[23]

On April 9, 1865 General Lee surrendered. On April 26, 1865 Confederate forces in North Carolina gave up their arms. For the men of the First Regiment, the war was essentially over. There were still gun battles with bands of roaming guerillas who attacked groups of freedmen and their schools and churches, but the big war had ended. Three months before the regiment was mustered out, Turner wrote a long letter dated June 29, 1865 to the Adjutant General of the Army. It is presented here in full because it represents so much of his work and feelings for the regiment:

Sir, I have the honor to submit the following report, as embracing the moral and religious condition of my regiment.

After we left the Fort of Richmond, and started on the Fort Fisher expedition, our campaign was so constant and uncertain, and being a part of the time detailed on extra duty, which subjected our religious exercises to so many disappointments, I thought it unnecessary to forward any more reports, untill so much of our active duties, should be over, as would enable us to have some assurrance, that our religious efforts and plans would not always be thwarted by unavoidable disappointments.

During this intermedium, however, we have had preaching, prayer meetings, and other moral or religious exercises, as frequently, as circumstances would permit, so much so, that no one could frame for an excuse, that his identity with sin, was founded upon the ground, that he was not taught better.

But for the last six weeks, our regimental church, has been systematically carried on, and I believe beneficaly disposed of. It gives me great pleasure to still acknowledge the religious integrity of several in the regiment, as well as the profound anxiety manifested by several others, who are yet strangers to Christ, in obtaining the pearl of Great Price.

Should it please God to let us remain in our present quarters for a reasonable time, surrounded with our present favorable conveniences, I cherish the hope, that many will be added to the lists of the faithful, and many others, if not actually purged by Grace, brought to so comprehend their future destiny, as to lay the base of a reformatory course of action. Upon the whole moral and religious aspects of the regiment, will tally quite favorable with any in the service.

Having constantly kept the subject of education before our soldiers, I flatter our literary success unequalled considering our time and chance. But at present, all literary efforts must remain at a partial stand still, owing to want of books, to supply the heavy demand, for whom it appears almost impossible to procure them.

Had my repeated application for leave of absence, been granted, I intended to have supplied this want, even at my own expense. But as it was not granted I hope it will not be an outrage upon the right of Petition, to most respectfully request, that you have my regiment furnished with at least (500) five hundred spelling books.

The most of these books too, should be of the advance kind, as a large portion of the Troops, who can read and write some, need to be much better drilled in spelling. And hundreds for whom I had gotten books, had them destroyed in their knapsacks, by the sinking of a boat in the Cape Fear River. I claim this favor for my regiment, upon the ground, that she is the mother of colored Troops, and that in nine battles, regardless of skirmishes, she has never faltered, give way, or retreated, unless ordered by the General Commanding. Her record for bravery, courage, or invincibleness difies the redicule of the world. I challenge mortal man to stain her career with one blot of cowardice. Therefore as a means to make brave soldiers, good and intelligent citizens, I must respectfully ask for 500 spelling books. I hope this application may meet a speedy and favorable consideration.

The health of our regiment is excellent at this time. Military decorum and soldierly deportment, are peculiarly characteristic of our officers as a general thing. I have the honor to be your servant.

Henry M. Turner[24]

Writing to the *Recorder* from Roanoke Island, North Carolina, Private William Brown related how the regiment spent July 4, 1865 the first celebration of national independence since the guns had fallen silent and first on which the specter of slavery no longer haunted the land:

It may be that some of your readers would be pleased to know how we spent the Fourth of July on Roanoke Island. I am a very poor writer, but I hope you will excuse all defects.

About sunrise there were 36 cannons fired, which sounded very much like war times, and appeared to arouse the very fish in the waters. The band then played several airs, and every body seemed to be alive. About 9 o'clock our Regiment turned out, the soldiers marching to the music of the drum corps, and then halting in front of head quarters, where the old flag was flung to the breeze amid the cheers of the assembled multitudes.

By this time about 3500 persons had collected. The regiment then stacked arms, and our most worthy and industrious chaplain, H. M. Turner, came along with his little wife by his side, who, by the way, appears to be a noble woman. Taking his position in front under a shade tree, he delivered one of the finest orations, I can safely say, that was ever heard on this island. Mr. Turner has always been the idol of our men, he goes with us every where in cold or heat, battle or sickness, he is always there, and every time he has something new to say. I could not realize that I had ever heard him before.

In his address to the Fourth, he reviewed the history of the country from the discovery by Columbus, and spoke on slavery from its inaugurating until it was destroyed by the proclamation of our lamented President. He concluded by paying the nation's flag a glorious tribute; he said the extremities of color, white and black in this country, had made it the world's theatre, and that every despotic nation under heaven should yet dance to American music, and that Daniel's stone made it the regulation in 1776, and would make its last when the whole world would be one great republic, and that as soon as God would knock down the wall of prejudice between the whites and blacks, sectional divisions would crumble into dust throughout the entire Globe. He handled his subject in a masterly manner, and the secessionists that heard him looked wild at its conclusion. Every body then returned to their homes, and the rest of the day went off quietly.[25]

When the regiment mustered out in September, Turner returned with the men to Washington. He spoke at the gala reception the regiment received (see Chapter 5). His former church home, Israel Bethel had gained a new pastor and had lost none of its activist vision and passion. The church's 1864 petition to the House and Senate had demanded the "unconditional right of the colored male citizen to the ballot box" and had garnered wide notice.[26]

Turner's attention had turned firmly toward the South in any case. This was part of the great mission that he had dreamed of since boyhood. "Oh, how the foul curse slavery has blighted the natural greatness of my race." He saw the immense problems of millions of freedmen as requiring the "special attention" of all blacks who could make positive contributions. Turner would concentrate his own efforts in "preaching, lecturing, and establishing schools, literary societies." By December 1865 he had been briefly appointed chaplain of the 138th USCT and then an agent of the Freedmen's Bureau in Georgia. He resigned after encountering bias and hostility from local whites.

By 1868 he had served briefly in the Georgia legislature. It would be his work on behalf of the AME church that made him legendary. He personally helped bring thousands of African Americans in Georgia to this denomination. After he made bishop in the early 1880s, Turner authored books and articles on African Methodism, was president of Morris Brown College and became the leading exponent of emigration to Africa prior to Marcus Garvey. His advocacy of black cultural and religious nationalism made him a precursor of individuals like Malcolm X and Stokely Carmichael (Kwame Toure). He was truly as his colleague Reverdy Ransom said "an epoch-making man."

Bishop H.M. Turner of the A.M.E. church.

CHAPTER IV

DEEP ROOTS, STRONG BRANCHES

"I am so proud to have his blood running through my veins"

Ruby M. Thomas

The first time she saw the large, old photograph of the stern, unsmiling man in a uniform, it frightened her.

"His eyes seemed to follow me around the room. When I was 4 or 5 years old, I would often visit my grandfather, William Henry Brown, at his home in Nanjemoy, Maryland. It was an old very quiet house, often dark, and we could move about only with the help of kerosene lamps. There was no electricity. We called his house the '*Home Place*' because it had been in the family for so many years. It was the house that my great-grandfather built. I was a curious child always walking through the house. I remember the kitchen had a wood stove. And in the living room over the fireplace hung this large picture of a man in a uniform. In the evening shadows by the light of an old lamp the picture looked spooky," Ruby M. Thomas, recalled with a smile.

"I remember asking my grandfather who is he? I can still hear the pride in his voice as he told me the soldier in that picture is my father and your great-grandfather who fought in the Civil War. I often reflect back to his words and remember how proud he was of his father. The picture now hangs in my living room representing now six generations of Brown history. That soldier in the large portrait wearing a distinguished Civil War uniform was Charles Henry Brown, in the United States Colored Troops, First Regiment," Thomas said.

Mrs. Thomas, who now is in her 50's, ironically has worked most of her government career in the field of equal employment opportunity with several government agencies. She wonders if she is carrying on her great-grandfather's quest for equality with more modern day approaches instead of a violent war.

"I guess in my early teenage years I started learning more about my family. My grandfather was a quiet man," Thomas said. "He spoke few words and often did not want to talk about the past so I obtained little information from him. He probably saw me as just a kid wanting to hold a grown-up conversation with them. Yes, I was one of those kids that asked a million questions. What is this, why are you doing that, explain

Ruby Thomas and Family (from left) Gerald Datcher, Tammi Miles (Ruby & James's daughter), Ruby Thomas and James Thomas

this, etc. Surely, my grandfather must have viewed me as a 'motor mouth.' But it was more than that. Early I realized the importance of learning about my family roots. He did not realize at that time he was only making me much more curious. My grandfather, William Henry Brown died on his 77th birthday in 1967 when I was 16 years old and taking with him a great deal of our family history," Thomas recounted.

Just shortly before her grandfather died, he sold the *"Home Place"* and Thomas hopes one day to purchase it and restore it to its grandeur. She later learned that there is a creek that runs through the property and it is appropriately named "Willie Brown Creek." "My great-grandfather must have played a major role in the naming of the creek in order for it to be named after my grandfather. All the local folk fondly called my grandfather by his nickname 'Willie.' I am going to assume that my grandfather must have enjoyed playing and fishing in the creek as a young boy for my great-grandfather to feel the need to name the creek after his son," Thomas insisted.

Her grandfather moved into another family house and fortunately he brought with him many very old photographs of probably family and friends which he stored in an old World War I chest. And of course he brought the portrait of Charles Henry Brown. "Thank goodness for my aunt Dorothy Brown Carroll" Thomas said with glee, "because she was a reservoir of information and blessed with a wonderful memory. She was able to name some of the people in the photographs." But Thomas saddened as she thought about the other pictures with nameless faces and wonders which ones are her relatives. Carroll also shared some stories about the different furnishings that she remembered in the *"Home Place."* Most of which Thomas still has today. "The old oil lamp, Victorian-style drum table, and worn bibles with the birth date of my grandfather are just some of the items that I truly cherish and will pass on to members in the family" Thomas added.

In the early 1980's Thomas found the time to begin unearthing new information about Charles Henry Brown located at the National Archives. She began by sorting through the thousands of pension records of black

Civil War veterans. She had no clues to help in her search other than his name and his wife's name. She did not know the regiment in which he had served or his exact dates of service.

For many hours each weekend she patiently examined the microfilm records of every Charles Henry Brown who had served in the United States Colored Troops (USCT) between 1862 and 1866.

"My daughter Tammi, who was in elementary school at the time, was with me the night I found my great-grandfather's actual records," Thomas remembered. "We were both real excited and hugged each other with joy. The discovery fired up my enthusiasm. I began interviewing relatives and finding relatives that I did not know existed. I spent a couple of years talking with every elderly person in the Nanjemoy region. During my trips, my husband James, who also grew up in the region, provided lots of information about the community, its people, and proved to have excellent videotaping skills," she recalled.

Over the years Thomas has slowly, painstakingly from a variety of public and private sources uncovered and pieced together a profile of her great-grandfather's family life and his military service in the Civil War.

Charles Henry Brown enlisted in Company I of the First Regiment, United States Colored Troops on June 28, 1863 at "Mason's Island, Virginia," a wooded, swampy 75-acre island in the middle of the Potomac River at Washington, D.C. The USCT was the segregated organization of black troops in the Union Army during the Civil War. Black troops were initially paid less than white troops and even given a segregated manual of marching and fighting instructions. The regiment had moved to that location primarily because of the hostile reception many of the city's white citizens had given its formation. Troops from a Massachusetts unit stationed in the city had to be called to guard the site of one enlistment meeting from troublemakers.

At a recruiting station near Capitol Hill in Washington, D.C. recruits had to huddle in the open at night and set up sentries armed with sticks to keep the curious and the hostile at bay. Many blacks and whites in the city still considered the conflict between the North and South "a white man's war."

The First Regiment, USCT, formally mustered into Federal service in June 1863, was not the first unit of black troops to fight during the Civil War. Black troops were organized unofficially by local Union military officials to fight Confederate forces as early as the spring and summer of 1862 in South Carolina. That same year, other unauthorized black regiments were organized in Kansas and Louisiana. When these units were formally mustered into federal service they were, however, re-designated numerically. For example, the First South Carolina Volunteers became the 33rd Regiment United States Colored Troops.[1]

Recruiting drives for the troops began in April 1863 and progress was slow at first for several reasons. Washington was filled with southern sympathizers and northern bullies. There were reports of black soldiers from the unauthorized units being murdered after capture or sold into slavery. There was also a War Department ban on commissioning black officers.

Nevertheless, many black men ultimately decided to join the regiment in order to strike a personal blow against slavery; an institution which they considered "the sum of all villainy" and "the crime of crimes." Thomas believed her great-grandfather held such sentiments. "After going back and reading every pension affidavit and all the other documentation, it clearly appears that my great-grandfather enlisted as a slave. So there is no doubt in my mind that he enlisted to fight for his freedom and for the freedom of others" stated Thomas.

Thomas believed that Brown and several of his friends including Joseph Ross and Edward Lawson both of whom signed documents attesting to Brown's service connected disability, made a pact to escape from slavery and fight together. "They all enlisted in the First Regiment. Although precisely how they escaped from bondage in Charles County, and made their way to Mason's Island will always be a mystery," she indicated.[2]

B   1   **U.S.C.T.**

Charles Brown

, Co. *D* , 1 Reg't U. S. Col'd Inf.

Appears on
Company Descriptive Book
of the organization named above.

DESCRIPTION.

Age *2* years; height *5* feet *7½* inches.

Complexion *Brown*

Eyes *Blk* ; hair *Blk*

Where born *St. marys md*

Occupation *farmer*

ENLISTMENT.

When *June 28* , 186*3*.

Where *Masons Island Va*

By whom *Col Birney* ; term *3* y'rs.

Remarks : *Slave — Promoted*
to Corpl per R.S.O. no 129
aug 1/64. Promoted to
Sergt per R.S.O. no 21
April 1, 1865.
Sept 29 1865 mustered
out S.O. no 179 (@3) Hd.
Qrs. Dept. N.C.

Boyd

(383g)   Copyist.

Enlistment record of Charles Brown.

At the end of June 1863, five companies of the regiment all with new blue uniforms, brass buttons and polished muskets paraded through the city to attend a prayer service at the church of Henry McNeal Turner, who was to become the regimental chaplain. A leading recruiter for the regiment, Turner was also an AME pastor who was a proponent of black enlistment.[3]

After serving in North Carolina, the regiment, nearly 900 strong and under the command of Colonel John Holman, traveled to Portsmouth, Virginia. Just across the river in Norfolk, a rebel civilian, who had sworn to shoot the first white man he saw drilling black troops, murdered one of the regiment's officers, Lieutenant A.L. Sanborn. The assassin was hanged.

Five months later, the regiment engaged in its first battle. Part of a large Union Army expedition from Norfolk, Virginia, the regiment pushed into northeastern North Carolina. The regiment built a bridge, liberated a number of slaves and engaged in short sharp fire fights with Confederate raiders. According to an after action report, "Colonel Holman burned two of their camps between Elizabeth and Hertford, taking some of their property, such as horses, guns, provisions, and clothing...."

In the spring of 1864, the regiment was ordered westward where it participated in Union General Benjamin Butler's operations south of the James River and against Richmond and Petersburg, Virginia. During the battles in and around Wilson's Wharf, part of the regiment captured a Confederate "signal station party and equipments...." A sergeant and three men of the First USCT were killed.

During June, the regiment was hurled into the siege against Petersburg where the Union Army missed an early opportunity to capture this vital communications center. A report of a June 15 battle notes that the regiment was one of several units to "engage the enemy before Petersburg with considerable loss." Seventeen men of the regiment were killed, 114 men were wounded, 25 were missing in action.[4]

A battle report signed by General E.W. Hincks, the division commander, cites the First USCT as one of the five black regiments whose actions "affords conclusive proof that colored men, when properly officered and drilled, will not only make soldiers but the best soldiers of the line."

The regiment actually fought two battles on June 15, 1864: Baylor's Farm and near Petersburg, Virginia. Brown's company with the rest of the regiment remained in the trenches in front of Petersburg until the end of June. Regimental headquarters shifted briefly to Point of Rocks in early August and then returned to the field in front of Petersburg the same month.   The losses among the enlisted men, particularly the noncommissioned officers, meant that promising privates had to be found and elevated in rank.

On August 1, 1864, the regiment promoted the battle-hardened Brown to corporal. Brown was considered worthy enough to gain a set of double sky-blue stripes. The precise reason for his promotion, Thomas asserted, was because of the courage he showed in the assaults of the previous months.

On October 27, 1864, near the town of Fair Oaks, seven miles east of Richmond, Virginia, the regiment was ordered to search for the left flank of the Confederate line while the rest of its brigade advanced toward Richmond. After moving about a mile, the regiment met Confederate cavalry and artillery numbering between 1,500 and 2,000 men.

Colonel Holman ordered the regiment to charge across open ground through a rebel artillery barrage. "The First was exposed to a severe fire of musketry, grape shot, and canister but advanced gallantly across the open field and carried a part of the enemies [sic]" line, getting possession of two guns," wrote an officer who saw the battle.

The regiment failed to get additional support and was forced to withdraw from the Confederate emplacements. Several soldiers and one officer were seized trying to bring captured cannons back to the Union lines. Holman was severely wounded within 200 yards of the Confederate lines as he charged with the men of the First USCT. The casualties were 12 dead, 96 wounded, and 16 men were listed "missing in action."

Between December 1864 and January 1865, the regiment took part in two major assaults against Fort Fisher, the guardian of Wilmington, North Carolina, "the last gateway between the Confederate States and the outside world," according to one historian.

After a point-blank 36-hour naval bombardment, an amphibious landing, and desperate infantry fighting during the second assault, the *Star*, a Washington, D.C. newspaper reported that Fort Fisher, at the mouth of the Cape Fear River, was "Carried by Storm. Seventy-two guns captured and twenty-five hundred taken prisoners."[5]

On the nearly 30-mile march from Fort Fisher to Wilmington, a shell fragment struck Brown, now a sergeant, in the right leg below the knee. He refused to report himself wounded and gamely shifted most of his weight to his left leg. He and the rest of the regiment were in Wilmington on February 22, 1865, when the city was finally captured.

On April 26, 1865, all Confederate forces in North Carolina surrendered. The War was over for the First USCT, but 185 of its fellow soldiers would never return to civilian life. The regiment was formally mustered out of service on September 29, 1865.[6]

Thomas said her great-grandfather "returned to Charles County, Maryland as a hero." Upon his return he built a log cabin. Later, he constructed a beautiful two-story dwelling on land the family referred to as the *"Home Place."* Brown became a farmer and married Edith Ward and fathered four children named Andrew, Nancy, Emmanuel, and George. Thomas found the children's names in the census records. However, the details of their existence are a real mystery and it greatly puzzled her. "No one in Charles County knows of them or their children or their grand children, Thomas pondered. It truly is a puzzling mystery but I am determined to solve it. They have completely vanished, it seems, leaving no descendants." Fortunately, after more research, Thomas was

To any Minister of the Gospel authorized to celebrate Marriages in the District of Columbia, Greeting:

You are hereby Licensed *to solemnize the Rites of Marriage between*

Charles H Brown , *of* Charles County Md

AND

Lannie Moore , *of* do

if you find no Lawful Impediment thereto; and having so done, you are commanded to appear in the Clerk's Office of the Supreme Court of said District, and certify the same.

Witness *my hand and the seal of said Court, this* 27TH *day of* September, 1883.

R. J. Meigs , Clerk.

By J. Jay Camp , Assistant Clerk.

I, Rev. P. Lewis , Minister of Enon Church in Washington DC , *hereby certify that by authority of a license of the same tenor as the foregoing, I solemnized the marriage of the parties aforesaid on the* 27TH *day of* Sept , 1883 , *at* 1/2 St No. 220 , *in the District of Columbia.*

Rev. P. Lewis

Clerk's Office, Supreme Court of the District of Columbia.

I, J. R. Young Clerk of the Supreme Court of the District of Columbia, *hereby certify that the foregoing License and Minister's Certificate are truly copied from Originals of Record on file in said Office.*

Witness *my hand and the seal of said Court, the* 18TH *day of* February , 1896.

J. R. Young , Clerk.

By C. E. Williams , Assistant Clerk.

District of Columbia, to wit:

I, E. F. Bingham Chief Justice of the Supreme Court of the District of Columbia, do certify that the foregoing attestation by J. R. Young Clerk of the said Court, is in due form. Witness *my hand and seal, this* 18TH *day of* Feby , 1896.

Marriage record of Charles Brown and Lannie Moore.

able to obtain a bit more information about her great-grandfather's first wife. She died during childbirth in the year 1879 and was buried at the Mount Hope Baptist Church Cemetery located in Nanjemoy, Maryland. Brown was one of the handful of men who established Mount Hope Baptist Church. The church opened its doors for service on July 4, 1867. For many years Brown served on the church's trustee board. He helped the congregation erect a small brick church to house its services. The old church building was later used from the early 1900s through the 1950's as a schoolhouse, "Mount Hope Baptist Elementary School" for blacks. The church is still very much active today serving the community and observed its 135th anniversary in 2002. The church and the land were the pillars that supported the black community in Charles County, then predominately black. The church sits on a little mole and its graveyard overlooks most of Thomas's family members, including her great-grandfather who was the first person to be buried there. His tombstone clearly marks his grave.

In 1880, the country, although it produced impressive supplies of oats, wheat, rye and corn, was second in the state in tobacco production. More than 5 million pounds of the tall broad-leafed herb were raised on just 7,900 acres of land. For many years, the county seat was located at a prosperous town named Port Tobacco. Tobacco was king of the county and chief source of commerce and industry. Port Tobacco was also well known as a slave trading post. Janie Dent was nearly a 100 years-old when she shared a story with Thomas about how her father was about to be sold in Port Tobacco to another slave master before the War. The slave master changed his mind after he had sent him with others to be sold. Brown, still a slave, was given direct instruction by the slave master to take a horse and to take the note the slave master had written stating "don't sell John" to the slave trading station and bring John back. Dent recalls how her father often stated Brown arrived just seconds before her father was sold.[7]

Of the 1,400 farms in the county in 1880, nearly all of them had some acreage devoted to tobacco and mostly worked by black labor. A quarter of these farms were "rented for shares of products" otherwise known as

Widow's Declaration for Pension.

This Declaration may be Executed before a Justice of the Peace, Notary Public, Clerk of Court, or before any other person authorized to administer oaths for general purposes.

State of _Maryland_, County of _Charles_, ss:

ON THIS _16th_ day of _August_ A. D. one thousand eight hundred and ninety-_Seven_ personally appeared before me _a Justice of the Peace_ within and for the County and State aforesaid _Lannie Brown_ aged _37_ years, who, being duly sworn according to law, makes the following declaration in order to obtain the Pension provided by Acts of Congress granting pension to widows: That she is the widow of _Charles Brown_, (Soldier's name.) who enlisted under the name of _Charles Brown_ at _____ on the _27_ day of _June_ A. D. 18_63_, in Company _D_ _1st_ Regiment, _U.S.C.T._ the army; or vessel and rank, if in the navy.) Volunteers, in the war of _1861-5_ who _died of Phthisis result of disease of_ (State nature of wounds and all circumstances attending them, or the disease and manner in which it was incurred, in either case showing soldier's death to have been the sequence.) _lungs contracted while in the service_

on the _1_ day of _Nov._ A. D. 18_95_, who bore at the time of his death the rank of _____ in _aforesaid_ ("In the service aforesaid," or otherwise.) that she was married under the name of _Lannie Moor_ to said _Charles Brown_ on the _23rd_ day of _Sept_ A. D. 18_53_, by _Rev. Peter Lewis_ at _Washington D C_ there being no legal barrier to such marriage; that neither she nor her husband had been previously married _____ (If either have been previously married so state, and give date of death or divorce of former spouse.)

that she has to present date remained his widow; that the following are the names and dates of birth of all his legitimate children yet surviving who were under sixteen years of age at date of father's death, viz:

Rachel of soldier by _Lannie Brown_, born _Aug. 7_ 18_84_
_Wm. H._ of soldier by _"_ _"_, born _July 28_ 18_90_
Eugene M. of soldier by _"_ _"_, born _Apr. 11_ 18_94_
_____ of soldier by _____, born _____ 18___
_____ of soldier by _____, born _____ 18___
_____ of soldier by _____, born _____ 18___
_____ of soldier by _____, born _____ 18___

That she has not abandoned the support of any one of her children, but that they are still under her care or maintainance.

(For such children as are not under her care claimant should account.)

that she has not in any manner engaged in, or aided or abetted the rebellion against the United States; that _a_ prior application has been filed _under Act June 27, 1890. ct./ # 434 652_ (If prior application has been filed either by soldier or widow, so state, giving number assigned to it.) that she hereby appoints, with full power of substitution and revocation,

W. H. WILLS, of Washington, D. C.,

her attorney to prosecute the above claim; that her residence is No. _____ Street, _____ and her Post Office address is _Doncaster, Md._

Pratsey Moore   _Lannie X Brown_
Cora Douglas   (Mark)
(Two persons, who can write, must sign here.)   (Signature of Claimant.)

ATTY FILED.

Pension claim of Lannie Moore Brown.

sharecropping. After returning from the Civil War, Brown worked on such a 15-acre farm for a white man named Albin Price.

It was to this farm that he brought a 23-year old local girl named Lannie Moore after their marriage on September 27, 1883, in Washington, D.C. Brown was in his early 40's. The blissful couple had sailed back to Charles County the day after the ceremony on one of the steamboats that regularly plied the waters of the Potomac River.

Moore gave birth to her first child in 1884, a girl name Rachel. In 1890, Thomas's grandfather, William Henry was born, and four years later another son named Eugene was born. He died during childhood.

Decreasing yields of tobacco, fluctuating prices, and the backbreaking labor required by the temperamental plant began to affect Brown's income. Combined with these circumstances were the increasing pain and disability from his combat injury and his advancing years.

When he learned that Congress had liberalized the laws granting pensions to Civil War veterans who served in the Union Army, Brown felt forced to finally acknowledge the injury he had received a quarter of a century earlier.

On June 27, 1890, Congress passed a law granting pensions to veterans "who were incapacitated for the performance of manual labor, and providing for pensions to widows, minor children and dependent parents." Pensioners were entitled to receive a maximum of $112 a month.

Brown submitted his claim describing the nature, location and extent of his injury adding that he had also developed a painful "knot" in his left side. As a result of favoring his wounded leg, he suffered from rheumatism resulting from his service-connected injury. He stated that he was "disabled by pain and unable to work as formerly."

On August 1, 1891, he was examined in Washington, D.C. by doctors who refused his claim noting in their report that "he did not go on sick report for his wound and did his duty right along."

"My great-grandfather appeared to be a fighter not only for his country but for himself as well. He must have said to himself, I am going to keep trying until I die. He collected several affidavits from his fellow former soldiers who knew of his injury and prepared what appears to be sufficient documentation to justify receiving the military pension. He even obtained another examination in Washington, D.C. in March 1895," Thomas said.

This time, Brown received a more thorough examination. The doctors noted the 4-inch scar on his leg, and "apparent stiffness when starting to walk." But they classified him "not incapacitated for the performance of manual labor." They also noted that Brown suffered from "harsh breathing, coughing, bronchitis and catarrh," a chronic inflammation of the membranes of the nasal passages.

On Friday, November 1, 1895, Thomas's great-grandfather, Charles Henry Brown died at his home in Charles County. He never received his pension. However, he left behind a wife just as determined as he. On a form titled "Widow's Declaration for Pension," Moore listed Brown's cause of death as "phthisis" or pulmonary tuberculosis. It is clear Brown showed some of the symptoms of tuberculosis at his March examination. Thomas does not believe that the doctors informed Brown of his illness. He died the same year that X-rays, which would have shown his lung lesions, were discovered.

Lannie applied for a widow's and children's pension provided for in Section 3 of the 1890 law. As required, she listed all her possessions: one house, one cow, and one horse. Their total value was $50.00.

On November 2, 1896, she was finally granted the standard $8.00 a month for a widow and $2.00 a month for each of the three children. Earlier that same year she had bought the farm that she and Brown had sharecropped for 13 years. She paid Albin Price $40.00 for the land that

Ruby Thomas with picture of Charles Henry Brown.
She is holding his original discharge papers.

would become the "*Home Place*" for three generations of the Brown Family. Moore died there on March 21, 1931 after serving many years in the community as a capable and trusted midwife.

Thomas feels that her research has brought her closer to both her great-grandparents, but particularly to her great-grandfather. "Over the years, he has become not just a man in a picture hanging in my house wearing a Civil War uniform, he is truly my inspiration. In a strange way, sometimes I feel his strength which gives me the motivation needed to continue his quest for equality. I know he would be tremendously proud to know that his great-granddaughter is an Equal Employment Opportunity Director for a Federal agency and a Commissioner for Prince George's County, Maryland on the Human Relations Commission who is fighting a war against discrimination," she said with pride.

"I bet he would have been a perfect great-grandfather. One who would share about his past and I am sure he would also provide me with wonderful words of wisdom. I wish I had known him personally. But he has left behind a warm as well as touching history of himself. In my interview with Janie Dent, she described his good character. She helped me capture in my mind that he had been a great man. I could just visualize him as she colorfully described him in great detail. She recalled how he walked with a cane; he was short, dark complexioned and loved to make people happy. She indicated that he always carried candy in his pockets to hand out to the children on Sundays at church. She laughed when she told me how he would tease her and he had nicknamed her Little Nip. She recalled how he encouraged her to practice reading and writing everyday. Great-grandfather never received a formal education and could only sign his name with a large "X" on his military documents," Thomas recounted.

"I have a tremendous amount of pride knowing Charles Henry Brown was my great-grandfather. He was a man who had courage to fight in a war for his country, demonstrating an inner strength and determination to escape from slavery, knowing that education was important for success, believing in human equality and most importantly he loved his family and the Lord. I am so proud to have his blood running through my veins," Thomas said smiling.

"My goal with all the wonderful information I have obtained on my great-grandfather's life is to capture it in a novel, maybe titled '*Home Place*' Thomas asserted.

Thomas says she is continuing her journey into her great-grandfather's past. She described her voyage of discovery as "challenging, worthwhile, and one of the most rewarding life experiences I have ever undertaken."

CHAPTER V

BOUND FOR FREEDOM'S LIGHT

"You have been engaged in sustaining the country in its supreme trial, now let your actions be equally worthy in the time of peace."

President Andrew Johnson

Black, Copper, & Bright

Welcome Home for the 1st Regiment of Colored Volunteers, DC
written and dedicated to the same October 8, 1865

Beat the drums! Now they come
From the long campaign!
Shout the war-won veterans home
From many a gory plain!

CHORUS Hi veterans! Ho victors! Welcome home again!
The "Bonnie Blue" was won by you brave soldiers not in vain!
Fields of gore - twelve or more
Speak your praises now
Where midst battle's rage and war
Beigh chaplets graced your brow!

CHORUS Hi veterans! Ho victors! Welcome home again!
The "Bonnie Blue" was won by you brave soldiers not in vain!
Now at last. The war-closed past
And your valor known
We our kindly fortunes cast
In common with your own!

CHORUS Hi veterans! Ho victors! Welcome home again!
The "Bonnie Blue" was won by you brave soldiers not in vain!
Welcome home! Welcome home!
To our cheerful boad
Use brave freeman as you come
The ballot as the sword!

CHORUS Hi veterans! Ho victors! Welcome home again!
The "Bonnie Blue" was won by you brave soldiers not in vain!

John H. Holman Papers
Western Historical Manuscript Collection
Columbia-University of Missouri

News of the regiment's definite return fell like a fire-brand on the District. For weeks rumors of first one date and then another flitted through the air like mosquitos on a muggy August night in Swampoodle. The regiments' return was anticipated with special eagerness. Of the city's white volunteer units that enlisted for extended service, the two infantry regiments (combined in February, 1865) served locally as part of the Defenses of Washington with brief stints of combat in or near the city. Only the cavalry regiment was still in the field at the beginning of October 1865.[1] Only that unit and the First USCT were posted so far away. There had been little word from the officers and men of the First USCT for the past two years except for the occasional letter or newspaper account.

Reverend Turner's last wartime report to the *National Republican* summarized the accomplishments of the regiment and ended with this stirring conclusion:

> However terrific the fire of the enemy, however fearful the contest, or however much out-numbered by the foe, with all the threats of death, if captured, staring them in the face, they nevertheless stood to their post firm and unbroken, unless when thinned out by the deadly fly of the enemy's missils [sic].

> Regiments on their right and left have flagged and succumbed to the paralyzing effects of battle strife. But the fighting First, as we have been called, have in no instance dishonored the nation's glorious escutcheon. This has been the proud career of the fighting First through eleven engagements. And now, as the war is over, it will undoubtedly return when its time expires (next June, unless sooner discharged) to its friends and relatives in Washington, with a name unsullied with cowardice, while we have not escaped the fate common to all regiments, having a few bad men in our ranks, we have to all ordinary considerations escaped the fortune of cowards.

> Withal, there is not a man in our midst, officer or private, but feels it a special honor to acknowledge his identity with the 1st USCT.[2]

At the end of September at Israel Bethel, a committee of leading African American citizens was hurriedly established to host a formal greeting for the returning veterans. George F.T. Cook, who was chosen secretary, and the famed caterer James Wormley, who was selected treasurer, were among the members. The committee began work by first appointing subcommittees. There was one for arrangements and a finance subcommittee to collect funds.[3] Wormley opened his stately home at 15th and I Streets, N.W. for meetings of the finance committee. One of the first contributions Wormley turned in was $5.00 given to him by an "English gentleman, Mr. Austin three years ago, to be expended for the regiment." A thousand dollars was ultimately raised for the event.

There was also an escort subcommittee that arranged for a 50-man platoon which included several members of the regiment, "fully equipped" to accompany the regiment through the streets. The escort included several members of the regiment already invalided back to the city because of wounds received in battle. The location chosen for the event was Campbell Hospital which stood at the end of the city's northern rail line on Boundary Street (Florida Avenue) between 5th and 7th Streets, N.W.

The hospital was a converted cavalry barracks which had become a huge and bustling haven of care. From its windows, patients could look east along Boundary Street and see Finley Hospital at Kendall Green, near the school for the deaf. The Secretary of War gave permission for a building to be set aside at Campbell for the regimental "reception and collation."[4]

Finally, on the afternoon of October 8, 1865, the First USCT returned to Washington City. The crowd began to cheer wildly as the transport steamer docked at the Sixth Street wharf. Ladies waved their kerchiefs. Men doffed their caps. Children scampered and stretched their necks for better views. Dogs barked. And the regimental band struck up the "Red,

National Republican

LOCAL AFFAIRS.

—————

THE FIRST REGIMENT DISTRICT OF COLUMBIA COLORED TROOPS.

—————

Their Welcome Home—Enthusiastic Reception—They will be Feasted To-morrow.

The colored citizens of this city and the District are animated by a just pride in the fame of their brethren of the First District of Columbia Colored Troops, who arrived here yesterday afternoon by steamer from Fortress Monroe. They have been anxiously expected for several days past by those who have relatives and particular friends in the regiment, and a handsome fund has been raised to defray the expenses of the "fatted calf" and other luxuries to be provided at the grand banquet now being prepared by Mr. James Wormley, the famous caterer.

October 9, 1865 account of the regiment's welcome home.

White, and Blue." In respect for the Sabbath, "the regiment ...remained onboard the vessel...." according to the *National Republican,* "in order that religious services in our churches might not be disturbed by their marching through the streets. The men behaved in a manner reflecting high credit upon their discipline, and the officers appeared well both in their military deportment and the neatness of their dress."[5]

At 4:30 p.m. the mostly black crowd, swollen with churchgoers and latecomers and buoyed with proud anticipation, watched with noisy approval as the silent men in blue tramped down the gangplank and marched up Seventh Street of a city greatly changed from the one they had left two years, two months, and nine days earlier. Among the transformations, streetcars were now formally desegregated. African American witnesses could no longer be excluded from local or federal courts. They could also now carry the United States mail and attend the New Year's Day reception at the White House. Frederick Douglass' visit with Lincoln at his second inaugural reception in March 1865 gained national attention as had black lawyer John S. Rock's admission to practice before the Supreme Court that February.[6]

Thousands of black men, women, and children escorted the regiment north through the city to Campbell Hospital. The stars were out by the time the throng dispersed. Perhaps it was shortly after taps on this night that the regimental commander recorded his welcome home for the unit and then tucked it into his private papers. The next day, the men rested and prepared their uniforms and weapons for a long and eventful Tuesday.

Early on the morning of October 10, 1865, the regiment assembled its companies and Colonel Holman ordered his men to shoulder their arms and march toward the White House. Entering through the eastern gate the regiment formed double columns in front of the Executive Mansion. President Johnson came out reviewed the troops and addressed them for about 30 minutes.

The Boston *Evening Transcript* analyzed the significance of the White House speech with the following words:

The address of President Johnson to the regiment of colored troops, recruited in the District of Columbia, is really one of the remarkable events of the present time. That a President of the United States should devote an half hour to counseling those who, only four years ago, had no rights which white men were bound to respect - that he should enforce the idea of the Government being based upon the principle of equality, and speak of the dusky warriors before him as his countrymen, significantly indicated the position now occupied by the nation. It shows that the whole people have been advanced by the war to a point requiring only a few more progressive steps to insure the perfect recognition of the democratic idea as applied to men of every station, rank, and color.

The demonstration at Washington yesterday deserves additional force from the fact that the principal actor in it was a Southern man, born among the baleful influences of the "institution" and inheriting all its prejudices, but yet compelled by the logic of events to acknowledge the manhood of a race whom he had seen despoiled of every privilege. The secessionists of the South, in forcing the true Union men of that section to take sides against slavery, did, unwittingly, a great service to the country. It is to be hoped that the partially "reconstructed" advocates of Southern dominion will continue their unconscious efforts to bring the general Government into full sympathy with the demands of even-handed republican justice.[7]

This was the first event of this kind in the history of the United States. During his speech, Johnson thanked the men for their service and encouraged them to adopt habits of morality, industry, order and self-control. At times, however, his words were condescending, if not offensive. He wondered aloud "whether the colored race can be incorporated and mixed with the people of the United States - to be made a harmonious and permanent ingredient in the population.... Are the digestive powers of the American government sufficient to receive this element in raw shape, and digest it and make it work healthfully upon the system that has incorporated it? That is the question to be determined." To men who had just spent two years of their lives enduring shot and shell for their liberty, Johnson questioned whether they were ready: "...to give evidence to the world that you are capable and competent to govern yourselves ...establish the fact that you are fit and qualified to be free." Not only did he take the occasion to wonder aloud whether blacks could "be made to take their place and work harmoniously and congrusomely [sic] in our system" but, as if these men were children and not ex-slaves who had witnessed white men violate their mothers, sisters, and daughters, he counseled them with these words: "I have lived in a southern state and know the habits of your people under the influence of slavery and I conjure you to live virtuously and respect the marriage relation. Be honest, moral, and industrious." This is your country as well as anybody else's country, he told them, "this country is founded upon the principles of equality, and the standard by which persons are to be estimated is according to their worth." Johnson encouraged them to "...do something by your example in civil life as you have done in the field."[8]

Johnson's words, however, were further proof of the "complete revolution of sentiment" noted by General Grant in his memoirs, by several members of Congress, and southern political conservatives. In 1862, Johnson, as military governor of Tennessee, had favored confiscation of and redistribution of rebel property to "honest and industrious men." He had also warned that "treason must be made odious, and traitors must be punished and impoverished."[9]

By the final year of the year of the war, the one-time tailor, alcoholic, and slaveholder from Tennessee had spun on a political dime, renounced his earlier positions, and embraced the doctrine of restoring his native region and its white citizens to their prewar prominence. Blacks would not be slaves again, not quite. Those who stayed that is. Johnson now favored black emigration. And he emerged in short order as a foe of black civil rights, the Freedmen's Bureau, and efforts to redistribute abandoned rebel farmlands to ex-slaves. In speech after speech beginning shortly after Lincoln's death, Johnson essentially told African Americans to be

Campbell Hospital.

quiet, know their place and wait to be led by a white "Moses." Johnson reserved that role for himself. Johnson's dislike for dealing with all but the most servile of blacks was illustrated at Lincoln's inaugural in March 1865. Frederick Douglass described it. "I was standing in the crowd by the side of Mrs. Thomas J. Dorsey when Mr. Lincoln touched Mr. Johnson, and pointed me out to him. The first expression which came to his face, and which I think was the true index of his heart, was one of bitter contempt and aversion. Seeing that I observed him, he tried to assume a more friendly appearance; it was too late. It was useless to close the door when all within had been seen."[10]

Johnson exhibited less obvious personal distaste while reviewing the District's black regiment that October day. Even his speech could not dampen the enthusiasm of the occasion. The troops cheered the best of the president's words. When he finished, the regimental band played. The soldiers marched back to Campbell Hospital.

The regiment arrived back at the hospital about 20 minutes before one. They were ordered to form in close columns near the main office by the music stand and given the command to stack arms. The band played another selection. A Mr. Bowker introduced an old friend, George F.T. Cook. He had helped organize the regiment. And, he had, as the *National Republican* pointed out "...made the presentation of a flag to the regiment before their departure to the field - a flag of which ...nothing but the staff remains."[11]

Cook described the services of the regiment, the exhilaration of victory and the anguish for the men who had lost their lives in service of their country. He concluded his words with a stirring reminder of the upcoming struggle for black enfranchisement, how some former friends who had helped in the work to end slavery were now deserting them, publicly doubting the right of African Americans to vote, even those who had bravely borne the rigors of battle. He pointed to the regiment's tattered banners insisting that enough allies remained ready for the next great contest: to obtain the vote. His brief speech drew great applause. The 30 year-old Cook and his older brother John, Jr., still operated the school founded by their father, the Reverend John F. Cook, Sr. In 1868, George F.T. Cook would become superintendent of the District's (and Georgetown's) black schools, a position he would occupy until 1900.[12]

Reverend W.G. Raymond next took the stand. In 1863 Jane Grey Swisshelm had described him and his speaking style:

> A close communion, revival Baptist preacher, full six feet high, with a square face full of determination; but slightly indebted to colleges for his gifts; apt in preaching to wander from the direct line of the subject to relate incidents in his own experience; confident of his ability to charge a battery or get up a revival; with a voice perfectly lion-like and a most powerful frame - he is a formidable specimen of a Yankee soldier.[13]

Raymond spoke with a certain paternal pride of how he had followed proudly his regiment's progress and his expectations of its success had been fully realized. He recounted the early difficulties met in raising the unit and concluded on the hopeful note that he had no doubt that sooner or later the men would secure their full rights. Neither he nor Rev. J.D. Turner had been idle since the regiment had left town. Using their contacts on Capitol Hill, they had been floating bills and memorials through Congress in a thus far futile attempt to obtain $800.00 to be split evenly between them, as compensation for recruiting the regiment. By the time of the speech, however, Turner had been dead for several months. Raymond, without success, continued to press the claim on behalf of himself and Turner's heirs.

A Mr. Bliss stepped up and read the names of those persons who had contributed funds toward the raising of the regiment. He thanked Brigadier General John H. Martindale, who was military governor of the district of Washington while the regiment was being organized, for providing troops to protect the black recruits. He urged the veterans to petition Congress for suffrage.

Chaplain Turner came forward to introduce Colonel Holman, their "father" whom he claimed, in a rhetorical flight of fancy, the rebels feared as much as they did the seven-headed dragon. Turner related that Holman was the senior colonel in the entire United States Colored Troops and should have been made a major general. He recollected that Holman, however, had told him "...he wanted only to have the privilege of taking the regiment home and restoring its brave men to their wives and children, their fathers and mothers, and brothers and sisters."

Holman moved forward to thunderous cheering and applause from his men. He looked out over the ranks of blue and said simply that he took pride in returning this brave regiment, which had never disgraced itself, to their friends, and on behalf of his officers and men he thanked the gentlemen of the committee for the flattering reception they had received. Sergeant George Hatton presented Holman with "a beautiful wreath with a handsome centerpiece of flowers."

The regiment was dismissed for 30 minutes while the banquet was set. One of the hospital's long dining halls was reserved for the feast. Even so, it was not large enough to accommodate all the men at once. They were divided into two shifts of about 400 each.

As each man filed into the long hall he saw a sumptuous meal catered by James Wormley. The tables were piled high with mouth-watering sides of beef, racks of lamb and mutton, whole roasted pigs, hams, and chickens and more, each garnished with red, white, and blue trimmings.

The *National Republican* reported:

> The seats of honor for the officers and guests were elaborately adorned with evergreens and flags of our Union. The old festoons that ornamented the hall have turned a nice yellow - the evergreens having become ever-dry - but they afforded a not unpleasant contrast to the fresh garlands and bouquets which were prepared especially for this occasion.

The officers had bouquets of immortelles presented to them, and Col. Holman was favored with a wreath of the same suspended across his breast. The tables bore a rich load of comestibles prepared in Wormley's best style, and when our reporter left the scene, hungry soldiers were doing ample justice to the repast.[14]

The celebration spread throughout the hospital as a huge crowd again engulfed the barracks and grounds. Gospel tunes sung with great fervor climbed from the throats of several groups invited to the reception. After the banquet, unmarried soldiers strolled with their sweethearts. The married men kissed their wives and played games with their children with the joyous abandon only peace could bring.

October 12, 1865 was the final day for the First USCT. The regiment assembled for a final photograph by Alexander Gardner. An associate of Matthew Brady, Gardner photographed many battles and used his craft to aid Allen Pinkerton's intelligence work. His office stood on the corner of 7th and D Streets, N.W.

Colonel Holman issued his final message to his men:

Headq'rs U.S. Colored Troops
Washington, D.C., October 12, 1865

Circular
This regiment is now paraded for the last time, and its existence as an organization will end this day. Upon the arrival of the paymaster, company officers will superintend the payment of their companies, and see that good order is preserved. As fast as the men receive their discharges they will be passed out of the enclosure by the guard, when all responsibility over them on the part of their company officers will cease.

The colonel commanding earnestly calls upon every soldier of the regiment after their discharge to conduct themselves as honorable men and citizens of a great and free country. Accept of the good advice of his Excellency, the President of the United States, and of your friends, who have honored you with a bountiful and hearty reception. It is with regret that he is obliged to say that there has been connected with this regiment a few bad men, but the good character of the many, and their brilliant deeds upon the field, completely obscures their bad conduct and renders them necessary of no further notice; further than that, he calls upon them for the last time for their own good to reform and become good men.

As he has labored for you in the past, so will he labor for you in the future; and whenever a discharged soldier of this regiment, whose character is good, requires a letter of recommendation from him, he can always procure it by letter.

The officers of this regiment, who have so nobly sustained themselves, and performed their duties under so many disadvantageous and trying circumstances, require no commendation from the colonel commanding. It cannot add to their renown. He can only thank them for the manner in which they have aided and sustained him as their commanding officer.

By command of Colonel John H. Holman.
N. L. Bishop, Adjutant.[15]

The officers and men lined upon columns in front of the paymaster received their soldier's pay and were offered the opportunity to purchase their arms and equipment for six dollars. Most men paid the money to keep these mementoes of their military service. As the men shook hands, passed out of hospital grounds and dispersed, the only event to mar the festivities occurred. The next day the *Star* described what happened under the caption:

Murder at Campbell Hospital. - Yesterday afternoon, as the First U.S. Colored Regiment were leaving their quarters at Campbell Hospital, they having been paid off and discharged, one of them, Jacob Clark of Company D, shot a colored woman, who had followed the regiment from North Carolina causing her death in a few minutes, the ball having passed through her neck. Just before the shooting took place Clark was seen in company with the woman, (whose name last night could not be ascertained), and they appeared to be angry with each other, and some parties heard him say "You have not been any comfort to me." As soon as the report was [heard] Lieut. P. B. Bergiven, the Military Commandant of the hospital, hastened towards the spot and seeing the accused walking away hurriedly, arrested him. Clark stated that he had shot the woman but that he had not done it purposely. He was at once taken before the woman, who was dying, and she identified him as the man who shot her, and stated that he did it intentionally. Lieut. Bergiven took charge of the corpse and prisoner, with such witnesses as he could find until the Coroner would hold an inquest. Clark belongs to the northern part of the city.[16]

At the inquest the next day, it was established that the shooting occurred about 2:45 p.m. and had been done by Jacob Clark. After reviewing the evidence and testimony, the jury ruled that the unknown black woman came to her death at Clark's hands. He was quickly brought before a justice who after further examination handed down a charge of murder. Clark was placed in jail.

SERVICE, SACRIFICE, AND STRUGGLE

"Of the 1,000 men who composed the regiment when it left the city only 220 have returned." noted the *National Republican* when the regiment returned. "Since going into the field it has received 480 recruits, and the present number of the regiment is 790." The only field officer of the original complement who returned with the regiment was the quartermaster, Lieutenant Sylvester H. Birdsall.

The regiment returned to the District with the following officers:

Colonel John H. Holman, Commanding
Lieutenant Colonel, Giles H. Rich, (promoted from lieutenant)
Major, Henry S. Perkins
Surgeon, Jacob B. Weist
Assistant Surgeon, Samuel A. Bell
Adjutant, Nathan L. Bishop
Quartermaster, Sylvester H. Birdsall
Chaplain, Henry M. Turner, colored
Band Master, Second Lieutenant George F. Miller

The following is a list of the company officers:

Company A - Captain, H. M. Van Winkle; First Lieutenant, Elam G. Beeman

Company B - Captain, Edward Simonton; First Lieutenant, Horace B. Whitcomb; Second Lieutenant, George P.Miller

Company C - Captain, Charles A. Hill; First Lieutenant, Ethan J. Weidman

Company D - Captain, Henry Ward; First Lieutenant, William H. Kilpatrick; Second Lieutenant, Thomas W. Miller

Company E - Captain, Frederick Pyne; First Lieutenant, George H. Sands

Company F - Captain, Henry H. Brown; First Lieutenant, Robert P. Parker; Second Lieutenant, Harry G. Williams

Company G - Captain, Hiram G. Thompson; First Lieutenant, Edward L. Randall; Second Lieutenant, C. Meech Woolsey

Company H - Captain, Wellington G. Sprague; First Lieutenant, George O. Sanderson; Second Lieutenant, S. S. Mann

Company I - Captain, William H. Davis; First Lieutenant, Frank Otto

Company K - Captain, G. Hiram Holmes; First Lieutenant, Nicholas Larney[17]

Most of the officers in the regiment at its mustering out did not remain in the District. Among Holman's papers at the University of Missouri is a roster of the regiment's commissioned officers with the colonel's "recommendations and remarks and their forwarding addresses." Holman placed the notation "an efficient and valuable officer" by each name, except for First Lieutenants Ethan Weidner and Nicholas Larney. He recorded that both were "addicted to overuse of intoxicating drinks." Holman placed no comments by Second Lieutenant George Miller's name - the regimental band master - or that of Chaplain Turner.

The majority of the officers gave forwarding addresses in various parts of New England, Pennsylvania, or the Midwest. First Lieutenant Samuel Bell, an assistant surgeon, was shown with an address of Alexandria, Virginia. Larney and Miller listed Washington, D.C. Holman listed Chealsea, Massachusetts but, like several other officers, he did not remain there long. He received a brevet promotion to brigadier general in 1865 for "gallant and meritorious service." He left the military that year. By 1869 he had returned to his old trade, and was supervising construction of the United States Custom House in Astoria, Oregon. In 1871 he began superintending the construction of the United States Custom House at Knoxville, Tennessee. Made of fine East Tennessee marble, the building

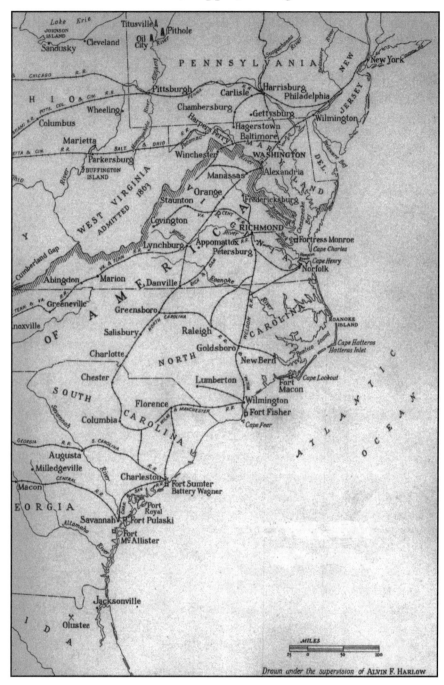

Map of major areas of regimental recruitment and operations.

still stands at what is now 314 West Clinch Avenue. The structure is now home to the East Tennessee Historical Center. In 1876 he applied for and began receiving a pension. Holman died in St. Louis, Missouri on June 26, 1883.[18]

Among the officers that received brevet elevations to the next higher ranks at the end of the war were Major Henry S. Perkins, Captain Henry Ward, and Captain Edward Simonton. Simonton remained in uniform until 1870 when he was discharged at his own request. Sylvester A. Birdsall left the service and on December 29, 1865 received a commission as surveyor of customs for Camden, New Jersey.[19]

The regiment participated in a number of small engagements and in the following major battles:

> Wilson's Wharf, May 24, 1884; Baylor's Farm, June 9, 1864; Petersburg, June 15, 1864; Deep Bottom, September 29, 1864; Fort Harrison, September 30, 1864; Fair Oaks, October 27, 1864; Fort Fisher (No. 1) December 25, 1864; Fort Fisher (No. 2) January 15, 1865; Sugar Loaf, N.C., February 18, 1865; Wilmington, N.C., February 20, 1865; Cox's Bridge, March 24, 1865.

They were among the "picked men" in the attack on Fort Fisher and fought bravely. They helped to secure Goldsboro, Raleigh, and were part of the Union forces in the area when General Johnston surrendered to General Sherman. The regiment received favorable mention in dispatches from such Union generals as Benjamin Butler and William H.F. "Baldy" Smith.

After the war the following story of love and trust emerged and was chronicled by Richard Devens Miller in *The Pictorial Book of Anecdotes and Incidents of the War of the Rebellion:*

Faith and its Reward

Not far from the Capitol in Washington lived an old Negro woman, whose only boy enlisted, in the spring of 1864 in the Negro regiment organized in that city. He took part in the action of July 30 in front of Petersburg, and was one of those who fell wounded near the famous crater. "Badly wounded and in the hands of the rebels," was the word that came to his mother. That was in August. The autumn months came and went in secession, but brought no further word of this only son of his mother and she a widow. Her friends and his friends generally believed him dead. It did not seem probable that he had survived his wounds yet no one had the heart to say as much to his poor old mother.

She continually said "I trust in de good Lord." She did not appear to think it possible her boy would die. Much effort was made in the latter half of November and the first half of December to get word from him, but all to no avail. "Some one ought to tell his mother," was often remarked among those who were interested in the case, yet no one spoke discouragingly to her. Who could do it? She wondered why she did not hear from him, she never wearied in devising crude and simple plans for communicating with him. About the middle of December, or a little later she was heard to say, "De Lord he will pervide an' I shall hear from him bime-by." That was on a Tuesday. The next Thursday afternoon he opened the door of his old mother's little house, and walked in and threw his arms around her neck. Wasn't that a royal Christmas gift for the trustful old soul? Half an hour later she burst into the house of friends who had aided her, with only "my boy's come, my boy's come!" He had not been wounded, but was taken prisoner and sent to the Libby Prison.

The enlisted men of the regiment had undergone the greatest change during the years of the war. Before the Emancipation Proclamation opened the door to their military service the men had been mostly farmers and laborers but there was also an amazingly diverse range of skilled trades represented. And it is presumed that most of these veterans returned to livelihoods with which they were familiar, as did Charles Brown profiled in Chapter Four:

OCCUPATION	TOTAL	OCCUPATION	TOTAL
ARTIST	1	HARNESS MAKER	1
BAKER	4	HOSPITAL STEWARD	1
BARBER	19	HOSTLER	20
BLACKSMITH	21	HOUSE SERVANT	4
BOATMAN	5	HUCKSTER	3
BOOK BINDER	1	LABORER	327
BRICKMAKER	6	MARINE	1
BRICK MASON	1	MASON	3
BRICKLAYER	4	MESSENGER	1
BUTCHER	15	MILLER	1
CAR HAND	1	NURSERYMAN	1
CARPENTER	20	OX DRIVER	1
CAULKER	1	OYSTER CATCHER	1
CHIMNEY SWEEP	1	OYSTERMAN	2
CHORE BOY	2	PAINTER	3
CIGAR MAKER	1	PLASTERER	5
CLERK	1	PORTER	2
COACHMAN	6	ROPE MAKER	1
COAL HEAVER	2	SAILOR	22
COOK	14	PRINTER	1
COOPER	1	SALOON WAITER	3
COTTON INSPECTOR	1	SCHOOL BOY	1
CUTLER	1	SEAMAN	1
DRIVER	1	SERVANT	4
DRUGGIST	1	SHOEMAKER	9
DYER	1	STEVEDORE	1
ERRAND BOY	2	TAILOR	1
FIELD HAND	11	TEAMSTER	28
FIREMAN	1	TOBACCONIST	3
FISHERMAN	3	UMBRELLA MAKER	1

FARMER	406	WAGONER	1
FOUNDRYMAN	1	WAGONING	1
GARDNER	4	WAITER	121
GIN WRIGHT	1	WATERMAN	2
GUN SMITH	1	WHITEWASHER	1
HACKMAN	3	WOOL SPINNER	1

Among the 1200 men whose names appear on the regiment's rolls, enlisted men specified 72 different occupations. The numbers above cover more than 90 percent of the unit's members.

The cost of victory was steep. There were still members of the regiment lying in army hospitals up and down the Atlantic seaboard recovering from sickness or their wounds. Others were discharged, crippled for life by battle. Jesse Reader, a private from Charles County, Maryland, was a sharpshooter who was struck in the left knee by a rebel minie ball. His leg was amputated in March 1865. By August 1865 he was being treated at Summit House Army Hospital in Philadelphia, Pennsylvania. His medical records note that at the time of his transfer to the hospital "his stump was nearly healed" and his general health was good. He received a disability discharge in November 1865 and returned to the arms of Colbert Reader, his father, in Charles County.

Never far from the thoughts of the officers and men who returned were memories of their comrades "who were sleeping their last long sleep" and "whose only honest epitaph was that they had done their duty well." The First USCT had lost four officers and 67 enlisted men killed or mortally wounded. One officer and 113 enlisted men lost their lives from disease. These men are buried all over the East Coast from New York to North Carolina. Only a few are buried in cemeteries in or near the District. Private Jerry Jones died of ascites, (dropsy of the abdomen) and phthisis on February 16, 1865, at Harewood Hospital which stood near what is now the Soldier's Home.

Several men from the First USCT were originally buried at the Freedmen's Cemetery in Alexandria, Virginia. At least some of these

Veterans of the First USCT at the 1915 G.A.R. encampmanet at Washington, D.C. John P. Quander is seated on the front row second from right.

graves are believed to have been among those relocated to Alexandria National Cemetery in 1865. In the Cypress Hill National Cemetery in Brooklyn, New York, rests Private Josiah Brown. He died of typhoid fever on July 24, 1864. His wife Mary and the rest of his family lived at North Point in Baltimore, Maryland. A large number of the regiment's casualties rest at Hampton National Cemetery in Hampton, Virginia. Rudimentary mortuary practices required immediate burial close to where the soldiers died.

Casehardened by the severity of battle, most of the men had somehow still carved out time to devote to the gentler pursuit of knowledge. Letter by letter, line by line, page by page, the men had unlocked the secrets of "reading, writing, spelling, and ciphering." Approximately 100 enlisted men could read and write when they joined the First USCT. At the time the regiment was mustered out, three times that number could read and write. "At the beginning of their service one half of the non-commissioned officers could read and write but at the end of the war, nearly all the non-commissioned officers could read and write. At the mustering out date there were only 24 sergeants and 61 corporals." Throughout the history of the regiment there had been a total of 56 sergeants and 128 corporals.[20]

Education effectively elevated their awareness of and desire for the right to vote. The exodus from bondage to liberty was a reality. Now the time had come to press for the elective franchise, what Douglass called "that glorious insignia of citizenship." The vote was also the keystone of the new social and political contract that African Americans intended to establish between themselves and whites in the District. Other parts of the contract included securing and expanding public education for African Americans, establishing opportunities for employment in the city government, and, a greater voice in local affairs. In April 1864, 2,500 African Americans had signed a petition to Congress demanding the ballot in city matters. Resolutions and petitions continued. In 1866, a group of black men at the 15th Street Presbyterian Church asked Congress to grant "impartial suffrage" without regard to race. In January of the following year a national convention of colored soldiers and sailors presented a resolution to the Senate which advocated blocking "...the admission of any state or territory into the Union, whose constitution makes any distinction among citizens thereof on account of color." Senator Timothy O. Howe of Wisconsin referred the resolution to a joint committee and saw to it that the resolution was printed.

Most whites in the District had no intention of sharing power with blacks. Angry and bewildered at the pace of change, the insistence of black demands, and the expansion of their population, whites were also repulsed at the looming possibility of congressional activists ramming civil equity laws down their throats. And this battle was set to occur in an increasingly severe post-war economic recession.

The celebrations for the return of the First USCT had barely ended when the city council, in the fall of 1865, issued a declaration reflecting the sentiment of the average white voter:

> The white man, being the superior race, must... rule the black.... Why he is black and we white, or why we the superior and he the inferior race are matters past our comprehension. It, then, becomes a civil as well as a Christian duty to weigh his capacity for advancement in civil rights, and the only test by which his claim to the right of suffrage can best be ascertained will be by a comparison with the white race under like circumstances.
>
> If it took the ancient Briton a thousand years to emerge from his only half-civilized condition... to reach the point to qualify him for the exercise of this right, how long would it reasonably take the black man, who but about two hundred years ago was brought from Africa....[21]

The mayor and city council were able to discredit another black suffrage petition after finding that fewer than 30 percent of the 2,500 signatories were property owners. Local politicians also attempted to deny the right of veterans of the First USCT to the ballot. W. W. Moore, the President of the Board of Aldermen spuriously claimed "Of the Negroes residing here in 1861 and 1862, ...not one hundred entered the service of the United States, but those who did go were refugees and contrabands who came here to seek bread and who were taken possession of by men of their own color, and sold into the service of the United States."[22]

In fact, blacks in the District were credited with sending 3,269 men (the equivalent of three regiments) to war-time military service representing a higher proportion of their population than the number (13,265) credited to local whites. Moreover, District blacks were also shown to have paid taxes on property worth over $1,225,000, built and maintained 21 churches, 20 Sabbath schools, and operated 30 civic and benevolent societies and groups.[23]

In December 1865, the political authorities of Washington and Georgetown arranged for a plebiscite on black suffrage "to ascertain and make known the opinion of the people of the two cities upon a subject so immediately affecting their welfare as a community." The vote, of course, was limited to qualified white males. The Washington vote: 6,556 - the largest, with only two exceptions, ever attained in the city - was resoundingly negative; only 35 votes were cast in favor of extending the elective franchise to African Americans.

In Georgetown the tally was 813 against and only one in favor; this turnout was greater than the average vote cast during the preceding annual election. In sum, the results were 7,369 against and only 36 in favor.[24] Douglass thought white voters "would at any time during the great war for union and liberty, have preferred [Jefferson] Davis to Lincoln, Lee, and Grant." President Johnson would use the results of these votes time and again in his efforts during the next two years to block the black franchise in the nation's capital.

Black aspirations would again need powerful allies. African Americans looked to Capitol Hill and found their friends Stevens, Wade, Sumner and a handful of others to help them in their battle. Wade first introduced a bill "to regulate the elective franchise in the District of Columbia" in the

Senate where it stalled and then died not passing until the end of the year.[25] In January 1866, Stevens finagled the measure through the House but around both men surged near hysterical resistance to black suffrage. It is popular today to believe that with the surrender at Appomattox came immediate public recognition of black valor and acceptance and understanding of the expectations of African Americans. The evidence shows otherwise.

Between 1865 and 1869 popular votes in New York, New Jersey, Ohio, Michigan, Connecticut, and Pennsylvania revealed firm opposition to the idea of the black American voter. Democrats in Pennsylvania, Steven's own state, issued a resolution on March 5, 1866 that read in part: "The white race alone is entitled to the control of the Government of the Republic, and we are unwilling to grant the Negroes the right to vote." Democrats in Delaware expressed similar feelings in a resolution which opposed the vote for blacks in the District saying that such measures had "their unqualified disapprobation." State Republicans were against black District voters but consented to Congress' authority over the city as long as there was no "attempt to enforce Negro suffrage upon the states." Although a northern state, Delaware had retained slavery until it was abolished by the 13th Amendment. Through a variety of means, blacks in the state were prevented from voting from 1873 until 1897 despite the 14th and 15th Amendments to the Constitution. Frank Blair, an anti-black former Union general who was the Democratic candidate for vice-president in 1868, called black suffrage bills "atrocious measures" and labeled their proponents in Congress "vindictive" usurpers who would let loose "a host of ignorant Negroes... to strip the white race of its birthright...."[26]

In December 1866, District black suffrage bills finally made their way through the House and the Senate, and over the President's veto on January 8, 1867. He had made his position clear on that previous January 31 when he characterized such bills "ill-timed, uncalled for, and calculated to do great harm" resulting in a race war and "certain extermination of the Negro population." But Congress had trumped both the President and the District's political leadership. Universal manhood suffrage arrived 19

John P. Quander, a veteran of the regiment, is wearing the black uniform of the Grand Army of the Republic. Organized in 1866, the G.A.R. was a volunteer organization of men who had served in the Union Army or Navy during the Civil War.

months before Congress approved the 14th Amendment and more than three years before ratification of the 15th Amendment to the Constitution. And the final law was free of educational and property qualifications. The new statute banned racial distinctions but limited the franchise to males. Women, paupers, minors, convicted criminals, and former rebels could not vote.

On March 18 voter registration began. One of the first locations was the 19th Street Baptist Church, an African American church, then in the first ward. The *National Intelligencer* reported that 180 blacks and 152 whites signed up.[27] Observing the rapid pace at which the blacks were registering compared to that of whites, the paper noted what it considered an ominous trend: "With such a showing as this, what supreme folly it is for the white voters to refuse to register! In the first, second, and third wards scarcely one-half of the names on the poll list one year ago will be upon the rolls under the new order of things, because the white voters held back and would not be registered."

One of the reasons whites were initially slow to register appears to have been that they did not want jury duty with African Americans. At the end of the registration period, the *National Intelligencer* estimated 8,240 white and 7,271 African American voters on the rolls; a slender city wide majority easily capable of being overturned if progressive whites joined blacks. In addition, there were actual black majorities in the first and second wards. In the third ward, a potential political stalemate existed because the white majority was only 15 votes and in the fifth and seventh wards the white edge varied from only 122 to 247 votes respectively. To the consternation of the Democrats and the joy the Republicans, the African American vote was now a powerful new reality in municipal politics. The first golden age of the black vote was about to begin.[28]

On June 3, 1867, blacks and whites, civilians and voters lined up at the polls. Aware of the historical importance of the event, African Americans behaved with decorum and purpose. In some wards, they rose before

1st Regiment, United States Colored Infantry

athan Adams ★ Samuel Adams ★ Winfield S. Adams ◆ Daniel Addison ◆ George Addison ★ Hamilton Addison ★ Theodore Ad
muel Allen ● William Allen ● Amos Anderson ★ Carey Anderson ★ Cornelius Anderson ★ George Anderson ★ John Anderson
★ Edwin Bailey ★ George W. Bailey ★ Harry Bailey ★ Henry Bailey ★ Thomas Bailey ★ Austin Baker ★ George Baker ★ William Bake
W. Banks ★ Henry Banks ★ John Banks ★ Manuel Banks ★ Robert Banks ★ William Banks ★ James Barber ★ Peter Barlow ★ Geo
ates ★ George W. Bates ★ Martin Bates ★ Armisted Baur ★ Armstead Baur ★ John H. Bauston ★ George Bean ★ Samie A. Bean ★ Will
ett ★ Charles Berkely ★ George Berkely ● James Berry ● William Berry ★ Joseph Bett ★ Jerry Beufort ★ Wyatt Beverly ★ Charles
er Bolden ● Robert Bolden ★ Peter Bonam ★ Armstrad Bond ★ David Boney ★ John Bonn ★ John Bony ◆ John Boom ★ Will
len ★ Abraham C. Bowers ★ Albert Bowie ★ Collumbus Bowie ★ Isaac Bowie ★ John Bowie ★ Nathan Bowling ★ Philip Bowman ★
r W. Briggs ★ Benjamin B. Brisbane ★ Edward Briscoe ★ Frank Briscoe ★ Joseph Briscoe ★ George Brisko ★ Henry Britman ★
Brooks ★ Robert Brooks ★ William Brooks ★ Albert Brown ● Alexander Brown ● Andrew Brown ★ Charles Brown ● Charles H. Bro
. Brown ★ John Henry Brown ★ John T. Brown ★ Josiah Brown ★ Lewis Brown ★ Matthias Brown ★ Nelson T. Brown ★ Robert
George Bryan ★ Jacob Bryan ★ Joseph. W. Bryant ★ William Robert Buchanan ★ Frederick W. Buck ★ Dennis Budd ★ Osamel
Burns ★ Walter Burns ★ Abram Burr ★ Robert Burt ★ Risdon Butcher ★ Alfred Butler ★ Benjamin Butler ★ Charles Butler ●
Daniel J. Canner ★ Curtis Cannon ★ Albert Carroll ★ Benjamin Carroll ◆ George Carroll ◆ Henson Carroll ★ Robert Carroll ◆ W
illiam D. Carter ★ William H. Carter ★ William S. Carter ★ William W. Carter ★ Philip Cartlet ★ Bernard Casanova ★ James C.
Daniel Chase ★ David E. Chase ★ Edward P. Chase ★ Henry Chase ★ Samuel Chase ◆ Shark Checney ★ James Chew ★ John Che
Clay ★ Ellis Claygrett ◆ Isaac Clayton ★ Pell Clefton ★ William Clifton ★ Enoch Colbert ★ Henry Cole ★ Joseph Coleman ★ Le
★ John Combash ★ Wallace Coners ★ James Conley ★ William Conley ★ Daniel J. Conner ★ Frank Cook ★ James E. Cook ★ Jam
Corsay ★ Wesley Coster ◆ George O. D. Courcey ★ Private Cox ★ Thomas Cox ★ Thomas Henry Cravens ★ William H. Crawfor
ond Crutchfield ◆ Joseph Cubbage ★ John Cumbash ◆ Henry Cure ★ Willoughby Curry ★ George Curtis ★ James Curtis ◆ John Cu
is ★ Joseph Davis ● Lorenzo Davis ★ Nehemiah Davis ★ Nelson Davis ★ Robert Davis ★ Thomas Davis ★ William Davis ★ Willi
orge W. Demby ★ George Denby ★ Albert Dennison ★ Henry Desheilds ★ Frederick Devann ◆ Peter Devann ◆ William Dicker
y Dixon ★ Richard Dixon ◆ William Dixon ● Thomas Dockett ● Edward Dorsey ★ Silas Dotson ◆ Jacob Douglas ★ Amos Douglas
s Dudley ★ Humphrey Duette ◆ Charles Duff ★ George Dunmore ◆ Gabriel Dutcher ★ Henry Dwin ◆ Thomas W. Dyson ★ Clifford

Regimental Plaque at the African American Civil War Memorial.

allies could hardly fail to be aware these African Americans overwhelmingly voted the Republican ticket. Nearly a century of white voter privilege had been overturned.

The next day, sour grapes issued forth from the old line politicians who had been turned out of office by callused black hands that had once cut tobacco but had now cut short their political careers. Moore, who had tried to sully the reputation of the First USCT, vented in his last official speech. He reviewed the "humiliating events of the last few days resultingfrom the unjust and oppressive experiment of Congress in enfranchising hordes of ignorant Negroes lately redeemed from slavery who are utterly unqualified for the exercise of the high office conferred upon them."

Racist words from people like Moore, however, failed to quench the joy that black voters felt that day. One of them, John V. Givens, recalled that election day made him proud and happy that he and other members of his race "had met the enemy at the polls on Monday and defeated him." One of the members of the winning slate of candidates to the Board of Aldermen, John R. Elvans complimented the African American voters and assured them that the election "...forever settled in Washington the question of discrimination on account of color." He also said he believed that "in a few short years, possibly in one short year, you men of color will be among our legislators and our jurors."

Elvans' prediction came true the next year. In 1868 the initial fruits of black suffrage became evident when John F. Cook and Carter Stewart, a barber, became the first African Americans elected to municipal office in the District. And on the frontline of this battle as he was during so many as a soldier was a member of the First USCT, Sergeant Major George W. Hatton. He had been elected secretary of two of the many republican clubs established in the wake of the passage of the Negro suffrage bills. He was nominated in 1869 for a seat on the city council representing ward four, the only black to receive such an honor. But he declined the nomination. He ran successfully for the seat in 1869 and served in the administration of Sayles J. Bowen, a white republican with a long record of support for local African American causes. During his term in office, Bowen helped implement Congressional edicts to eliminate the words "white" and "colored" from city ordinances and establish fines for anyone violating public accommodation laws on the basis of race. Hatton nevertheless openly broke with Bowen when he disagreed with him on policy and fiscal matters.[31] After a year-one term on the city council, Hatton decided not to run again.

Like Hatton, many veterans of the First USCT became leaders in their communities, churches, and schools. Charles Brown helped found Mt. Hope Baptist Church in Charles County, Maryland when he returned home after the war. Many veterans also joined branches of the Grand Army of the Republic, an organization of Civil War veterans and like John P. Quander, who had been a corporal in Company G, attended periodic reunions for years to maintain ties with battlefield comrades. He died in 1921.

THE LEGACY OF THE FIRST USCT

The valor of the regiment in battle earned for its members the highest claim on American citizenship. They offered their lives in defense of justice, humanity, and freedom. As the historian C.M. Green remarked in *The Secret City*: "The pride colored men took in wearing the United States uniform and fighting for their country would sustain them in the trying years to come and inspired in their descendants of the next four generations a sense of special distinction."

The regiment, however, left much more than pride and inspiration; it left behind tangible achievements and institutions that exist in the District today. The record of the First USCT forever demolished white objections to the service of African Americans in the city's militia, and it solidified and affirmed their martial spirit, desire, and potential. During the summer of 1864, after the regiment had proved itself, two proposals came forward suggesting that black residents be encouraged to form a volunteer militia organization to defend the District. The proposal that John W. Forney of the *Chronicle* offered on July 20 drew an interested response from the

Army's adjutant general's office. The office requested that Major General C.C. Augur, commander of the local military district, provide officers and enlisted men "as necessary to aid in the organization and instruction of the association." With troops and equipment in short supply, the Army apparently changed its mind.

In response to a similar idea about the same time from R. A. Armstrong, the Army indicated on July 29 that "the interests of the service would not be promoted by the organization of a regiment for the special services proposed by you."[32] Congress had already removed racial restrictions from its 1862 militia bill and again in 1867, the same year black suffrage came to the District. With those conditions removed, the way was clear for the establishment of black units; the earliest of which were the Butler Zouaves, named after General Butler and the Stanton Guards who chose their name in honor of Lincoln's second Secretary of War. Other units followed in the 1880's. In 1891 the units were reorganized into the First Separate Battalion which ultimately led to today's District of Columbia National Guard.[33]

The return of the regiment released into the local population hundreds of men keenly familiar with regulations, organizational structure, and the preservation of law and order. They were excellent job candidates when, in July 1869, the Washington police force hired its first black policemen, Calvin C. Caruthers and Charles C. Tillman. David E. Chase who joined the force in 1872, was probably the same David E. Chase, a native Washingtonian, who was a member of Company E of the First USCT. He served as a patrolman for three years. From 1867, Congress had required that all candidates for the police be honorably discharged veterans. The late 1860's and the 1870's were important periods of reorganization and expansion and most of these early African American policemen built records of fidelity and courage.[34] Every time a black police officer goes on duty today that heritage of service and devotion is affirmed and renewed.

Light After Darkness, an 1896, *"Pocket History of the Negro Race,"* was written by R.C.O. Benjamin whom *The Washington Bee,* a black newspaper, called "...a scholar, he is a model speaker. His command of language is perfect and almost unlimited. His presence on the platform is fine and his delivery graceful. He carries his audience from tears, to peals of hearty laughter; then to an attentive silence that is remarkable." In writing of the service of black troops during the Civil War, Benjamin, who was also Chairman of the Board of Trustees of the Alexandria, Virginia Normal and Industrial School and who was undoubtedly inspired by the deeds of the First USCT, described the services of black Civil War soldiers:

> their iron nerve, patriotic valor, incomprehensible courage, indubitable heroism, their sufferings and privations, their long marches and stubborn fights, their impregnable alignments, the terrible changes endured and made for the freedom of their race and to keep the Government from being torn in twain, called forth from the Chief Magistrate the assertion that no braver men than they ever stood before as brave an enemy; and during the long night of war not a traitor in black skin was ever found." Never did a race in all history of wars merit such a tribute.[35]

The story of the First USCT was told and told again in the ensuing decades. The hallowed deeds of these men served to inspire the post-Civil War generation of African Americans who had not been born under the slavery's lash. In October and November 1915, *The Washington Bee* began to carry advertisements for a series of "historical charts and historic pictures" drawn and sold by M.C. Maxfield, a local black artist living at 1229 First Street, N.W. For a quarter, you could purchase a likeness of Lincoln, Grant, Sumner, or Douglass. Among the 38 different subjects were famed abolitionists, Union generals, and a dozen black soldiers from several regiments of the United States Colored Troops, including the First USCT. Picture No. 20 was that of "Hopkins and Henderson, 1st U.S. Col. Regt." While no known copies of the Maxfield pictures have survived, regimental records confirm the existence of a Sergeant Charles Henderson of Alexandria, Virginia and a Private Robert Hopkins, a native of the District.

According to the *Bee*, the artist wanted "to honor the colored race" and his pictures had a five-fold "requisite" purpose: "For home and office ornament, for veneration to our patriotic benefactors, for the truth of history for newspaper articles, for patriotic sentiment from all our libraries, for imparting patriotic history not heretofore easy of access." The newspaper wanted the pictures and biographies "...in the homes of everybody... and in every colored home but they should be in the schools as well. The colored child knows but little of the great colored men of the race."

Colonel Holman in his final speech at Campbell Hospital had this to say about the men with whom he had served for the past two years:

> Many a hardship have you undergone, but, it was the price of liberty, and as much as you have suffered I full well knew you were prepared to offer still greater sacrifices for the maintenance of human rights. How stands it today? Jefferson Davis is a criminal in the hands of justice, and his fancied slave empire scattered to the 4 winds of the earth. The humblest soldier that stands before me today would not exchange positions with this dark traitor in the hands of justice who 4 years ago was the proud aristocrat of the slave power.... Our work is nearly finished and let us be content. There need be no misgivings about the future. Those wise statesmen, who have carried us safely through this struggle will take good care that your kindred receive the benefit of the victory gained by the force of your arms.[36]

Holman's words are a fitting conclusion to this episode in the saga of Lincoln's great "broken shackle" army. The battle to enlist the emancipated, to help his freeborn brother to volunteer was one of the noblest and far reaching endeavors of the American Civil War. The resultant victory was a golden hour in the life of the District of Columbia and the nation.

Service and Freedom.

AFTERWORD

The 1st Regiment, United States Colored Infantry organized in the District of Columbia May 19 to June 30, 1863, like so many other regiments of the United States Colored Troops, suffered the dangers of combat with the enemy and the humiliation of discrimination by their white comrades in arms. But on May 24, 1864, in the battle at Wilson's Wharf, along the banks of the James River, the 1st USCT made a singularly unique contribution to the legacy of the United States Colored Troops (USCT) in the Civil War. In this battle, the actions of the 1st USCT silenced for the duration of the war the critics who insisted that black troops were not capable of fighting exclusively on their own without major support by white troops. General Edward A. Wild, an abolitionist from Massachusetts, who commanded the 1st Brigade that consisted of the 1st U.S. Colored Infantry, was thrilled with his men's performance. "Within my own command, all behaved steadily and well," he said. "[They] stood up to their work like veterans... [against a force] at least double my own, and probably triple." The New York Times correspondent who watched the battle rhapsodized that "the chivalry of Fitzhugh Lee and his cavalry division was badly worsted in the contest last Tuesday with negro troops, composing the garrison at Wilson's Landing." Even Confederate Major General Fitzhugh Lee, nephew of General Robert E. Lee later admitted that his troops had "found a foe worthy of their steel." Sergeant George W. Hatton of the 1st U.S. Colored Infantry, recorded the performance of his regiment at Wilson's Wharf for posterity, by noting that "the heroism displayed by the gallant boys of the 1st needs no comment, for they have won for themselves unfading laurels, to be stamped on the pages of history." C.R. Gibbs' history is a testament to the honor that the 1st USCT has passed on to all of us who love freedom.

> Asa Gordon,
> Secretary-General
> Sons & Daughters United States Colored Troops

DOCUMENTS

To Col. Holman
(undated letter)
Commander of 1st Col
Reg of D.V.

We the undersigned regularly ordained ministers of the Gospel, are well acquainted with the Rev. Henry McNeal Turner, and take pleasure in recommending him for your grove consideration. He is a regularly ordained minister of the African M. E. Church and in good standing. He is fully qualified, both in a literary and theological point of view, to fill the position with profit to the regiment. He was the first in Washington, to advocate publicly, the enlisting of colored soldiery.

He can but be loyal.

Therefore we recommend him as a fit person, to perform the duties of Chaplain to the 1st Col. Regt. of D.V.

Jacob P. Hamer   Benj T. Tanner
Pastor of John Wesley Church   Pastor of Ebenezer Church

David Smith   Jos. A. Handy
Pastor of Good Hope Church   Pastor, Union Bethel

                                        John T. Hurburt
                                        Pastor, E. St. Chapel

M 1819 Compiled Service Record of Reverend Henry McNeal Turner.

Letter

Pastor of a Washington, D.C., African Methodist Episcopal Church to the
Secretary of War

Washington

August 1ˢᵗ 1863

Dear Sir,   Having been connected with the movement of raising colored
troops, from its commencement in this city,
    And having by repeated Solicitations, concluded to go as the chaplain
of the first colored regiment, the organization was commenced in my
church,
    And having at the request of cols Birney and Holman sent in my
application, endorsed by five regularly ordained ministers,
    And having been kept in suspense for some time, expecting the position
of chaplain, from the promises made by the above named colonels, and the
desire expressed by the Soldiers, and several of the officers of Said
regiment,
    Your honor would greatly relieve me, by informing me ONCE FOR
ALL whether it is the intention of the government to have colored
chaplains or not,
    By answering this questain, leasing your honor, you will settle my own
mind on the subject, and enable me to inform my congregation what they
may depend on your humble servant.

H M Turner

H. M. Turner to Hon. E. M. Stanton, 1 Aug. 1863, filed with T-18 1863,
Letters Received, ser. 360, Colored Troops Division, RG 94 [B-44].
Quoted in *"Freedom."*

Letter

Secretary of the Treasury and an Illinois Congressman to the Secretary
of War

[Washington, D.C.] Sep. 4,, [1863]

Dear Sir, Allow me to introduce the Revd H. M. Turner, the colored
minister of whom I spoke the other day, and whom you said you would
direct to be appointed Chaplain of a Colored Regiment. He has been very
useful in raising the first Colored regiment raised here & Sent to North
Carolina and thinks he could be useful in raising the tone of the men now
forming the second. Yours truly

S P Chase
O Lovejoy

S. P. Chase and O. Lovejoy to Hon. E. M. Stanton, 4 Sept. [1863], filed
with T-18 1863, Letters Received, ser. 360, Colored Troops Division, RG
94 [B-44]. Quoted in *"Freedom."*

Headquarters 1st U.S. Colored Troops
Camp Near Portsmouth, VA
January 3, 1864

Regimental Order No. 69

By order of the Brigadier General Commanding Norfolk and Portsmouth, this regiment has been detailed as the Provost Guard of Portsmouth.

In announcing this order the colonel commanding desires to congratulate the men of his command upon the great progress made by them since their enlistment into the service of the United States. When this regiment was formed, it was confidently asserted that it was not possible for a colored man to make a soldier. Many obstacles were put in their way; but by their attention to duty, and by soldierly bearing, the men of this command have overcome these obstacles, have received the commendations of the Commanding General, and have been appointed to Provost Guard of the city of Portsmouth.

The colonel commanding desires also to impress upon officers, non-commissioned officers and privates of his command, the great importance of maintaining the good reputation which this regiment now enjoys among the officers of this District; of observing the strictest care that no improprieties take place; that no outrages are committed upon citizens; remembering that the offenses of one man will be visited upon the entire regiment, and that by the misconduct of one man while on duty in town the whole command may be relieved from duty there and sent into the field.

By order of Colonel John H. Holman, Commanding
Myron W. Smith, Adjt.

M858, Roll #3, Volumes 4 and 5, 1864 [2300].

Letter

wilson Creek   Va   May 25th 1864
dear wife   I take the pleasant opportunity of writeing to you a few lines to
inform you of the Late Battle we have had   we was a fight on Tuesday
five hours   we whipp the rebls out   we Killed $200 & captured many
Prisener   out of our Regiment we lost 13 Thirteen Sergent Stephensen
killed & priate out of Company H & about 8 or 10 wounded   we was in
line Wednesday for a battele But the rebels did not Appear   we expect an
Attack every hour   give my love to all & to my sisters give my love   to
Miss Emerline tell John Skinner is well & sends much love to her. Joseph
H Grinnel is well & he is as brave a lion   all the Boys sends there love
them   give my love to Miss Missenger   You must excuse my short Letter
we are most getting ready to go on Picket   No more from your Husband
Ruphus Wright

Ruphus Wright to dear wife, 25 May 1864, filed with affidavit of
Elisabeth Wright, 21 Aug. 1865, Letters & Orders Received, ser. 4180,
Norfolk VA Asst. Subasst. Comr., RG 105 [A-7945], Quoted in *Freedom.*

Affidavit

Norfolk [Va.] August the 21 1865
This is to certify That Elisabeth Wright Appeared Before me J W Cook
Notary and Counsiler Fore The Freedmen In This Department By
Permission Of Maj General Miles And Swore to The Fowling Statements
and the Said Testimony Was Confermed By Seargant Frank Turner 5th
Sergant Co [I] Wich Said Decased Belong to Captain William Brazzee
Col John Holman Commanding Regiment 18 Armey Core Maj B F Butler
commanding   Having Stated That Her Husband Was Killed in June 1864
Before Petterburgh Rufus Wright And She The Said Widdow-Elisabeth
Wright has Never Received Pay Or Allowances From the Goverment And
know Ask to Receive The Pay That May Be Due The Said Rufus Wright

Her Husband   I have The Honnor To Remain Your Most Obedient Servant

Elisabeth   her mark x Wright
Witness his mark   Frank x Turner

P.S. The Papers in Testimony I here With Enclose To Be Retured with you convenience

Affidavit of Elisabeth Wright, 21 Aug. 1865, Letters & Orders Received, ser. 4180, Norfolk VA Asst. Subasst. Comr., RG 105 [A-7945]. Endorsements. The enclosures mentioned are the marriage certificate and letters printed above. Private Rufus Wright died in the U.S. General Hospital at Ft. Monroe, Virginia, on June 21, 1864, of an abdominal wound received in action at Petersburg on June 15. (Service record of Rufus Wright, 1st USCI. Carded Records, Volunteer Organizations: Civil War, ser. 519, RG 94 [N-40].) Quoted in *Freedom.*

Report of Col. John H. Holman, First U.S. Colored Troops,
of operations June 15.
Headquarters First U.S. Colored Troops,
Camp in the Field, June 20, 1864

Sir: I have the honor to report the movement of the troops under my command in the engagement with the enemy and the assault upon his works before Petersburg on the 15th instant:

Pursuant to orders from division headquarters, I moved from City Point at 2 a.m. on the 15th instant with the following command: First U.S. Colored Troops, Lieutenant-Colonel Wright; Fifth Massachusetts Cavalry, Colonel Russell; two companies Fourth Massachusetts Cavalry, Lieutenant-Colonel Washburn, and Captain Choate's battery. My troops composed the second line in the charge upon the enemy's works, encountered about five miles from City Point. Colonel Russell was wounded in the charge, and was obliged soon after in consequence to retire. The command of that regiment then devolved upon Major Weld. After the rout of the enemy at this point the First United States was ordered in the advance, with directions to clear the way for the advance of the column, and upon arriving at the bridge, about one mile, where the enemy had been previously intrenched, and deploy to the right of the road. From this point the enemy's pickets were engaged and quickly driven in, and the high ground, which was desired for the position of our batteries, secured. This was about 9 a.m. Seven companies of the First United States were subsequently deployed upon this line. About this time Colonel Washburn was relieved from my command, as was also Captain Choate's battery. The Fifth Massachusetts Cavalry were partially held in reserve and partially deployed upon the left flank to protect that part of the line and give notice of any movement of the enemy in that direction. The enemy opened and kept up a destructive fire from his artillery and sharpshooters upon my skirmish line, which could not be returned with much effect, as he was well protected by his intrenchments. About 5 p.m. I was informed that the assault would soon be ordered by the skirmish line only. I made such dispositions of my command as seemed to me best suited to insure success. At 6 p.m. I received the order from General Hinks to make the assault with the skirmish line. I immediately ordered Colonel Wright, First U.S. Colored Troops, to advance upon the enemy's works; at the same time I ordered the captain commanding two companies of the Fifth U.S. Colored Troops, whose men were deployed as skirmishers on the left, to make a determined assault upon the enemy's works in his front in connection with the First United States. Those two companies did not advance for what reason I am not aware. At the same time I dismounted and took immediate command of two companies of the First United States on the left near the Jordan Point road. The ground upon the left covering the approach to the works in my front was found to be covered with timber and brush, and exceedingly difficult to cross. The right of the line under Colonel Wright, having smooth ground to advance over, reached and carried the enemy's works known as Battery No. 6 before I had very much advanced through the brush and timber on the left. I moved forward the two companies on the left as fast as possible, and received the fire from the gun known as Battery No. 9 when within fifty yards, and carried the battery from the front, the enemy running to Battery No. 10, which was still stubbornly held, when opportunely the Fourth United States, who had entered the enemy's works farther to the right, came down upon their flank and carried the position.

Great credit is due Lieutenant-Colonel Wright, commanding First U.S. Colored Troops, and all the line officers and men under his command; also to the commanding officer of the Fifth Massachusetts Cavalry for the prompt obedience to the orders communicated to him.

For further details the report of Lieutenant-Colonel Wright, together with a diagram of the enemy's position, is herewith forwarded. Particular attention is called to that part of Lieutenant-Colonel Wright's report relative to the inefficiency of the stretcher corps.

Much to my surprise I received notice about 9 o'clock the next day that some of the wounded had not been removed from near Battery No. 8, which fact I immediately communicated to the adjutant-general.

I am, captain, with much respect, your obedient servant,

JOHN H. HOLMAN,
Colonel, Commanding.

O.R. 51/1: 263-265.

Letter

October 14, 1864

My dr wife
i take this opportunity to right you A few lines to let you know that I am
well at this time and i hope these lines will find you the same. i am at the
front of the lines ten miles from Rich: And so-far we have had a quiet time
and Comfortable quarters an no fighting. Yet we took the Steam Boat on
the 8 day of October an was on water till tuesday the [illegible] we started
from camp casey, an went to Washington an from there to pinne point an
from there forbes manor an from there to city point an from there to Deep
Bottom an there we got off the boat an marched 6 miles to the front an
joind the first united states colored infntry. Company E. i am there at this
time an we are drilling four in day on the right wing of the line not far
from where we was the hard fight on the 13 day when we whip them an
captured ten hundred rebels prisners an there is about three thousand
rebels Cum over since we bein there we see the rebels every day give my
love to all the inquiring frien and keep the mos for you an children an the
Beloved for my old friends. No more at present. Direct your letter to the
first colord united states infntry Company E in care of Captain William
"D" Parlatt an I will git it.

                                              [signed] Daniel

Brooks your

                                                        effecnit

husBand

Note: Private Daniel Brooks was a free-born African American whose
family resided in Kent County, Maryland in 1864. He enlisted at
Baltimore, Maryland on September 27, 1864. This document is located
in Brooks' compiled service record.

M1819 Compiled Service Record of Daniel Brooks.

Letter

May 10, 1865

Sir,

Your letter of May 2nd is received and i must hasten to reply i am so poor that I cannot pay for the transportation of the body of my only and Dearest son. now but oh sir if you only could send him home to his poor mother. the Blessings of the God that made us all would remain with you and my thanks forever. he was my all. and oh in Heavens name your what[illegible] that i may bury it among. also send what things he Died from [illegible] of sir. when i tell you that i am in the 5th month of pregnancy. you will see what the importance i attach to having his body sent home to me. Oh i must see him one more and then farewell my Dear Hero son. Oh i beg his body and for the sweet Christ send it to me as soon as Possible after getting this send me word when we may look for it and be sure and not Disappoint me and may our Father reward you for it

As ye shall Deal with the matter of the Dearest? so shall the High and Holy one Deal with you in thy Dying Hour forgive all harshness for there is none meant

Yours in Deep sorrow and trouble

Mrs. Augusta A. Greely
North Haverhill Grafton County
New Hampshire

Note: Private Greely's body could not be sent to his mother. Mrs. Greely was responding to a letter from the Superintendent of McDougall Army Hospital near Ft. Schuyler in New York. Her son was buried on or about January 31, 1865 in Cypress Hill Cemetery, Long Island, New York. She received his personal effects: one overcoat, one blouse (shirt), and one vest on May 25, 1865.

M1819 Compiled Service Record of Horace Greeley.

Footnotes
Chapter I

1.   Jacob Dodson to Simon Cameron, April 23, 1861, T-817, Microfilm
      Publication M858, "The Negro In the Military Service of the United
      States, 1639-1886," Roll #1, Vols. 1 & 2, 1639-1862 [803]
      (hereinafter referred to as M858).   Also see Dodson to Simon
      Cameron, April 23, 1861 in War of the Rebellion: ...*Official Records
      of the Union and Confederate Armies* (128 vols., 1880-1901)
      (hereinafter cited as O.R.), Ser. 3, Vol I, p. 106.

2.   John Charles Fremont, *The Life of Colonel John Charles* Fremont,
      [New York, 1856] pps. 190, 215, 323.   Mary Lee Spence and
      Donald Jackson (eds.), *The Expedition of John_Charles Fremont,
      Vols. 1 and 2,* (Chicago, 1973).   C. R. Gibbs, *Black Explorers,*
      (Silver Spring, 1992) pps 108-110.   Also see Walter Colton, *Three
      Years in California* [New York, 1850] p. 377.   John C. Van Tramp,
      Prairie and Rocky Mountain Adventures, [Columbus, 1870] p. 415.

3.   The *Revised Code of the District of Columbia* (1857), Part 1, Title
      VIII, Chapter 14, Section 1, p. 107, limits military duty to: "Every
      able-bodied male citizen between the ages of eighteen and forty-five
      residing in their District, and not exempt by law...."

4.   Simon Cameron to Jacob Dodson, April 27, 1861, M858, op. cit
      [806].

5.   *Douglass Monthly,* September 1861.

6.   "Special Report of the Commissioner of Education on the Condition
      and Improvement of Public Schools in the District of Columbia," p.
      195.

7.   Margaret Leech, *Reveille in Washington 1860-1865,* (New York,
      1941) p. 236.

8. Colored Census of 1860 - Territories, M858, op. cit [395].

9. Charles Summer's speech to the Republican Convention at Worcester, Massachusetts, September, 1861; quoted from the *Congressional Globe* in M858, op. cit. [824].

10. *Congressional Globe,* 37 Cong., 37 Cong., 2 session, July 5, 1862, p. 3127.

11. Unknown to Christian A. Fleetwood, April 12, 1862, Christian A. Fleetwood Papers; Library of Congress quoted in James M. McPherson's, *The Negro's Civil War,* (New York, 1965) p. 45.

12. *Anglo-African,* April 19, 1862, McPherson, op. cit.

13. Elizabeth Keckley, *Behind the Scenes,* [New York, 1868] pps. 111-112. E.E. Hale, "How to Use Victory," *Atlantic Monthly,* Vol. XXX, No. LXXV (January 1864): p. 765.

14. William B. Hesseltine, *Lincoln and the War Governors,* [New York, 1948] p. 203.

15. Quoted in William Wells Brown, *The Negro in the American Rebellion,* (Boston, 1867), p. 114.

16. *Roster of the Fifty Fourth Massachusetts Infantry,* compiled by George F. McKay, n.p., n.d., pps. 371, 372, 387.

17. Norwood P. Hallowell, *The Negro as a Soldier in the War of the Rebellion,* [Boston, 1897], p. 8. Hallowell was colonel of the 55th Regiment Massachusetts Volunteers.

18. April 8, 1863. April 23, 1863. April 25, 1863. April 26, 1863. Abraham Lincoln Papers, Library of Congress.

19.   M858, Roll #2, Vol. 3, Parts 1 & 2 - 1863 [1234]. Also see Robert Ewell Greene, *Black Defenders of America,* [Chicago, 1974] p. 387.

20.   Francis Heitman, *Historical Register and Dictionary of the United States Army 1789-1903* [Washington, DC, 1903] p. 818. Frederick H. Dyer, *Compendium of the War of the Rebellion* [Des Moines, 1908] pps. 1439, 1559. Samuel P. Bates, *History of Pennsylvania Volunteers,* 1861-5, 5 Vols., [Harrisburg, 1869-71] p. 754.

21.   Horace Greely, *The American Conflict,* [Hartford, 1866] p. 527.

22.   Jacob Bruner Papers, #MSS0994, "The African American Experience in Ohio," Ohio Historical Society.

23.   Quoted in Fawn M. Brodie, *Thaddeus Stevens, Scourge of the South,* [New York, 1959] p. 160.

24.   *Christian Recorder,* July 19, 1862; February 7, 1863. *Harper's Weekly,* December 12, 1863

25.   Benjamin Quarles, *The Negro in the Civil War* [Boston, 1953] p. 247: "...the ladies in the nation's capital presented a regimental flag to the First District Colored Volunteers. Designed by D. B. Bowser, a colored artist of Philadelphia, the flag portrayed the Goddess of Liberty, her foot on a serpent's head, handing a musket to a Negro soldier." Quarles places the event on or about August 14, 1863. The regiment had left the city by that time. Bowser designed several non-regulation regimental flags for black units including the 6th and 24th USCT. Army regulations provide for the issuance of two stands of colors: a set of Stars and Stripes and a blue United States regimental flag.

26.   Leech, op. cit. p. 254.

27.   The *Liberator,* June 12, 1863, Quoted in McPherson, op. cit., p. 179.

28. William Wells Brown, op. cit., p. 274.

29. The address is based on news accounts. William Gant's compiled service record lists his mother as living on G street.

30. "Addresses of the Hon. W. D. Kelly, Miss Anna E. Dickinson, & Mr. Frederick Douglass, at a mass meeting..." Philadelphia, July 6, 1863 for the promotion of colored enlistments, African-American Pamphlet Collection, Library of Congress, Call No. E540. N3 K3., 8 pps.

31. Dudley T. Cornish, *The Sable Arm,* [Lawrence, 1987] p. 210.

32. M858, op. cit. [1234][1246][1376].

33. *Christian Recorder*, June 20, 1863.

34. Horatio Nelson Taft Diary, June 29, 1863, Library of Congress.

35. Arthur J. Larsen (ed.), *Crusader and Feminist: Letters of Jane Grey Swisshelm,* [St. Paul, 1934] p. 241.

36. Justin Kaplan (ed.), *Walt Whitman: Poetry and Prose,* [New York, 1982], pps. 1181-1184. John H. McElroy (ed), *The Sacrificial Years,* [Boston, 1999] pps. 48, 63, 93, 153. The September date must be in error. The unit had been transferred out of the area by that time.

37. Dyer, op. cit., p. 1723.

38. Washington *Evening Star,* October 15, 24, & 26, 1863. *Harper's Weekly,* November 7, 1863. The Abraham Lincoln Papers at the Library of Congress contain several letters on Wright. Lincoln ordered Dr. John P. Gray, Director of the New York State Lunatic

Asylum and an editor of the *American Journal of Insanity* to examine Wright. Gray concluded that Wright was sane. Lincoln approved Wright's execution.

Footnotes
Chapter II

1.   J. F. Trow (printer), *Hints on the Internal Improvement of North Carolina*, [New York, 1854] pps. 15, 36, 37, 40, 42. J.D.B. DeBow, *The Industrial Resources*, [New Orleans, 1852] pps. 458, 463, 464, 569. Alexander C. Brown, *The Dismal Swamp Canal*, [Norfolk, 1967] pps. 45, 48, 53, 71-77. *Harpers Weekly*, September 28, 1861.

2.   James Dabney McCabe, *The Great Republic* [Philadelphia, 1871] pps. 563, 606. Richard Edwards, *Statistical Gazetteer of the State of Virginia*, [Richmond, 1855], pps. 95, 97, 131, 133, 325, 327. Also see Henry Wadsworth Longfellow's poem, *The Slave in Dismal Swamp* (1842) and Harriet Beecher Stowe's second antislavery novel, *Dred: A Tale of the Dismal Swamp* (1856) Bland Simpson, *The Great Dismal*, [Chapel Hill, 1998] p. 71. The author estimated that over a thousand slaves took refuge in the swamp.

3.   Thomas R. Butchko, *On the Shores of the Pasquotank*, [Elizabeth City, 1989], pps. 13, 14, 36, 329. Joseph T. Wilson, *Black Phalanx*, [Hartford, 1887] p. 469. Thomas P. Kettell, *History of the Great Rebellion*, [Hartford, 1866] pps. 207, 256, 342, 361. Also see: Fred W. Mallison, *The Civil War on the Outer Banks* [Jefferson, 1998], and John W. Hinds, *Invasion and Conquest of North Carolina*, [Shippensburg, 1998].

4.   To Major C.T. Christensen, Asst. Adjutant General New Orleans, dated July 18, 1864, quoted in Herbert Aptheker, *To Be Free*, [New York, 1969]. p. 212.

5.   The six serving in hospitals in the city were Charles B. Purvis (who contracted typhoid while serving at Camp Barker), Alpheus Tucker,

John Rapier, William Ellis, Anderson R. Abbott, and William Powell. John V. DeGrasse served briefly as an assistant surgeon with the 35th U. S. Colored Infantry. Alexander T. Augusta (breveted a Lieutenant Colonel on March 13, 1865) was attacked and beaten while in uniform twice in Baltimore, refused streetcar service in the District, denied surgeons pay for a year, and while with the 7th USCT, as senior surgeon at Camp Stanton near Benedict, seven of his subordinate white surgeons serving with black units wrote to Lincoln to complain about being placed under the command of a black man. See Quarles, op. cit. pps. 203-204, 234. Rayford Logan and Michael Winston (eds), *Dictionary of American Negro Biography*, [New York, 1982] pps 19, 20, 168, 507, 508.

6. Richard Edwards, *Statistical Gazetteer of the State of Virginia*, [Richmond, 1855] pps. 35, 57, 99, 113, 146, 148, 241, 321, 327, 345, 383. Horace Greeley, op. cit., pps. 16, 21, 453, 476-477. John Fletcher, *Studies On Slavery*, [Natchez, 1852] p. 157. R.T. Walker, *Virginia: A Geographical and Political Summary*, [Richmond, 1876] pps. 24, 63, 64, 94, 97, 132-144, 160-170.

7. C.W. Foster, Asst. Adjutant General to Hon. E.M. Stanton, Secretary of War, October 31, 1863, O.R. Miscellaneous Correspondence Union Authorities, p. 1115.

8. O. R. 29/1:911-912. Robert M. Browning, Jr., *From Cape Charles to Cape Fear...* [Tuscaloosa, 1993] pps. 127-128. Longacre, Edward. "Brave, Radical, Wild: The Contentious Career of Brigadier Edward A. Wild." *CW Times Illus* 19 (Jun 1980): pps. 8-19.

9. Edward A. Wild to George H. Johnston, December 28, 1863. Benjamin F. Butler to Hon. Edwin Stanton, December 31, 1863. Butler Papers, Library of Congress.

10. Christian A. Fleetwood Diary, Wednesday, April 27, 1864, Christian A. Fleetwood Papers, Library of Congress.

11. *Christian Recorder,* May 28, 1864. In April, while stationed in North Carolina, Hatton had written, "Though the Government openly declared that it did not want the negroes in this conflict, I look around me and see hundreds of colored men armed and ready to defend the Government at any moment; and such are my feelings, that I can only say, the fetters have fallen -- our bondage is over."

12. George W. Williams, *A History of Negro Troops* [New York, 1969] pps. 240-243. Simonton, Edward, "The Campaign Up the James River to Petersburg." In *Glimpses of the Nation's Struggle* (MOLLUS, MN, Vol. 5). St. Paul, MN: Review Pub Co, 1903. pps. 481-95. Greeley op. cit., pps. 574, 584. Kettel, op. cit. pps. 530, 532, 768. *Cleveland Gazette,* March 26, 1887.

13. *Daily Morning Chronicle,* May 30, 1864.

14. Carpenter, Rev. W. Spencer, "Negro Soldier's Contribution in the Wars of the U.S.," *AME Church Review,* Jan. 1913, Vol. 29, No. 3, pps. 215-224.

15. Simonton, ibid.

16. O.R. 50/1: 265-266. See William Swinton, *Campaigns of the Army of the Potomac* [New York, 1882] for a discussion of the Army's failure to occupy Petersburg on June 15, 1864.

17. William Fox, *Regimental Losses* [Albany, 1888] p. 450, Bryce Suderow. "The Battle of the Crater: The Civil War's Worst Massacre,*C.W. History*, Vol. 43, No. 3, September 1997, pps. 219-224.

18. *Christian Recorder,* July 16, 1864. George Hatton's father was Henry Hatton who was living in the District at the time of his son's enlistment.

19. Virginia M. Adams, *On the Altar of Freedom* [New York, 1992] pps. 117-120. Herbert Aptheker, *A Documentary History of the Negro People* [New York, 1951] pps. 482-484.

20. John H. Holman Papers, Western Historical Manuscript Collection - Columbia, University of Missouri.

21. Fox, op. cit., p. 458.

22. R.J.M. Blackett (ed.), *Thomas Morris Chester, Black Civil War Correspondent* [New York, 1989] pps. 99, 171, 176, 178-80, 182, 185-186

23. Greeley, op. cit., pps 9, 14, 16, 708-714. Kettell, op. cit. pps 601, 679, 687-690, 696-700, 710. General John Ames, "The Victory at Fort Fisher," *Overland Monthly and Out West Magazine,* Vol. 9, Issue 4, pps. 323-332, Oct 1872, San Francisco.

24. Ulysses S. Grant, *Personal Memoirs* [New York, 1886], Chapter LXIX. Alexander Stephens, *A Constitutional View of the Late War,* [Philadelphia, 1868] pps 582-583. Kettell, op. cit., 734-736. *Cleveland Gazette,* Feb. 22, 1890, "General Sherman and AfroAmericans." Dallas T. Ward, *The Last Flag of Truce* [Franklington, 1914] 16 pps. See also, Reverend L.R. Ferebee, *A Brief History of the Slave Life...* [Raleigh, 1882] pps. 5-11 for the story of blacks living near the Outer Banks during the war.

Footnotes
Chapter III

1. Various sources conflict over whether the year of Turner's birth was 1833 or 1834. Turner's military records give 1833. See for example

William Simmons, *Men of Mark: Emminent, Progressive, Rising* (1887) pp.806-819 and Rayford Logan and Michael Winston (eds). *Dictionary of American Negro Biography* (New York, 1982), pp. 608-609.

2.   Simmons, ibid, p. 807.

3.   Bergman and Bergman, *Chronological History of the Negro in America,* (New York, 1969), p. 138. Also see Herbert Aptheker, *American Negro Slave Revolts,* (New York, 1993), pp. 237, 241; Eugene Genovese, *Roll, Jordan, Roll* (New York, 1976) p. 400-401.

4.   Simmons, ibid, p. 808.

5.   Benjamin T. Tanner, *An Apology for African Methodism* (1867).

6.   Simmons, ibid, p. 809

7.   Henry M. Turner, cited in Simmons, ibid. p. 809.

8.   Quoted in *Journal of Negro History* Vol., XLI, No. 1, January 1976, "Documents - The Quest for Freedom" pps. 94-97.

9.   William Wells Brown, *Rising Sun* (Boston, 1874) pps. 506-507.

10.   *The Daily National Republican,* April 15, 1862.

11.   *Eighth Census: Statistics of the U.S., 1860*; Volume I and II. See Melvin R. Williams' essay in *Records of the Columbia Historical Society of Washington D.C.,* Volume 50, pps. 172-179. George Washington Williams, *History of the Negro Race in America*, 1619-1880: [New York, 1883] pps 182, 183, 192, 193, 196, 197, 206-209.

12.   *Christian Recorder,* October 4, 1862.

13. "Reminiscences of the Proclamation of Emancipation," *AME Church Review,* Vol. 29, Number 3, January 1913, pps. 211-215.

14. *Christian Recorder*, January 10, 1863.

15. General Orders No. 15, May 4, 1861, and No. 47, August 3, 1861, Adjutant General's Office, *Official Records,* ser. 3, Vol. I: 154, 382. In 1862, The word "Christian" was eliminated to make way for Jewish chaplains. Added was the requirement that a chaplaincy candidate had to present either a recommendation from an authorized ecclesiastical body or a testimonial signed by not less than five accredited ministers belonging to the candidate's denomination.

16. Warner B. Armstrong, "Union Chaplains and the Education of the Freedmen" *Journal of Negro History* (April 1967), pps. 104-115. Edwin S. Redkey, "Black Chaplains in the Union Army," *Civil War History*, 33 (Dec. 1987), pps. 334, 338, 350.

17. Quoted in Berlin, *Black Military Experience,* p. 359, RG 694, Chaplain H. M. Turner to Hon. E. M. Stanton, 30 June 1864, T-334, 1864. Letters Received, ser. 12, [K-2].

18. R. J. Blackett, (ed), op. cit. p. 154.

19. *Christian Recorder*, August 8, 1864; August 5, 1865.

20. John Blassingame, *"The Union Army as an Educational Institution for Negroes 1862-1865,"* Journal of Negro Education (Spring 1965), 34, pps 152-159.

21. *"Private and Official Correspondence of Gen. Benjamin F. Butler,"* Volume V, pps. 546-547, n.p., 1917.

22. Redkey, Edwin S., ed. "Rocked in the Cradle of Consternation." [Journal of Henry W. Turner] *Am Heritage* 31 (Oct/Nov 1980): pps 70-79.

23. *Christian Recorder*, February 4, 1865, Quoted in McPherson, op. cit. pps. 210-211.

24. Quoted in Berlin, op. cit. pps 626-627, RG 94. Chaplain Henry M. Turner to Adjutant General U.S. Army, 29 June 1865, T-736 1865, Letters Received, ser. 12, [K-537]. Endorsements.

25. *Christian Recorder*, July 22, 1865. Quoted in Redkey, op. cit. pps 174-174.

26. Herbert Aptheker, *And Why Not Every Man,* (New York, 1961) pps. 255-258.

Footnotes
Chapter IV

1. Thomas Wentworth Higginson, *Army Life in a Black Regiment* [Boston, 1890]. Dudley Taylor Cornish, *The Sable Arm,* [Lawrence, 1987], pps 71-76, 88-89, 133-138, 193-195, 201-202. See also Susie King Taylor, *Reminiscences of My Life in Camp,* [Boston, 1902].

2. Edward Lawson enlisted as a 19 year-old private in Company H. Joseph Ross does not appear on regimental rolls.

3. Simmons, ibid. *Harper's Weekly,* December 12, 1863. Edwin S. Redkey, *Respect Black,* [New York, 1971], *Cleveland Gazette,* October 14, 1893.

4. Fox, op. cit., p. 450.

5. Washington *Evening Star,* January 17, 1865.

6. Washington *Evening Star,* April 24, 29, 1865. *Tabular Analysis of the Records of the U.S. Colored Troops and Their Predecessor Units in the National Archives of the United States,* National Archives and Records Service, General Services Administration [Washington, 1973] pps. 5, 20.

7. John W. Bear, *The Life and Travels of John W. Bear,* [Baltimore, 1873] p. 281, gives a revealing glimpse of racial politics in post war Charles County. Also see George Alfred Townsend, *The Life, Crime and Capture of John Wilkes Booth,* [New York, 1865] pps. 42, 52. Charles County, Maryland's early history is examined in Jean B. Lee's, *The Price of Nationhood,* [New York, 1994].

Footnotes
Chapter V

1. Dyer, op. cit., pps. 1018-1020.

2. *National Republican,* September 4, 1865.

3. *Evening Star,* October 7, 1865. *National Republican,* September 26, 1865.

4. *National Republican,* September 28, 1865.

5. *National Republican,* October 9, 1965. I have identified two dozen Civil War-era songs with that obviously patriotic title, "Red, White, and Blue." Which version was played that day at the wharf is unknown at present. *Evening Star,* October 9, 1865.

6. Quarles, op. cit., pps. 258, 259, 313.

7. *National Republican,* October 13, 1865.

8. *National Republican,* October 10, & 20, 1865.

9.   George Fort Milton, *Age of Hate, Andrew Johnson and the Radicals,* [New York, 1930], p. 111ff. Also see the *Nashville Press,* February, 1863 on its comments on Johnson's remarks during his tour of northern cities.

10.   Frederick Douglass, *Life and Times...,* [Hartford, 1881], p. 370. In a February 20, 1863 speech in Indianapolis, Indiana, Johnson said: "I have lived among negroes all my life and I am for this Government with slavery under the Constitution as it is. I am for the Government of my father with negroes, I am for it, without negroes. Before I would see this government destroyed, I would send every negro back to Africa disintegrated and destroyed." A February 1866, White House meeting with a group of firm and articulate black leaders including Douglass and George Downing also rankled Johnson. After the meeting he snarled to an aide: "Those d_d sons of b_s thought they had me in a trap." Of Douglass, Johnson said "...just like any nigger... would sooner cut a white man's throat than not."

11.   *National Republican,* October 10, 1865.

12.   Logan and Winston, op. cit., p. 123.

13.   Swisshelm, op. cit., p. 231.

14.   *National Republican,* October 10, 1865.

15.   *National Republican,* October 13, 1865.

16.   *Evening Star,* October 13, 1865.

17.   *National Republican,* October 9, 1865.

18.   John Holman Papers. University of Missouri.

19. *Journal of the Executive Proceedings of the Senate of the United States,* Vol. 14, December 29, 1865, p. 500.

20. Warren A. Innis, *The History of the 1st and 7th United States Colored Troops,* M.A. thesis, Howard University, 1962, pps. 60-76.

21. Constance M. Green, *The Secret City,* [Princeton, 1967], p. 76.

22. Green, op. cit., p. 77.

23. *Nation,* January 25, 1866, II:98.

24. Green, op. cit., p. 77.

25. *The Biographical Encyclopaedia of Ohio of the Nineteenth Century,* [Cincinnati, 1876], p. 416. Green, op. cit., p. 77. William Horatio Barnes, History of the Thirty-Ninth Congress of the United States. [New York, 1868], pps. 50-94.

26. O.D. Case & Company, *The American Yearbook and National Register for 1869,* [Hartford, 1869], p. 273. Edward McPherson, *Political History of the United States During the Period of Reconstruction,* [Washington, 1876], p. 123. Amy H. Hiller, "The Disfranchisement of Delaware Negroes in the Late Nineteenth Century," *Delaware History,* Vol. XIII, No. 2, October, 1968, pps. 124-153.

27. *National Intelligencer,* March 23, April 2, 12, 15, 1867.

28. *National Intelligencer,* March 23, April 1, 5, 15, 20, & May 7, 1867.

29. Green, op. cit., p. 77-81, *Washington Post,* October 23, 2000.

30. Washington *Evening Star,* June 3, 1867. *Washington Post,* October 23, 2000.

31.   Keith Melder, *City of Magnificent Intentions,* [Washington, D.C., 1997], pps. 188-194.

32.   M858, Roll #3, Vols. 4 and 5, [269], [2724].

33.   Green, op. cit., 130, 164. Martin K. Gordon, *The Black Militia in the District of Columbia,* Records of the Columbia Historical Society, Vol. 48, 1971-72, F.C. Rosenberger (ed), [Washington, 1973], pps. 411-420.

34.   Kenneth G. Alfer, *Law and Order in the Capital City,* George Washington University Studies, George Washington University, Washington, D.C., September 1970, Chapter Five.

35.   R.C.O. Benjamin, *Light After Darkness...,* [Xenia, 1896], African American Perspectives: Pamphlets from the Daniel A.P. Murray Collection, 1818-1907. Library of Congress.

36.   John H. Holman Papers, University of Missouri.

Notes on Sources

Three primary sources form the core of this book and are found at the National Archives on microfilm: M1819, Compiled Military Service Records of Volunteer Union Soldiers Who Served With The United States Colored Troops, First United States Colored Infantry, Rolls 1-19; Record Group 94, M858, The Negro In The Military Service of the United States, 1639-1886, Rolls 1-5, Volumes 1-7; and M594, Compiled Records Showing Service of Military Units in Volunteer Union Organizations.

M1819 contains the compiled service records consisting of both a jacket-envelope for each soldier, labeled with his name, rank, and unit, and several information cards. Information from muster rolls, regimental returns, descriptive books, and other records was copied verbatim onto cards. A separate card was prepared each time an individual name appeared on the document. A typical jacket often contains card abstracts of entries found in original records relating to the soldier and original documents relating solely to that soldier. Examples of the latter include enlistment papers, substitute certificates, casualty sheets, death reports, prisoner-of-war memorandums, and correspondence.

Unique to the records of the United States Colored Troops (USCT) are deeds of manumission, oaths of allegiance, proof of ownership, certificates of monetary award, and bills of sale. These items appear most frequently in units recruited in the border states of Kentucky, Missouri, and Maryland. These states remained in the Union but were slave states. Jackets and cards include a section labeled "bookmark," which was reserved for cross-references to other records relating to the individual or his unit. The service records are arranged by arm of service, thereunder numerically by regiment or independent battalion or company, and thereunder alphabetically by name with the records of enlisted men. Some men have only one card on file. This usually means that they were not formally taken up on the regiment's rolls. The rank that I listed for each man in the appendix was the highest his records indicated that he had attained, however briefly. If an individual served in more than one unit, which was typical for USCT officers, there will be a separate service record for each unit in which he served.

M858 is a microfilmed reproduction of the seven volumes (eight bound parts) of records compiled for publication by the Colored Troops Division of the Adjutant General's Office. There are several items on the First USCT.

M594 contains microfilmed copies of records showing the histories of military organizations that served during the Civil War. The records relate to stations, movements, or activities of each unit or part of it. For the First USCT, their regimental and company returns from June 1863 to August 1865 are available. There is also field and staff and detachment muster roll information from June or July 1863 to August 1865.

Useful as well were several chapters of the official records of the Union and Confederate armies. This multi-volume series published between 1880-1901 by the Government Printing Office contains, among other things, the formal reports of all military operations in the field with related correspondence and orders.

Also of importance was the John H. Holman Papers, part of the Western Historical Manuscript Collection at the University of Missouri at Columbia. Holman was the colonel of the regiment. The papers in this collection comprise two folders of correspondence covering the years 1861-1876. The correspondence pertains to Holman's military service in Missouri, his service with the First USCT, and personal matters.

Original spellings have been retained throughout the book except in cases of possible unintelligibility. I relied primarily on data included on the company descriptive book cards. The spellings of names may vary slightly from those found in the Civil War Soldiers and Sailors System. The records listed above are a treasure trove of African American experiences during the Civil War. They are full of not only military history, but also humor, pathos, and the interminable struggle of African Americans to survive, build, and be free.

Roster

Commissioned Officers

	Date of Commission	Disposition

COLONEL
Holman, John — May 22, 1863 — Promoted to Brigadier General March 13, 1865.

LIEUTENANT COLONELS
Martin, George G. — — Dismissed December 31, 1863.
Rich, Giles H. — October 13, 1864
Wright, Elias — — Promoted August 15, 1864, to Colonel, 10th U.S.C.T.

MAJOR
Perkins, Henry — April 29, 1864 — Promoted to Brevet Lieut. Colonel March 13, 1865.

CAPTAINS
Bennett, William T. — — Promoted April 14, 1864, to Lieut. Colonel 102nd U.S.C.T.
Boyden, Stephen A. — — Discharged November 17, 1864.
Brazie, William R. — — Promoted October 25, 1864, to Major 5th U.S.C.T.
Brown, Henry H. — January 1, 1865
Davis, William H. — January 2, 1865
Hill, Charles A. — May 28, 1865
Holmes, C. Hiram — May 28, 1865
Houston, William W. McB. — — Killed at Fair Oaks, VA, October 27, 1864.
Parlin, William D. — — Resigned March 17, 1865.
Payne, Frederick — May 28, 1865
Rice, Judson E. — — Killed in action at Fair Oaks, VA, October 27, 1864.
Simonton, Edward — May 28, 1865 — Promoted to Brevet Lieut. Colonel March 13, 1865.
Sprague, Wellington G. — October 7, 1863 — Promoted to Brevet Lieut. Colonel March 13, 1865.
Thompson, Hiram P. — October 26, 1864
Van Winkle, Henry M. — April 29, 1864
Ward, Henry — July 14, 1863 — Promoted to Brevet Lieut. Colonel March 13, 1865.

FIRST LIEUTENANTS
Beeman, Elam C. — June 28, 1863
Birdsall, Sylvester H. — June 13, 1863

	Date of Commission	Disposition
FIRST LIEUTENANTS (con't)		
Bishop, Nathan .	November 14, 1863	
Brisbane, Benjamin L.		Resigned April 17, 1864.
David, John A.		Dismissed December 22, 1863.
Eagle, Clifford F.		Resigned March 8, 1865.
Foster, William E.		Resigned January 8, 1864.
Kilpatrick, William H.	September 2, 1863	
Larney, Nicholas	November 25, 1861	
Otto, Frank	October 26, 1861	
Parker, Robert P.	July 27, 1861	
Randall, Edward L.	October 13, 1861	
Rice, Lewis B.		Resigned November 28, 1864.
Sanderson, George O.	May 28, 1865	
Sands, George H.	May 28, 1865	
Smith, Myron W.		Died October 4, 1864, of wounds received at Fillmore, VA.
Weidner, Ethan J.	May 28, 1865	
Whitcomb, Horace G.	May 28, 1865	
SECOND LIEUTENANTS		
Bailey, Marcellus		Promoted August 22, 1863, to First Lieut. and Adj't 4th U.S.C.T.
Barr, Charles		Died February 22, 1865, of wounds received at Town Creek, near Wilmington, NC.
Bean, Samuel		Discharged January 13, 1864.
Buck, Frederick W.		Dismissed June 19, 1865.
Burnham, Nathan		Discharged August 31, 1864.
Day, Henry M.		Dismissed January 31, 1864.
Kellogg, Norton P.		Promoted November 25, 1864, to First Lieut, 6th U.S.C.T.
Krosen, James C.		Discharged October 4, 1865.
Mann, Samuel S.	August 8, 1865	
Martin, Abraham		Appointment revoked August 26, 1865.
Miller, George F.	August 25, 1865	
Miller, Thomas W.	July 27, 1865	
Sanborn, Anson		Murdered in Norfolk, VA July 11, 1863.
Sterling, Wallace G.		Resigned August 16, 1864.
Sykes, Charles R.		Resigned January 15, 1864.
Williams, Henry G.	July 14, 1865	
Woolsey, C. Meech	August 29, 1865	
CHAPLAIN		
Turner, Henry M.	September 10, 1863	
SURGEONS		
Weist, Jacob R.	November 3, 1863	

	Date of Commission	Disposition

SURGEONS (con't)

Willoughby, Henry W.   Discharged July 31, 1864.

ASST. SURGEONS

Bell, Samuel A.   June 30, 1865

Crawford, William H.   Dismissed August 21, 1864.

Pettyjohn, J.B.

Pryor, William   Appointment revoked November 28, 1863.

HOSPITAL STEWARD

Sands, Charles V.

NAME	HIGHEST RANK	COMPANY	AGE AT ENLIST	OCCUPATION	DATE OF ENLIST	PLACE OF ENLIST	BIRTHPLACE
Abrams, William	Pvt.	Co. D	21	Farmer	6/14/1863	Mason's Island, VA	Smithville, MD
Adams, Henry	Pvt.	Co. D	28	Laborer	9/30/1864	Harford, NY	Valopraso, Chilli
Adams, James T.	Sgt.	Co. D	24	Gardener	6/14/1863	Mason's Island, VA	Washington, DC
Adams, John Q.	Cpl.	Co. C	21	Farmer	6/8/1863	Washington, DC	Howard County, MD
Adams, Samuel	Pvt.	Co. C	19	Shoemaker	6/8/1863	Washington, DC	Detroit, MI
Adams, Winfield S.	Pvt.	Co. D	18	Waiter	6/14/1863	Mason's Island, VA	Washington, DC
Addison, Daniel	Pvt.	Co. D	18	Laborer	6/14/1863	Mason's Island, VA	Prince George's County, MD
Addison, George	Pvt.	Co. F	22	-	7/9/1864	Mason's Island, VA	Prince George's County, MD
Addison, Hamilton	Pvt.	Co. D	23	Farmer	9/26/1864	Ellicotts Mills, MD	Fairfax, VA
Addison, Theodore	Pvt.	Co. H	17	Laborer	7/6/1863	Baltimore, MD	Montgomery County, MD
Alexander, James	Cpl.	Co. C	20	Carpenter	6/8/1863	Washington, DC	Baltimore, MD
Alexander, William	Sgt.	Co. E	23	Farmer	7/3/1863	Mason's Island, VA	Fredericksburg, VA
Alexandria, William	Sgt.	Co. I	23	Druggist	6/28/1863	Mason's Island, VA	Washington, DC
Allen, Daniel	Cpl.	Co. G	30	Miller	6/25/1863	Mason's Island, VA	Prince George's County, MD
Allen, George	Cpl.	Co. G	21	Laborer	6/25/1863	Mason's Island, VA	Frederick City, MD
Allen, Jacob	Pvt.	Co. K	40	Waiter	7/1/1863	Mason's Island, VA	Baltimore, MD
Allen, Joseph	Pvt.	Co. K	22	Laborer	7/1/1863	Mason's Island, VA	Richmond, VA
Allen, Peter	Pvt.	Co. A	24	Farmer	3/7/1865	Wilmington, NC	Brunswick County, NC
Allen, Randall	Pvt.	Co. D	27	Carpenter	3/2/1865	Wilmington, NC	Wilmington, NC
Allen, Richard	Pvt.	Co. F	20	-	6/21/1863	Mason's Island, VA	Washington, DC
Allen, Samuel	Pvt.	Co. I	21	Bricklayer	7/12/1863	Washington, DC	Alexandria, VA
Allen, Samuel	Sgt.	Co. I	22	Waiter	6/28/1863	Mason's Island, VA	Washington, DC
Allen, William	Pvt.	Co. H	18	Laborer	6/27/1863	Mason's Island, VA	King William, VA
Allen, William	Pvt.	Co. K	21	Farmer	6/30/1863	Mason's Island, VA	Virginia
Andrews, Andrew	Pvt.	Co. H	49	Cook	7/6/1863	Mason's Island, VA	Washington, DC
Anderson, Cornelius	Pvt.	Co. D	35	Laborer	9/26/1864	Wilmington, DE	Cann Co, DE
Anderson, John	Pvt.	Co. E	25	Farmer	6/17/1863	Mason's Island, VA	Pohick Church, VA
Anderson, John A.	Pvt.	Co. H		Butcher	7/6/1863	Mason's Island, VA	Washington, DC
Andrews, William H.	Pvt.	Co. C	26	Plasterer	6/8/1863	Washington, DC	Philadelphia, PA
Annison, Page	Cpl.	Co. H	39	Farmer	6/27/1863	Mason's Island, VA	Caroline County, VA
Arno, John	Sgt.	Co. A		Tobacconist	5/19/1863	Washington, DC	St. Pierre, Martinique Island, WI
Artist, Joseph	Pvt.	Co. D	18	Farmer	10/26/1863	Cox's Point, VA	Southhampton County, VA
Ashton, Charles	Pvt.	Co. H	22	-	6/27/1863	Mason's Island, VA	
Bailey, Edwin	Pvt.	Co. E	20	Teamster	6/17/1863	Mason's Island, VA	Wilmington, DE

Name	Rank	Co.	Age	Occupation	Date	Enlistment Place	Residence
Bailey, George W.	Sgt.	Co. I	20	Bricklayer	6/28/1863	Mason's Island, VA	St. Mary's County, MD
Bailey, Henry	Pvt.	Co. I	18	Carpenter	6/28/1863	Mason's Island, VA	Suffolk, VA
Bailey, Harry	Pvt.	Co. I	32	Farmer	6/28/1863	Mason's Island, VA	Prince George's County, MD
Bailey, Thomas	Sgt.	Co. E	20	Coachman	6/17/1863	Mason's Island, VA	Fairfax County, VA
Bailey, William	Pvt.	Co. K	20	Waiter	6/28/1863	Mason's Island, VA	Hartford, CT
Baker, Austin	Sgt.	Co. G	24	Tobacconist	6/25/1863	Mason's Island, VA	Brunswick, VA
Baker, George	-	Co. B	20	Laborer	9/28/1864	Ellicotts Mills, MD	Rappahannock County, VA
Baker, William	Cpl.	Co. K	18	Waiter	6/30/1863	Mason's Island, VA	New York City
Ball, Lewis (Luccius)	Pvt.	Co. F	19	Waiter	6/21/1863	Mason's Island, VA	Northumberland Co., VA
Ball, William H.	Pvt.	Co. A	22	Farmer	7/12/1863	Mason's Island, VA	Richmond, VA
Ballet, Hanson	Pvt.	Co. H	20	Farmer	6/27/1863	Mason's Island, VA	Alawack County, VA
Banks, Alexander	Sgt.	Co. B	19	Coachman	7/2/1863	Mason's Island, VA	New Bern, NC
Banks, Barnett	Pvt.	Co. G	18	Laborer	9/23/1864	Ellicotts Mills, MD	Culpepper County, VA
Banks, Bradley	Pvt.	Co. F	19	Farmer	5/16/1864	Wilson's Wharf Landing, VA	Charles City Co., VA
Banks, George W.	Pvt.	Co. F	16	Waiter	6/21/1863	Mason's Island, VA	Baltimore, MD
Banks, Henry	Pvt.	Co. C	20	Farmer	7/2/1863	Mason's Island, VA	Richmond County, VA
Banks, John	Sgt.	Co. H	34	Waiter	6/27/1867	Mason's Island, VA	Washington, DC
Banks, Manuel	Pvt.	Co. I	33	Farmer	6/28/1863	Mason's Island, VA	Caroline County, VA
Banks, William	Pvt.	Co. E	20	Laborer	9/16/1864	Mason's Island, VA	Staunton, VA
Barber, James	Pvt.	Co. K	28	Laborer	6/30/1863	Frederick, MD	Rockville, MD
Barlow, Peter	Pvt.	Co. G	23	Laborer	9/26/1864	Mason's Island, VA	Richmond, VA
Barnes, George W.	Pvt.	Co. G	22	Farmer	7/7/1864	Frederick, MD	Howard County, MD
Barnes, Richard	Pvt.	Co. F	46	Laborer	12/13/1863	Ellicotts Mills, MD	Hertford County, NC
Barnett, James	Pvt.	Co. G	21	Farmer	5/27/1864	Portsmouth, VA	Anne Arundel County, MD
Barney, Bazil	Pvt.	Co. E	34	Farmer	9/27/1864	Ellicotts Mills, MD	Carroll County, MD
Barry, Columbus	Pvt.	Co. E	16	Waiter	6/17/1863	Baltimore, MD	Washington, DC
Bates, George W.	Pvt.	Co. K	20	Laborer	4/15/1865	Mason's Island, VA	Barnwood, SC
Baur, Armstead	Cpl.	Co. F	30	Laborer	6/21/1863	Wilmington, NC	Norfolk County, VA
Bauston, John H.	Sgt.	Co. F	28	Barber	6/21/1863	Mason's Island, VA	Gettysburg, Adams County, PA
Bean, George	Pvt.	Co. G	21	Laborer	6/25/1863	Mason's Island, VA	Brinetown, MD
Bean, William H.	Pvt.	Co. B	17	Laborer	5/19/1863	Mason's Island, VA	Leonardtown, MD
Beauford, Jerry	Pvt.	Co. E	26	Farmer	7/3/1863	Washington, DC	Southhampton County, VA
Bell, Harry	Musician	Co. E	19	Waiter	6/8/1863	Washington, DC	Washington, DC
Bell, Perry	Drummer	Co. C			6/8/1863	Washington, DC	Washington, DC
Belt, Thomas	Pvt.	Co. D	23	Laborer	6/14/1863	Mason's Island, VA	Prince George's County, MD
Belts, Joseph	Pvt.	Co. H	19	Butcher	6/27/1863	Mason's Island, VA	Georgetown, DC
Berkeley, Charles	Pvt.	Co. E	18	Nurseryman	6/17/1863	Mason's Island, VA	Culpepper C.H., VA
Beckley, George	Pvt.	Co. H	21	Waiter	6/27/1863	Mason's Island, VA	Fairfax County, VA
Berry, James	Pvt.	Co. A	23	Boatman	5/19/1863	Washington, DC	Pittsburg, PA

Berry, James	Pvt.	Co. I	45	Laborer	9/26/1863	Wilmington, DE	Dover, DE
Berry, William	Pvt.	Co. E	23	Farmer	6/17/1863	Mason's Island, VA	Prince William County, VA
Beverly, Wyatt	Cpl.	Co. E	23	Waiter	6/17/1863	Mason's Island, VA	Caroline County, VA
Bias, Charles	Pvt.	Co. C	22	Farmer	6/8/1863	Washington, DC	Talbot County, MD
Bland, George	Sgt.	Co. B	24	Farmer	5/17/1863	Washington, DC	Fauquier County, VA
Blankam, Jonas	Cpl.	Co. D	23	Farmer	6/14/1863	Mason's Island, VA	Page County, VA
Blankam, Joseph	Pvt.	Co. K	25	Laborer	6/30/1863	Mason's Island, VA	Page County, VA
Boggs, Gabriel	Pvt.	Co. K	33	Laborer	6/21/1863	Mason's Island, VA	Spotslyvania County, VA
Bohannan, Robert	Pvt.	Co. F	22	Farmer	6/21/1863	Mason's Island, VA	Madison County, VA
Bolden, Peter	Pvt.	Co. C	23	Farmer	6/25/1863	Mason's Island, VA	Prince George's County, MD
Bolden, Peter	Pvt.	Co. G	20	Farmer	3/8/1865	Mason's Island, VA	Southampton County, VA
Bonam, Peter	Pvt.	Co. A	18	Farmer	3/9/1865	Mason's Island, VA	Hanover County, VA
Boney, David	Pvt.	Co. C	27	Farmer	6/30/1863	Wilmington, NC	Dublin County, NC
Bowey, John	Pvt.	Co. K	17	Waiter	5/19/1863	Wilmington, NC	Washington, DC
Boom, John	Pvt.	Co. B	21	Painter	9/26/1864	Mason's Island, VA	Barbados, West Indies
Boon, John	Pvt.	Co. C	24	Oysterman	6/21/1863	Washington, DC	Norfolk, VA
Borden, Benjamin	Pvt.	Co. F	20	Farmer	6/8/1863	Baltimore, MD	Annapolis, MD
Boston, George	Pvt.	Co. C	25	Hostler	6/28/1863	Mason's Island, VA	Washington, DC
Boston, Nathaniel	Cpl.	Co. G	19	Laborer	6/8/1863	Washington, DC	Prince George's County, MD
Boswell, John	Pvt.	Co. C	19	Waiter	6/17/1863	Mason's Island, VA	Loudon County, VA
Boswell, Phillip	Sgt.	Co. E					
Boulden, Robert	Pvt.	Co. A	20	Waiter	5/19/1863	Washington, DC	Lynchburg, VA
Bouy (Bowie), John	Pvt.	Co. B	29	Farmer	6/25/1863	Mason's Island, VA	Prince George's County, MD
Bowden, John	Pvt.	Co. B	18	Laborer	5/19/1863	Washington, DC	Prince George's County, MD
Bowers, Abraham	Pvt.	Co. C	35	Barber	9/6/1864	Mason's Island, VA	Providence, RI
Bowie, Albert	Pvt.	Co. I	22	Farmer	6/28/1863	Washington, DC	Prince George's County, MD
Bowie, Issac	Pvt.	Co. F	38	Caulker	7/9/1864	Windsor, VT	Baltimore, MD
Bowie, John	Pvt.	Co. B	24	Teamster	9/24/1864	Mason's Island, VA	Washington, DC
Bowman, Philip	Pvt.	Co. F	21	Farmer	7/10/1863	Ellicotts Mills, MD	Kent County, MD
Bowser, Issac	Pvt.	Co. I	38	Huckster	9/28/1864	Baltimore, MD	Washington, DC
Boyd, Alfred	Pvt.	Co. F	12	Waiter	6/21/1863	Mason's Island, VA	Alexandria, VA
Boyd, Lewis	Pvt.	Co. G	21	Waiter	6/25/1863	Baltimore, MD	Henry County, VA
Boyle, Richard	Pvt.	Co. G	18	Farmer	9/24/1864	Mason's Island, VA	Charles City County, VA
Braxton, Jesse	Pvt.	Co. B					
Brenth, George	Pvt.	Co. A	20	Farmer	5/12/1864	Mason's Island, VA	Port Tobacco, MD
Brice, Martin	Cpl.	Co. K	26	Waiter	5/19/1863	Ellicotts Mills, MD	Baltimore, MD
Briggs, Archer	Sgt.	Co. A	23	Farmer	6/30/1863	Wilson's Landing, VA	Frankfort, VA
Briscoe, Edward	Sgt.	Co. D	20	Butcher	5/19/1863	Mason's Island, VA	Alexandria, VA
Briscoe, Edward	Sgt.	Co. D	20	Butcher	6/14/1863	Mason's Island, VA	Charles County, MD

Name	Rank	Company	Occupation	Age	Date	Enlistment Place	Residence
Briscoe, Joseph	Pvt.	Co. I	Dyer	38	6/28/1863	Mason's Island, VA	Baltimore, MD
Brisks, George	Pvt.		Laborer	43	10/11/1864	Buffalo, NY	Maryland County, MD
Britt, William	Pvt.	Co. D	Laborer	18	6/14/1863	Mason's Island, VA	Norfolk, VA
Britman, Henry	Pvt.	Co. D	Laborer	18	9/26/1864	Frederick, MD	Maryland
Britton, Ira	Pvt.	Co. G	Farmer	28	6/25/1863	Mason's Island, VA	Birkie County, NC
Brackett, Issac	Pvt.		Farmer	25	2/22/1864	Cortland, NY	Tyrell County, NC
Brodly, John	Pvt.	Co. A	Sailor	37	5/19/1863	Washington, DC	Baltimore, MD
Bragden, John F.	Sgt.	Co. D	Waiter	20	6/14/1863	Mason's Island, VA	Washington, DC
Bronson, Frederick	Pvt.	Co. H	Farmer	29	6/27/1863	Mason's Island, VA	West Miller, VA
Brookins, Philip	Pvt.	Co. B	Laborer	30	5/19/1863	Washington, DC	King & Queen County, VA
Brooks, Cyrus	Cpl.	Co. F	Waiter	28	6/21/1863	Mason's Island, VA	Baltimore, MD
Brooks, David R.	Pvt.	Co. D	Laborer	18	6/14/1863	Mason's Island, VA	Charles County, MD
Brooks, Daniel	Pvt.	Co. E	Farmer	33	9/27/1864	Baltimore, MD	Kent County, MD
Brooks, Joseph	Pvt.	Co. H	Laborer	32	3/14/1865	Syracuse, NY	Culpepper, VA
Brooks, Peter	Pvt.	Co. A	Laborer	39	5/19/1863	Washington, DC	Washington, DC
Brooks, Robert	Cpl.	Co. D	Laborer	20	6/14/1863	Mason's Island, VA	Fredericksburg, VA
Brooks, William T.	Pvt.	Co. B	Waiter	24	5/19/1863	Washington, DC	Prince George's County, MD
Brown, Albert	Sgt.	Co. H	Miller	22	6/27/1863	Mason's Island, VA	Fairfax County, VA
Brown, Alexander	Pvt.	Co. D	Laborer	19	6/14/1863	Mason's Island, VA	Frederick County, MD
Brown, Andrew	Cpl.	Co. I	Farmer	20	5/31/1864	Ft. Powhatan, VA	Surry County, VA
Brown, Charles	Pvt.	Co. A	Laborer	20	5/19/1863	Washington, DC	Front Royal, VA
Brown, Charles	Pvt.	Co. G	Blacksmith	22	6/25/1863	Mason's Island, VA	Staten Island, NY
Brown, Charles F.	Sgt.	Co. B	Waiter	19	7/1/1863	Mason's Island, VA	Detroit, MI
Brown, Charles H.	Sgt.	Co. I	Farmer	26	6/28/1863	Mason's Island, VA	St. Mary's County, MD
Brown, Charles F.	Sgt.	Co. C	Shoemaker	24	7/22/1863	Mason's Island, VA	Prince George's County, MD
Brown, Charles W.	Pvt.	Co. K	Laborer	21	7/4/1863	Washington, DC	Maryland
Brown, Dennis	Pvt.	Co. H	Farmer	18	9/23/1863	Portsmouth, VA	Portsmouth, VA
Brown, Frederick	Pvt.	Co. I	Farmer	22	7/12/1863	Washington, DC	Culpepper, VA
Brown, Henry	Pvt.	Co. E	Teamster	21	6/1/1863	Washington, DC	Culpepper, VA
Brown, Henry	Sgt.	Co. F	Farmer	21	5/24/1864	Ellicotts Mills, MD	Montgomery County, MD
Brown, Henry	Pvt.	Co. H	Farmer		6/27/1863	Mason's Island, VA	Alexandria, VA
Brown, James	Pvt.	Co. A	Laborer	19	5/19/1863	Washington, DC	Frederick County, MD
Brown, James	Pvt.	Co. D	Laborer	18	9/26/1864	Wilmington, DE	Harford County, MD
Brown, James R.	Pvt.	Co. K	Laborer	21	9/23/1864	Wilmington, DE	Millington, MD
Brown, John	Pvt.	Co. A	Farmer	19	5/19/1863	Washington, DC	Anne Arundel County, MD
Brown, John	Cpl.	Co. F	Farmer	17	6/21/1863	Mason's Island, VA	Frederick City, MD
Brown, John	Pvt.	Co. G	Farmer	18	7/10/1863	Mason's Island, VA	Rockville, MD
Brown, John	Pvt.	Co. G	Laborer	20	7/9/1864	Ellicotts Mills, MD	Bladensburg, MD
Brown, John H.	Sgt.	Co. E	Waiter	20	6/17/1863	Mason's Island, VA	Prince George's County, MD

Name	Rank	Co.	Age	Occupation	Date	Place	Residence
Brown, John H.W.	Sgt.	Co. C	28	Barber	7/4/1863	Mason's Island, VA	Elizabeth, NJ
Brown, John T.	Cpl.	Co. F	20	Waiter	6/21/1863	Mason's Island, VA	Baltimore, MD
Brown, Josiah	Pvt.	Co. B	25	Laborer	5/19/1863	Washington, DC	Baltimore County, MD
Brown, Matthias	Pvt.	Co. E	19	Farmer	5/19/1863	Mason's Island, VA	Galesville, MD
Brown, Nelson T.	Pvt.	Co. K	25	Laborer	6/30/1863	Mason's Island, VA	Montgomery County, MD
Brown, Robert	Pvt.	Co. E	23	Farmer	5/17/1863	Wilson's Wharf, VA	Richmond, VA
Brown, Robert	Pvt.	Co. I	20	Farmer	5/19/1864	Wisn's Creek	Charles City County, VA
Brown, Robert	Pvt.	Co. I	25	Farmer	10/25/1864	Ellicotts Mills, MD	
Brown, Samuel	Pvt.	Co. G	20	Blacksmith	7/7/1863	Mason's Island, VA	Prince George's County, MD
Brown, Sidney	Pvt.	Co. C	19	Farmer	4/15/1865	Wilmington, NC	Robinson Co., NC
Brown, Solomon	Pvt.	Co. D	18	Laborer	9/29/1864	Wilmington, DE	Harford County, MD
Brown, William	Pvt.	Co. C	17	Farmer	9/26/1864	Wilmington, DE	Harford County, MD
Brown, William	Pvt.	Co. C	19	Farmer	9/26/1864	Baltimore, MD	Prince George's County, MD
Brown, William H.N.	Pvt.	Co. C	18	School boy	6/8/1863	Washington, DC	Winchester, VA
Brown, Winston	Pvt.	Co. D	18	Laborer	6/14/1863	Mason's Island, VA	Louisa County, VA
Bruce, Upton	Pvt.	Co. F	28	Farmer	5/30/1864	Ellicotts Mills, MD	Prince George's County, MD
Brumley, Bailey	Pvt.	Co. H		Farmer	6/27/1863	Mason's Island, VA	King & Queen County, VA
Bryan, George	Pvt.	Co.	30	Laborer	9/28/1864	Ellicotts Mills, MD	Accomack, VA
Bryan, Jacob	Pvt.	Co. K	40	Laborer	9/24/1864	Wilmington, DE	New Castle County, DE
Bryant, Joseph W.	Pvt.	Co. C	35	Farmer	6/8/1863	Washington, DC	Loudon County, VA
Budd, Dennis	Pvt.	Co. G	25	Wagoner	5/25/1864	Ellicotts Mills, MD	
Burginne, Alfred	Pvt.	Co. G		Farmer	7/9/1864	Ellicotts Mills, MD	Prince George's County, MD
Burjo, Josias	Sgt.	Co. D		Blacksmith	6/14/1863	Mason's Island, VA	Madison County, VA
Burk, James	Pvt.	Co. B	23	Coachman	5/19/1863	Washington, DC	Leesburg, VA
Burley, Richard	Pvt.	Co. K	20	Laborer	6/30/1863	Mason's Island, VA	King & Queen County, VA
Burnell, Issac	Pvt.	Co. I	19	Field Hand	7/12/1863	Washington, DC	North Carolina
Burnet, Henry	Pvt.	Co. I	21	Oyster Catcher	6/28/1863	Mason's Island, VA	Philadelphia, PA
Burns, John	Pvt.	Co. A	20	Farmer	5/19/1863	Washington, DC	Bedford, PA
Burns, Walter	Sgt.	Co. I	26		6/28/1863	Mason's Island, VA	
Burr, Abram	Pvt.	Co. I	23	Field Hand	7/12/1863	Washington, DC	Hyde County, NC
Burt, Robert	Pvt.	Co. B	19	Waiter	7/3/1863	Mason's Island, VA	Spotsylvania County, VA
Butcher, Risdon	Sgt.	Co. G	30	Laborer	9/26/1864	Wilmington, DE	Accomack County, VA
Butler, Alfred	Pvt.	Co. B	22	Farmer	5/19/1863	Washington, DC	Fauquier County, VA
Butler, Benjamin	Pvt.	Co. B	28	Laborer	5/19/1863	Washington, DC	Prince George's County, MD
Butler, Charles	Cpl.	Co. D	23	Laborer	7/9/1863	Mason's Island, VA	Washington, DC
Butler, Charles	Cpl.	Co. E	19	Farmer	6/17/1863	Mason's Island, VA	Prince William County, VA
Butler, George	Pvt.	Co. H	22	Farmer	6/27/1863	Mason's Island, VA	Charles County, MD
Butler, George	Pvt.	Co. I	23	Boatman	6/28/1863	Mason's Island, VA	Alexandria, VA
Butler, Stephen	Pvt.	Co. I	38	Farmer	6/28/1863	Mason's Island, VA	Charles County, MD

Name	Rank	Company	Age	Occupation	Date	Place	Location
Butler, William	Pvt.	Co. C	17	Laborer	7/4/1863	Mason's Island, VA	Washington, DC
Butler, William	Pvt.	Co. E	26	Waiter	6/17/1863	Mason's Island, VA	Charles County, MD
Butt, David	Pvt.	Co. F	44	Farmer	6/21/1863	Mason's Island, VA	Norfolk County, VA
Caesar, Julius	Pvt.	Co. G	19	Baker	6/25/1863	Mason's Island, VA	Alexandria, VA
Calhoun, Peter	Pvt.	Co. C	17	Laborer	6/8/1863	Washington, DC	Baltimore, MD
Campbell, James	Pvt.	Co. E	18	-	6/17/1863	Mason's Island, VA	Montgomery County, MD
Campbell, Matthew	Pvt.	Co. D	22	Laborer	6/14/1863	Mason's Island, VA	Charles County, MD
Campbell, Philip	Pvt.	Co. B	20	Farmer	5/19/1863	Washington, DC	Westmoreland County, VA
Cannon, Curtis	Pvt.	Co. G	17	Laborer	9/15/1864	Easton, MD	Henry County, NC
Carroll, Albert	Pvt.	Co. B	19	Waiter	5/19/1864	Washington, DC	Charles County, MD
Carroll, Benjamin	Pvt.	Co. A	19	Farmer	7/12/1863	Mason's Island, VA	Washington, DC
Carroll, George	Sgt.	Co. F	20	Laborer	6/21/1863	Mason's Island, VA	Alexandria, VA
Carroll, Henson	Pvt.	Co. F	21	Waiter	6/21/1863	Mason's Island, VA	Rockville, MD
Carter, Addison	Pvt.	Co. I	22	Laborer	6/28/1863	Mason's Island, VA	Northumberland Co., VA
Carter, Arthur	Pvt.	Co. B	18	Waiter	5/19/1863	Mason's Island, VA	Warrenton, VA
Carter, David	Pvt.	Co. K	15	Laborer	6/20/1863	Mason's Island, VA	Northern Neck, VA
Carter, Edward	Pvt.	Co. A	19	Laborer	5/19/1863	Mason's Island, VA	Fredericksburg, VA
Carter, Frank	Pvt.	Co. E	19	Laborer	6/17/1863	Washington, DC	Alexandria, VA
Carter, Frederick	Pvt.	Co. E	19	Carpenter	6/17/1863	Mason's Island, VA	Marlboro Forest, MD
Carter, George H.	Pvt.	Co. K	19	Laborer	6/30/1863	Mason's Island, VA	Washington, DC
Carter, Hezekiah	Pvt.	Co. I	19	Field Hand	6/28/1863	Mason's Island, VA	Northumberland Co., VA
Carter, Samuel	Sgt.	Co. E	18	Waiter	7/3/1863	Mason's Island, VA	Pittsburgh, PA
Carter, William D.	Pvt.	Co. D	18	Laborer	6/14/1863	Mason's Island, VA	Northumberland Co., VA
Carter, William H.	Pvt.	Co. E	18	Farmer	7/3/1863	Mason's Island, VA	Richmond, VA
Carter, William S.	Pvt.	Co. D	19	Laborer	6/14/1863	Mason's Island, VA	Madison County, VA
Carter, William W.	Pvt.	Co. C	24	Farmer	6/8/1863	Washington, DC	Denton, MD
Cartlet, Phillip	Pvt.	Co. A	35	Waiter	5/19/1863	Washington, DC	Pensacola, FL
Cassells, James	Pvt.	Co. B	18	Servant	7/2/1863	Mason's Island, VA	Suffolk, VA
Casson, Andrew	Pvt.	Co. B	30	-	12/1/1863	Norfolk, VA	-
Chamberlain, Christopher	Pvt.	Co. I	25	Field Hand	6/28/1863	Mason's Island, VA	King & Queen County, VA
Champ, Daniel	Pvt.	Co. H	20	Ox Driver	6/27/1863	Mason's Island, VA	Loundon County, VA
Chaney, James	Cpl.	Co. I	16	Waiter	6/28/1863	Mason's Island, VA	Baltimore, MD
Chaney, Lane	Pvt.	Co.	26	Farmer	9/29/1864	Baltimore, MD	Baltimore County, MD
Chaney, William	Pvt.	Co. G	28	Sailor	6/28/1863	Mason's Island, VA	Talbot County, MD
Chase, Daniel	Pvt.	Co. A	21	Farmer	7/12/1863	Mason's Island, VA	Blow County, VA
Chase, David E.	Pvt.	Co. E	19	Waiter	6/8/1863	Washington, DC	Washington, DC
Chase, Henry	Pvt.	Co. G	27	Laborer	6/25/1863	Mason's Island, VA	Montgomery County, MD
Chase, Samuel	Cpl.	Co. H	23	Sailor	7/6/1863	Mason's Island, VA	Baltimore, MD
Cheeney, Sharp	Pvt.	Co. C	25	Teamster	6/8/1863	Washington, DC	Lancaster County, VA

Name	Rank	Co.	Age	Occupation	Date	Enlistment Place	Birth/Residence
Chew, Samuel	Pvt.	Co. D	38	Laborer	6/14/1863	Mason's Island, VA	Nottingham, MD
Chew, John	Cpl.	Co. I	27	Field Hand	6/28/1863	Mason's Island, VA	Caroline County, VA
Chew, William H.	Sgt.	Co. K	18	Artist	6/30/1863	Mason's Island, VA	Washington, DC
Claggett, Thomas	Pvt.	Co. E	25	Farmer	6/8/1863	Washington, DC	Montgomery County, MD
Clark, Hannibal H.	Pvt.	Co. G	22	Farmer	6/25/1863	Mason's Island, VA	Maryland
Clark, Jacob	Pvt.	Co. D	18	Laborer	6/14/1863	Mason's Island, VA	Washington, DC
Clark, John L.	Sgt.	Co. G	29	Carpenter	6/25/1863	Mason's Island, VA	Washington, DC
Clark, Leonard	Pvt.	Co. I	28	Field Hand	6/28/1863	Mason's Island, VA	Charles County, MD
Clark, Richard N.	Pvt.	Co. G	22	Laborer	6/25/1863	Mason's Island, VA	Washington, DC
Clark, Robert P.	Cpl.	Co. G	21	Farmer	6/25/1863	Mason's Island, VA	Prince George's County, MD
Clark, Samuel	Pvt.	Co. I	18	Gun Smith	6/28/1863	Mason's Island, VA	Washington, DC
Clay, Henry	Pvt.	Co. I	18	Field Hand	7/12/1863	Washington, DC	Orange County, VA
Claygreth, Ellis	Pvt.	Co. K	22	Waiter	6/30/1863	Mason's Island, VA	Prince George's County, MD
Clayton, Issac	Pvt.	Co. H	17	Farmer	6/27/1863	Mason's Island, VA	Virginia
Clifton, William	Pvt.	Co. I	30	Laborer	9/26/1864	Mason's Island, VA	Kent County, DE
Colbert, Enoch	Pvt.	Co. D	28	Hostler	7/9/1863	Wilmington, DE	Prince George's County, MD
Coleman, Joseph	Cpl.	Co. K	41	Laborer	6/30/1863	Mason's Island, VA	Leesburg, VA
Coleman, Lewis	Pvt.	Co. I	20	Laborer	6/28/1863	Mason's Island, VA	Lancaster County, VA
Coleman, Minor	Pvt.	Co. I	17	Hostler	6/28/1863	Mason's Island, VA	Caroline County, VA
Coleman, William	Pvt.	Co. K	30	Laborer	6/30/1863	Mason's Island, VA	Fredericksburg, VA
Collins, Benjamin	Cpl.	Co. E	20	Coachman	5/17/1863	Mason's Island, VA	Hagerstown, MD
Collins, William	Sgt.	Co. G	23	Farmer	6/25/1863	Mason's Island, VA	Adams County, PA
Colson, Richard	Pvt.	Co. D	19	Laborer	6/14/1863	Mason's Island, VA	Fredericksburg, VA
Columbus, Christopher	Pvt.	Co. B	25	Laborer	5/19/1863	Washington, DC	Camden County, NC
Conley, James	Pvt.	Co. F	16	Teamster	6/21/1863	Mason's Island, VA	Washington, DC
Conley, William	Pvt.	Co. I	25	Teamster	6/28/1863	Mason's Island, VA	Philadelphia, PA
Conner, Daniel	Pvt.	Co. G	21	Brick Maker	7/8/1863	Mason's Island, VA	Prince William County, VA
Conway, Ewell	Cpl.	Co. E	20	Farmer	6/17/1863	Mason's Island, VA	Glocester, VA
Cook, Frank	Cpl.	Co. I	21	Coal Heaver	6/28/1863	Mason's Island, VA	Gettysburg, PA
Cook, James E.	Sgt.	Co. K	20	Laborer	6/25/1863	Mason's Island, VA	Carrol County, MD
Cook, James W.	Pvt.	Co. G	29	Laborer	9/29/1864	Frederick, MD	Georgetown, DC
Cook, John H.	Pvt.	Co. C	21	Laborer	7/8/1863	Mason's Island, VA	Prince George's County, MD
Cook, Richard	Pvt.	Co. C	23	Laborer	6/8/1863	Washington, DC	Loudon County, VA
Cooper, Alfred	Pvt.	Co. I	16	Field Hand	6/28/1863	Mason's Island, VA	Orange County, VA
Cooper, Henry	Pvt.	Co. A	22	Laborer	5/19/1863	Washington, DC	Washington, DC
Cooper, Shadrack	Pvt.	Co. I	19	Brick Maker	7/12/1863	Washington, DC	Caroline County, VA
Cooper, William	Pvt.	Co. G	19	Sailor	9/28/1864	Ellicotts Mills, MD	Lanks County, VA
Corbett, Issac	Pvt.	Co. H	18	Farmer	6/27/1863	Mason's Island, VA	Chucituck, VA
Corbin, Issac	Pvt.	Co. H	33	Farmer	6/27/1863	Mason's Island, VA	

Name	Rank	Company	Age	Occupation	Date	Place	Residence
Coster, Wesley	Pvt.	Co. G	25	Laborer	6/25/1863	Mason's Island, VA	Gates County, NC
Cox, Thomas	Pvt.	Co. K	19	Farmer	6/6/1864	City Point, VA	Prince George's County, MD
Cravens, Thomas H.	Pvt.	Co. E	16	Waiter	6/17/1863	Mason's Island, VA	Leesburg, VA
Crier, Thomas	Pvt.	Co. I	13	Painter	6/28/1863	Mason's Island, VA	Washington, DC
Cromedy, Alexander	Pvt.	Co. G	19	Farmer	4/15/1865	Wilmington, NC	Bladen County, NC
Cromedy, Evar	Pvt.	Co. D	19	Laborer	4/15/1864	Wilmington, NC	Bladen County, NC
Crosberry, Thomas	Pvt.	Co. E	30	Laborer	9/24/1864	Wilmington, DE	Kent, DE
Cross, Robert	Pvt.	Co. B	24	Laborer	5/19/1863	Washington, DC	Bladensburg, MD
Crummedy, Anthony	Pvt.	Co. G			4/15/1865	Wilmington, NC	
Crummedy, Rufus	Pvt.	Co. A		-		-	-
Crump, Israel	Pvt.	Co. E	19	Farmer	6/17/1863	Mason's Island, VA	Fairfax Courthouse, VA
Crump, Horace	Pvt.	Co. E	19	Farmer	6/17/1863	Mason's Island, VA	Alexandria, VA
Crutchfield, Edmund	Pvt.	Co. K	18	Laborer	6/30/1863	Mason's Island, VA	Fredericksburg, VA
Cubbage, Joseph	Pvt.	Co. E	27	Laborer	9/24/1864	Wilmington, DE	Kent, DE
Cumbash, John	Sgt.	Co. F	23	Farmer	6/21/1863	Mason's Island, VA	Frederick County, MD
Cure, Henry	Pvt.	Co. E	21	Farmer	6/17/1863	Mason's Island, VA	Elkridge, MD
Curry, Willoughby	Pvt.	Co. B	18	Farmer	9/21/1864	Baltimore, MD	Cumberland, VA
Curtis, George	Pvt.	Co. A	19	Farmer	7/12/1864	Mason's Island, VA	Baltimore County, MD
Curtis, James	Pvt.	Co. G	21	Hostler	6/25/1863	Mason's Island, VA	Washington, DC
Custis, John	Pvt.	Co. I	21	Butcher	7/12/1863	Washington, DC	Accomack County, VA
Dad, William A.	Cpl.	Co. A		-	5/19/1863	Washington, DC	-
Dangerfield, Beverly	Pvt.	Co. K	37	Laborer	6/30/1863	Mason's Island, VA	Spotsylvania County, VA
Dangerfield, James W.	Pvt.	Co. K	26	Laborer	7/4/1863	Washington, DC	Spotsylvania County, VA
Darcy, Frank	Pvt.	Co. G	18	Farmer	6/25/1863	Mason's Island, VA	Leonardtown, MD
Davenport, Frank	Pvt.	Co. H	25	Foundryman	6/27/1863	Mason's Island, VA	Fredericksburg, VA
Davis, Albert	Pvt.	Co. H	18	Shoemaker	6/27/1863	Mason's Island, VA	Culpepper County, VA
Davis, Charles	Pvt.	Co. I	22	Laborer	7/12/1863	Washington, DC	Louisa County, VA
Davis, Henry	Pvt.	Co. B	18	Laborer	5/19/1863	Washington, DC	Washington, DC
Davis, Henry	Pvt.	Co. G	21	Farmer	6/25/1863	Mason's Island, VA	Middlesex County, VA
Davis, John	Pvt.	Co. F	28	Plasterer	6/21/1863	Mason's Island, VA	Washington, DC
Davis, Joseph	Pvt.	Co. A	31	Laborer	7/12/1863	Mason's Island, VA	Washington, DC
Davis, Joseph	Sgt.	Co. I	26	Sailor	6/28/1863	Mason's Island, VA	Washington, DC
Davis, Lorenzo	Pvt.	Co. B	28	Painter	5/19/1863	Washington, DC	Randolph County, MD
Davis, Nehemiah	Pvt.	Co. G	18	Laborer	9/25/1864	Wilmington, DE	Caroline County, VA
Davis, Nelson	Cpl.	Co. C	25	Laborer	6/18/1863	Washington, DC	Baltimore, MD
Davis, Robert	Pvt.	Co. C	21	Laborer	6/8/1863	Washington, DC	Prince George's County, MD
Davis, William	Pvt.		-		-	-	-
Day, Edward N.	Pvt.	Co. I	31	Cook	6/28/1863	Mason's Island, VA	Oxon Hill, MD
Day, James	Pvt.	Co. K	21	Mason	6/30/1863	Mason's Island, VA	North Carolina

Name	Rank	Co.	Age	Occupation	Date	Enlisted	Birthplace
Day, John F.	Cpl.	Co. I	25	Plasterer	6/28/1863	Mason's Island, VA	Charles County, MD
Deadman, Henry	Pvt.	Co. G	21	Farmer	6/25/1863	Mason's Island, VA	Glouchester County, VA
Dean, William	Pvt.	Co. H	19	Farmer	6/27/1863	Mason's Island, VA	Sowden County, VA
Dean, William	Pvt.	Co. K	37	Laborer	9/24/1864	Wilmington, DE	Kent County, DE
Decoursay, George O.	Sgt.	Co. F	20	Barber	6/21/1863	Mason's Island, VA	Cecil County, MD
Delany, Richard	Pvt.	Co. G	21	Farmer	6/25/1863	Mason's Island, VA	Prince George's County, MD
Demby, George	Pvt.	Co. I	21	Laborer	9/26/1864	Wilmington, DE	Smyrna, DE
Dennison, Albert	Pvt.	-	-	-	6/8/1863	Mason's Island, VA	-
Desheads, Henry	Pvt.	-	20	Laborer	9/29/1864	Ellicotts Mills, MD	Jefferson County, VA
Devann, Frederick	Pvt.	Co. I	21	Farmer	3/3/1865	Wilmington, NC	Hanover County, NC
Devann, Peter	Pvt.	Co. I	19	Farmer	3/3/1865	Wilmington, NC	Hanover County, NC
Dickinson, James	Pvt.	-	26	Laborer	10/8/1864	Buffalo, NY	Cincinnati, OH
Dickinson, William	Pvt.	Co. B	19	Laborer	5/19/1863	Washington, DC	Nelson County, VA
Diggs, Phillip	Pvt.	Co. K	16	Farmer	6/30/1863	Mason's Island, VA	Washington, DC
Diggs, Robert	Pvt.	Co. D	23	Farmer	5/19/1863	Washington, DC	Lower Marlboro, MD
Diggs, Thaddeus	Pvt.	Co. F	18	Waiter	7/10/1863	Mason's Island, VA	Portsmouth, VA
Diggs, Wilson	Cpl.	Co. H	24	Waiter	7/17/1863	Mason's Island, VA	Prince William, VA
Dison, Washington	Pvt.	Co. A	23	Laborer	5/19/1863	Washington, DC	Marcy County, MD
Dixon, George	Cpl.	Co. A	22	Waiter	5/19/1863	Washington, DC	Near Long Bridge, VA
Dixon, Henry	Pvt.	Co. I	16	Laborer	6/28/1863	Mason's Island, VA	Alexandria, VA
Dixon, Richard	Cpl.	Co. A	25	Laborer	5/19/1863	Washington, DC	Fauquier County, VA
Dixon, William	Cpl.	Co. E	40	Laborer	7/3/1863	Mason's Island, VA	Caroline County, VA
Dixon, William	-	Co. E	18	Farmer	3/15/1865	Wilmington, NC	Charleston, SC
Dockett, Thomas	Cpl.	Co. G	20	Blacksmith	6/25/1863	Mason's Island, VA	Prince George's County, MD
Dorsey, Edward	Pvt.	Co. C	31	Farmer	6/8/1863	Washington, DC	Montgomery County, MD
Dotson, Silas	Pvt.	Co. F	24	Waiter	6/21/1863	Mason's Island, VA	Washington, DC
Douglass, Jacob	Pvt.	Co. K	25	Laborer	7/4/1863	Washington, DC	Prince George's County, MD
Douglass, Amos	Cpl.	Co. E	26	Farmer	6/17/1863	Mason's Island, VA	Warrenton, VA
Douglass, Daniel	Pvt.	Co. B	19	Laborer	5/19/1863	Washington, DC	Prince William County, VA
Douglass, James H.	Cpl.	Co. K	38	Driver	6/30/1863	Mason's Island, VA	Washington, DC
Douglass, Noah	Cpl.	Co. H	25	Farmer	6/27/1863	Mason's Island, VA	Loudon County, VA
Douglass, William	Sgt.	Co. I	36	Waterman	6/28/1863	Mason's Island, VA	Washington, DC
Drawhorn, Frank	Pvt.	Co. I	21	Farmer	4/9/1865	Faison Station, NC	Bladen County, NC
Drawhorn, Thomas	Pvt.	Co. C	-	Farmer	4/9/1865	Faison Station, NC	Bladen County, NC
Driver, Robert	Pvt.	Co. I	19	Laborer	6/28/1863	Mason's Island, VA	Fredericksburg, VA
Ducket, Pins	Pvt.	Co. I	28	Hostler	7/1/1863	Mason's Island, VA	Nottingham, MD
Dudley, James	Pvt.	Co. B	19	Waiter	7/4/1863	Mason's Island, VA	Newbern, NC
Duette, Humphrey	Pvt.	Co. K	23	Carpenter	7/4/1863	Mason's Island, VA	Southhampton County, VA
Duff, Charles	Pvt.	Co. G	20	Laborer	7/8/1863	Mason's Island, VA	Baltimore, MD

Name	Rank	Co.	Age	Occupation	Date	Location	Residence
Dunmore, George	Pvt.	Co. H	18	Waiter	6/27/1863	Mason's Island, VA	Washington, DC
Dutcher, Gabriel	Pvt.	Co. F	17	Waiter	6/21/1863	Mason's Island, VA	Washington, DC
Dwin, Henry	Sgt.	Co. C	45	Carpenter	6/8/1863	Washington, DC	Henderson County, NC
Dyson, Thomas W.	Pvt.	Co. I	20	Farmer	6/28/1863	Mason's Island, VA	Prince George's County, MD
Easton, Charles	Pvt.	Co. E	13	Waiter	6/17/1863	Mason's Island, VA	Baltimore, MD
Edmons, Richard	Pvt.	Co. B	18	Waiter	5/19/1863	Mason's Island, VA	Washington, DC
Edwards, Hezekiah	Cpl.	Co. H	22	Laborer	6/27/1863	Mason's Island, VA	Washington, DC
Edwards, James	Cpl.	Co. A	28	Waiter	5/19/1863	Washington, DC	Frederick, MD
Edwards, Thomas	Pvt.	Co. H	22	Laborer	6/27/1863	Mason's Island, VA	Washington, DC
Ellis, Samuel	Pvt.	Co. A	20	Farmer	5/19/1863	Washington, DC	Prince George's County, MD
Elrod, James T.B.	Pvt.	Co. K	17	Waiter	7/4/1863	Mason's Island, VA	Jackson, TN
Elson, John	Pvt.	Co. D	20	Laborer	6/14/1863	Mason's Island, VA	Baltimore, MD
Ennis, Joseph	Cpl.	Co. C	25	Farmer	6/8/1863	Washington, DC	Westriver County, MD
Ennis, Thomas	Pvt.	Co. A	19	Laborer	5/19/1863	Washington, DC	Marble Forrest, MD
Evans, Hezekiah	Pvt.	Co. I	32	Laborer	6/28/1863	Mason's Island, VA	Frederick County, MD
Evans, John D.	Cpl.	Co. E	25	Laborer	6/17/1863	Mason's Island, VA	Manchester, VA
Everett, Charles	Sgt.	Co. C	33	Barber	6/8/1863	Washington, DC	Carswell County, NC
Farmer, Mason	Pvt.	Co. C	22	Cook	5/19/1863	Washington, DC	Stafford County, VA
Fausky, Dub	Pvt.	Co. G	22	Farmer	6/25/1863	Mason's Island, VA	Hide County, NC
Fawkes, Josiah	Cpl.	Co. E	24	Farmer	6/17/1863	Mason's Island, VA	Sylvester County, MD
Felton, Anthony	Pvt.	Co. F		Farmer	6/21/1863	Mason's Island, VA	Chowan County, NC
Felton, Calvin	Cpl.	Co. G	20	Farmer	6/25/1863	Mason's Island, VA	Simmons County, NC
Felton, Lewis	Pvt.	Co. G	20	Farmer	6/25/1863	Mason's Island, VA	Hurtfort, NC
Felton, Oliver	Pvt.	Co. G	21	Farmer	6/25/1863	Mason's Island, VA	Hurtfort, NC
Felton, Stephen	Pvt.	Co. B	20	Farmer	5/19/1863	Washington, DC	Heightford City, NC
Fennell, Sylvester	Pvt.	Co. A	19	Farmer	3/7/1865	Wilmington, NC	New Hanover County, NC
Ferguson, James R.	Pvt.	Co. I	21	Blacksmith	6/28/1863	Mason's Island, VA	Jefferson County, VA
Field, William	Pvt.	Co. F	18	Coal Heaver	7/12/1863	Washington, DC	Alexandria, VA
Fields, Gabriel	Cpl.	Co. F	24	Farmer	6/21/1863	Mason's Island, VA	Loudon County, VA
Fisher, Simon	Pvt.	Co. E	21	Waiter	6/17/1863	Mason's Island, VA	Loudon County, VA
Flamer, Joseph	Pvt.	Co. K	21	Teamster	6/28/1863	Mason's Island, VA	Baltimore, MD
Fletcher, George W.	Pvt.	Co. F	19	Teamster	6/21/1863	Mason's Island, VA	Washington, DC
Fletcher, Henry	Cpl.	Co. E	35	Waiter	6/17/1863	Mason's Island, VA	Prince George's County, MD
Fletcher, Samuel H.	Cpl.	Co. G	25	Shoemaker	6/25/1863	Mason's Island, VA	Upperville, VA
Foote, Henry	Pvt.	Co. H	19	-	6/27/1863	Mason's Island, VA	Anne Arundel County, MD
Forbes, Thomas	Pvt.	Co I	21	Waterman	7/12/1863	Washington, DC	Marlboro, MD
Ford, Edward	Pvt.	Co. A	20	Laborer	5/19/1863	Washington, DC	Marble Forrest, MD
Ford, Robert	Pvt.	Co. D	20	Farmer	6/14/1863	Washington, DC	St. Charles County, MD
Ford, Walter	Cpl.	Co. B	19	Carpenter	5/19/1863	Washington, DC	Leesburg, VA

Name	Rank	Company	Age	Occupation	Enlistment Date	Enlistment Place	Birthplace
Ford, William	Sgt.	Co. F	19	-	6/21/1863	Mason's Island, VA	Wilmington, DE
Forman, John	Pvt.	Co. K	18	Laborer	6/30/1863	Mason's Island, VA	Norfolk, VA
Foster, George	Cpl.	Co. E	18	Waiter	6/17/1863	Mason's Island, VA	Fairfax County, VA
Fox, Lewis	Pvt.	Co. I	22	Shoemaker	6/28/1863	Mason's Island, VA	Fredericksburg, VA
Franklin, James	Pvt.	Co. K	20	Laborer	6/21/1863	Mason's Island, VA	Anne Arundel County, MD
Franklin, John	Pvt.	Co. F	17	-	6/30/1863	Mason's Island, VA	Lewistown, PA
Freeman, Frank	Pvt.	Co. K	25	Laborer	7/9/1863	Mason's Island, VA	Page County, VA
Freeman, Samuel	Pvt.	Co. D	22	Bricklayer	5/19/1863	Washington, DC	Southhampton County, VA
Gaiter, William H.	Pvt.	Co. B	23	Farmer	7/10/1863	Mason's Island, VA	Frederick County, MD
Gallop, Samuel	Pvt.	Co. F	-	-			-
Gallsway, Henry	Pvt.	Co. A	25	Farmer	5/19/1863	Washington, DC	Prince George's County, MD
Gant, Frank	Pvt.	Co. B	23	Book Binder	5/19/1863	Washington, DC	Washington, DC
Gant, John	Pvt.	Co. K	19	Farmer	5/19/1863	Washington, DC	Marble Forrest, MD
Gant, Phillip	Pvt.	Co. D	19	Laborer	7/9/1863	Mason's Island, VA	Northumberland, MD
Gant, Thomas	Cpl.	Co. D	25	Farmer	7/9/1863	Mason's Island, VA	Prince George's County, MD
Gant, William	Pvt.	Co. D	22	Laborer	6/14/1863	Mason's Island, VA	Washington, DC
Gardner, Adam	Pvt.	Co. A	20	Laborer	5/19/1863	Washington, DC	Chesterfield Courthouse, VA
Garnet, Addison	Pvt.	Co. -	23	Sailor	12/7/1864	New York City	Virginia
Gatlin, Frederick	Pvt.	Co. F	26	Laborer	6/21/1863	Mason's Island, VA	Craven County, NC
Gatlin, Edmond	Pvt.	Co. B	28	Farmer	5/19/1863	Washington, DC	Gates County, NC
Gaylor, John	Pvt.	Co. F	25	Laborer	6/21/1863	Mason's Island, VA	North Carolina
Gibbs, George	Cpl.	Co. E	17	Laborer	6/17/1863	Mason's Island, VA	Alexandria, VA
Gibson, Amos	Pvt.	Co. H	21	Farming	7/6/1863	Baltimore, MD	Onslow, NC
Gibson, Andrew	Pvt.	Co. K	25	Laborer	9/24/1864	Faison's Depot	Caroline County, MD
Gibson, Calvin	Pvt.	Co. C	23	Farmer	4/9/1865	Mason's Island, VA	Marlboro, NC
Gibson, Charles	Pvt.	Co. H	16	Waiter	7/6/1863	Easton, MD	Rock Creek, MD
Gibson, Henry	Pvt.	Co. A	17	Laborer	9/27/1864	Mason's Island, VA	Harford County, MD
Gilbert, William	Pvt.	Co. D	21	Waiter	6/14/1863	Washington, DC	Washington, DC
Giles, Jacob	Pvt.	Co. A	22	Laborer	5/19/1863	Baltimore, MD	Prince George's County, MD
Giles, William	Pvt.	Co. K	40	Laborer	9/30/1864	Washington, DC	Harford County, MD
Goff, Manning	Pvt.	Co. K	30	Farmer	7/4/1863	Mason's Island, VA	Baltimore, MD
Goodwin, James	Pvt.	Co. E	20	Farmer	6/17/1863	Mason's Island, VA	Mount Pleasant, MD
Gordon, Carry	Pvt.	Co. H	33	Laborer	6/27/1863	Mason's Island, VA	Nansemond County, MD
Gordon, George	Pvt.	Co. G	17	Laborer	6/25/1863	Mason's Island, VA	Fortress Monroe, VA
Gordon, John	Sgt.	Co. I	21	Hostler	7/12/1863	Washington, DC	Winchester, VA
Gordon, Sandy	Pvt.	Co. G	19	House Servant	6/25/1863	Mason's Island, VA	Fauquier County, VA
Gordon, William	Pvt.	Co. C	25	Farmer	7/4/1863	Mason's Island, VA	Northumberland, MD
Goswell, George D.	Cpl.	Co. F	20	Coachman	12/17/1864	Tarrytown, NY	Newton, NY
Gould, Benjamin	Pvt.	Co. A	21	Laborer	5/19/1863	Washington, DC	Baltimore, MD

Name	Rank	Co.	Age	Occupation	Date	Location	Origin
Granbray, Justin	Pvt.	Co. H	38	Carpenter	8/17/1863	Washington, DC	Perquimans County, NC
Granison, Charles	Pvt.	Co. H	22	Laborer	6/27/1863	Mason's Island, VA	Georgetown, DC
Grant, William H.	Cpl.	Co. C	17	Farmer	6/8/1863	Washington, DC	Lenox, MA
Graves, David	Pvt.	Co. I	24	Farmer	5/31/1864	Ft. Powhatan, VA	Sussex County, VA
Gray, John	Pvt.	Co. D	18	Laborer	6/14/1863	Mason's Island, VA	Prince George's County, MD
Gray, John	Cpl.	Co. G	24	Farmer	6/25/1863	Mason's Island, VA	Alda County, VA
Gray, Luther	Pvt.	Co. K	18	Laborer	6/30/1863	Mason's Island, VA	Alexandria, VA
Gray, Stephen	Pvt.	Co. K	20	Laborer	6/30/1863	Mason's Island, VA	Fredericksburg, VA
Gray, Washington	Pvt.	Co. I	24	Farmer	6/281863	Mason's Island, VA	Prince George's County, MD
Gray, William	Pvt.	Co. H	27	Waiter	7/6/1863	Mason's Island, VA	Washington, DC
Grayson, Washington	Pvt.	Co. I	19	Farmer	6/28/1863	Mason's Island, VA	Stafford County, VA
Greely, Horace	Pvt.	Co. G	40	Farmer	6/25/1863	Mason's Island, VA	Onslow County, NC
Green, Andrew	Cpl.	Co. A	21	Waiter	7/12/1863	Washington, DC	Washington, DC
Green, Charles A.	Sgt.	Co. H	23	Waiter	6/27/1863	Mason's Island, VA	Georgetown, DC
Green, Erastus	Pvt.	Co. G	19	Shoemaker	6/25/1863	Mason's Island, VA	Rappahannock, VA
Green, George	Pvt.	Co. -	-	-	-	-	-
Green, Henry	Sgt.	Co. A	21	Mason	5/19/1863	Washington, DC	New Orleans, LA
Green, Henry	Cpl.	Co. D	18	Teamster	6/14/1863	Mason's Island, VA	Washington, DC
Green, Henry, 1st	Pvt.	Co. I	21	Farmer	6/25/1863	Mason's Island, VA	Prince George's County, MD
Green, Henry, 2nd	Pvt.	Co. J	21	Hostler	7/12/1863	Mason's Island, VA	Charlotte County, VA
Green, James	Cpl.	Co. C	18	Farmer	6/8/1863	Washington, DC	Charles County, MD
Green, James	Sgt.	Co. H	20	Farmer	7/6/1863	Washington, DC	Washington, DC
Green, John	Pvt.	Co. E	20	Farmer	6/17/1863	Mason's Island, VA	Hanover Court House, VA
Green, John, Wesley	Pvt.	Co. K	22	Laborer	6/30/1863	Mason's Island, VA	Baltimore, MD
Green, Robert	Pvt.	Co. E	20	Carpenter	6/17/1863	Mason's Island, VA	Savannah, GA
Green, Robert	Pvt.	Co. F	18	Teamster	6/21/1863	Mason's Island, VA	Baltimore, MD
Green, Robert H.	Sgt.	Co. I	26	Barber	6/28/1863	Mason's Island, VA	Falmouth, VA
Green, Scott	Pvt.	Co. H	21	Laborer	6/30/1863	Mason's Island, VA	Harrisburg, PA
Green, William	Pvt.	Co. C	18	Waiter	7/4/1863	Mason's Island, VA	Fredericksburg, VA
Greenfield, Daniel	Pvt.	Co. K	23	Laborer	6/30/1863	Mason's Island, VA	Sandusky, OH
Greggsby, Flem	Pvt.	Co. F	-	-	6/21/1863	Mason's Island, VA	-
Gregory, Lemuel	Pvt.	Co. G	21	Farmer	6/25/1863	Mason's Island, VA	Camden County, NC
Grey, James	Pvt.	Co. A	25	Waiter	7/12/1863	Washington, DC	King William County, VA
Greyson, James	Pvt.	Co. C	18	Waiter	6/8/1863	Washington, DC	New Bedford, MA
Greyson, William H.	Pvt.	Co. C	18	Laborer	6/8/1863	Washington, DC	Prince William County, VA
Griffin, John	Pvt.	Co. B	-	-	-	-	-
Griggsby, Tyler	Pvt.	Co. H	19	Farmer	6/27/1863	Mason's Island, VA	Fauquier County, VA
Griggsby, Alfred	Pvt.	Co. F	26	Teamster	7/10/1863	Mason's Island, VA	Loudon County, VA
Grimball, John	Sgt.	Co. C	34	Tailor	6/8/1863	Washington, DC	Charleston, SC

Name	Rank	Company	Occupation	Age	Date	Enlistment	Birthplace
Grinfer, Henry	Pvt.	Co. B	Farmer	20	7/1/1863	Mason's Island, VA	Beantown, MD
Grinnell, Joseph H.	Pvt.	Co. G	Waiter	20	7/8/1863	Mason's Island, VA	Washington, DC
Gutridge, Charles W.	Cpl.	Co. K	Carpenter	27	6/30/1864	Mason's Island, VA	Prince George's County, MD
Guy, Sewell	Pvt.	Co. G	Farmer	21	9/24/1864	Wilmington, DE	Hartford County, DE
Hagan, Robert	Pvt.	Co. E	Farmer	18	6/17/1863	Mason's Island, VA	Charles County, MD
Hailstock, John	Pvt.	Co. D	Farmer	29	6/14/1863	Mason's Island, VA	Charlottesville, VA
Haines, John	Pvt.	Co. A	Blacksmith	40	7/12/1863	Mason's Island, VA	King George County, VA
Haines, Maryland	Pvt.	Co. G	Farmer	32	6/25/1863	Mason's Island, VA	North Hampton Court House, NC
Hall, Andrew	Pvt.	Co. D	Farmer	18	6/14/1863	Mason's Island, VA	Prince George's County, MD
Hall, Henry	Sgt.	Co. H	Farmer	28	6/27/1863	Mason's Island, VA	Anne Arundel County, MD
Hall, Issac	Pvt.	Co. C	Farmer	24	6/8/1863	Washington, DC	Upper Marlboro, MD
Hall, Issac	Cpl.	Co. H	Butcher	18	6/27/1863	Mason's Island, VA	Montgomery County, MD
Hall, John	Pvt.	Co. D	Laborer	20	6/14/1863	Mason's Island, VA	Washington, DC
Hall, Thomas	Pvt.	-	Laborer	20	12/4/1863	Washington, DC	-
Hall, Thomas	Pvt.	Co. G	Farmer	26	9/29/1864	Albany, NY	Hurford County, MD
Hall, William H.	Pvt.	Co. C	Laborer	19	6/8/1863	Washington, DC	Pautexent, MD
Hamilton, Edward W.	Sgt.	Co. F	Waiter	19	6/24/1863	Mason's Island, VA	Alexandria, VA
Hammond, John	Pvt.	Co. H	-	26	6/27/1863	Mason's Island, VA	-
Hammond, John H.	Pvt.	Co. C	Farmer	-	9/22/1864	Baltimore, MD	Anne Arundel County, MD
Hampton, James	Pvt.	Co. K	Waiter	19	6/30/1863	Mason's Island, VA	Northumberland, MD
Harcomb, Samuel	Pvt.	Co. A	Farmer	19	5/19/1863	Washington, DC	Westminster, MD
Hardin, Nicholas	Pvt.	Co. A	Laborer	22	5/19/1863	Washington, DC	Nansemond County, VA
Harlan, Jacob	Pvt.	Co. I	Shoemaker	23	6/28/1863	Mason's Island, VA	Bedford, PA
Harley, George W.	Sgt.	Co. C	Laborer	21	6/8/1863	Washington, DC	Virginia
Harris, Addison	Pvt.	Co. I	Laborer	23	7/12/1863	Washington, DC	St. Mary's County, MD
Harris, Edward	Pvt.	Co. D	Laborer	30	7/9/1863	Mason's Island, VA	Middlesex, VA
Harris, George	Pvt.	Co. H	Farmer	18	6/27/1863	Mason's Island, VA	Fredericksburg, VA
Harris, John	Pvt.	Co. E	Laborer	21	6/17/1863	Mason's Island, VA	Georgetown, DC
Harris, John	Pvt.	Co. G	Saloon Waiter	17	7/10/1863	Mason's Island, VA	Washington, DC
Harris, Joseph	Pvt.	Co. G	Farmer	21	7/10/1863	Mason's Island, VA	Cambridge, MD
Harris, Thomas, James	Pvt.	Co. D	Waiter	22	6/14/1863	Mason's Island, VA	Williamsburg, VA
Harris, William	Pvt.	Co. E	Errand Boy	16	7/3/1863	Mason's Island, VA	Georgetown, DC
Harris, William	Pvt.	Co. F			7/10/1863	Mason's Island, VA	Baltimore, MD
Harrison, William H.	Pvt.	Co. A	Farmer	22	5/19/1863	Washington, DC	Surry County, VA
Harrison, Ephriam	Pvt.	Co. I	Farmer	22	5/31/1864	Ft. Powhatan, VA	Virginia
Harrison, Henry	Pvt.	Co. H	Farmer	18	6/27/1863	Mason's Island, VA	Washington, DC
Harrison, Joseph	Pvt.	Co. G	Laborer	18	9/26/1864	Frederick, MD	Frederick, MD
Harrison, Samuel	Pvt.	Co. C	Farmer	23	5/16/1864	Wilson's Landing, MD	Charles City County, VA
Harrison, William H.	Sgt.	Co. B	Porter	19	5/19/1863	Washington, DC	Bladensburg, MD

Name	Rank	Company	Occupation	Age	Date	Location	Residence
Harrison, William H.	Pvt.	Co. C	Farmer	19	5/16/1864	Wilson's Landing, MD	Charles City County, VA
Haskins, Reson	Pvt.	Co. I	Farmer	21	6/28/1863	Mason's Island, VA	Rockville, MD
Hatton, George W.	Sgt.	Co. C	Porter	21	6/8/1863	Washington, DC	Prince George's County, MD
Hatton, Henry	Cpl.	Co. E	-	22	7/3/1863	Mason's Island, VA	Prince George's County, MD
Hawkins, Alexander	Pvt.	Co. C	Farmer	27	6/8/1863	Washington, DC	Upper Marlboro, MD
Hayes, William	Pvt.	Co. C	Laborer	24	6/8/1863	Washington, DC	Nottingham, MD
Heath, Frank	Pvt.	Co. G	Blacksmith	22	6/25/1863	Mason's Island, VA	Page County, VA
Hebron, Samuel	Sgt.	Co. H	Farmer	28	7/6/1863	Mason's Island, VA	Anne Arundel County, MD
Hector, David	Pvt.	-	Laborer	43	2/12/1864	Bridgeport, CT	Shearon, CT
Hedgeman, Buck	Pvt.	Co. E	Laborer	18	7/3/1863	Mason's Island, VA	Thoroughfare Gap, VA
Henderson, Charles	Sgt.	Co. E	Farmer	22	6/17/1863	Mason's Island, VA	Norfolk, VA
Henry, Abram	Pvt.	Co. C	Laborer	29	6/8/1863	Washington, DC	Upper Marlboro, MD
Henry, Edward	Pvt.	Co. C	Laborer	20	6/8/1863	Washington, DC	Louisa County, VA
Henry, James	Pvt.	Co. H	-	20	6/27/1863	Mason's Island, VA	-
Henry, John	Pvt.	Co. E	Farmer	21	6/17/1863	Mason's Island, VA	Aldea, VA
Henry, John	Pvt.	Co. H	-	24	6/27/1863	Mason's Island, VA	-
Henry, Robert	Pvt.	Co. H	-	30	6/27/1863	Mason's Island, VA	-
Henry, William	Pvt.	Co. B	Farmer	18	7/3/1863	Mason's Island, VA	Port Tobacco County, MD
Henson, William	Pvt.	Co. E	-	18	6/17/1863	Mason's Island, VA	Washington, DC
Herbert, William H.	Pvt.	Co. C	Butcher	21	6/8/1863	Washington, DC	Washington, DC
Hewson, Joseph	Pvt.	Co. D	Laborer	18	6/14/1863	Mason's Island, VA	Eastern Shore, MD
Hicks, Henry	Sgt.	Co. A	Wool Spinner	22	5/19/1863	Washington, DC	New York City, NY
Hiles, Henry	Pvt.	Co. A	Laborer	20	5/19/1863	Washington, DC	Marlboro, MD
Hill, Frederick	Pvt.	Co. A	-	-	5/19/1863	Washington, DC	-
Hill, John	Cpl.	Co. D	Farmer	19	7/9/1863	Mason's Island, VA	Stafford County, VA
Hill, William	Pvt.	Co. F	Teamster	18	6/21/1863	Mason's Island, VA	Montgomery County, MD
Hill, William H.	Pvt.	Co. H	Brick Maker	29	7/6/1863	Mason's Island, VA	Washington, DC
Hillard, William	Pvt.	Co. K	-	-	6/30/1863	Mason's Island, VA	-
Hogins, James	Pvt.	Co. K	Laborer	29	6/30/1863	Mason's Island, VA	Fairfax County, VA
Holland, Jacob	Pvt.	Co. K	Laborer	28	6/30/1863	Mason's Island, VA	Norfolk, VA
Holland, John	Pvt.	Co. C	Farmer	25	4/9/1865	Faison's Depot	Augusta, GA
Holland, John	Pvt.	Co. F	Teamster	19	7/10/1863	Mason's Island, VA	Nansemond County, VA
Holland, Richard	Pvt.	Co. H	Sailor	23	6/27/1863	Mason's Island, VA	Norfolk, VA
Holliday, John	Pvt.	Co. I	-	21	6/28/1863	Mason's Island, VA	-
Holly, Robert	Pvt.	Co. B	Farmer	23	7/2/1863	Mason's Island, VA	Barhold Court House, SC
Holmes, Richard	Pvt.	Co. I	Laborer	18	6/28/1863	Mason's Island, VA	Alexandria, VA
Holmes, William	Pvt.	Co. B	Rope Maker	30	9/21/1864	Baltimore, MD	Baltimore, MD
Hopkins, Robert	Pvt.	Co. A	Cook	19	5/19/1863	Washington, DC	Washington, DC
Hopper, Moses	Pvt.	Co. B	Waiter	25	5/19/1863	Washington, DC	Norfolk, VA

Name	Rank	Company	Age	Occupation	Date	Enlistment	Birthplace
Horton, Daniel	Pvt.	Co. A	22	Farmer	5/19/1863	Washington, DC	Portsmouth, VA
Houston, William W.							
Howard, Alexander	Pvt.	Co. A	23	Farmer	5/19/1863	Washington, DC	Prince George's County, MD
Howard, Jackson	Cpl.	Co. I	30	Laborer	6/28/1863	Mason's Island, VA	Alexandria, VA
Hughes, Allen	Pvt.	Co. C	23	Farmer	6/8/1863	Washington, DC	Culpepper County, VA
Hughes, Charles	Pvt.	Co. E	17	Errand Boy	6/17/1863	Mason's Island, VA	Washington, DC
Hughes, John	Pvt.	Co. K	34	Laborer	9/26/1864	Wilmington, DE	Kent County, DE
Hughes, Samuel	Sgt.	Co. G	20	Servant	6/25/1863	Mason's Island, VA	Washington, DC
Humphrey, George	Pvt.	Co. C	29	Laborer	7/4/1863	Mason's Island, VA	Alexandria, VA
Hungerford, George	Cpl.	Co. B	39	Baker	5/19/1863	Washington, DC	King George County, VA
Hurley, Robert	Pvt.	Co. B	19	Farmer	7/1/1863	Mason's Island, VA	Leesburg, VA
Hutchins, Albert	Pvt.	Co. F	46	Farmer	6/21/1863	Mason's Island, VA	Mathis County, VA
Hymer, Samuel	Pvt.	Co. K	21	Laborer	6/30/1863	Mason's Island, VA	Martin County, NC
Ingraham, John	Pvt.	Co. G	49	Laborer	6/25/1863	Mason's Island, VA	Putnam County, GA
Inman, Luke	Pvt.	Co. C	20	Farmer	3/18/1865	Wilmington, NC	Georgia
Jackson, Allan	Pvt.	Co. I	21	Farmer	6/28/1863	Mason's Island, VA	Spotsylvania County, VA
Jackson, Charles	Pvt.	Co. E	20	Waiter	6/17/1863	Mason's Island, VA	Washington, DC
Jackson, Claiborne	Pvt.	Co. K	20	Laborer	6/30/1863	Mason's Island, VA	Loudon County, VA
Jackson, Daniel T.	Cpl.	Co. I	21	Cook	7/12/1863	Washington, DC	Baltimore County, MD
Jackson, Edward	Pvt.	Co. H	15	Waiter	6/27/1863	Mason's Island, VA	Washington, DC
Jackson, George	Pvt.	Co. E	18	Farmer	6/17/1863	Mason's Island, VA	Front Royal, VA
Jackson, George	Pvt.	Co. H	30	Farmer	6/27/1863	Mason's Island, VA	Loudon County, VA
Jackson, George	Pvt.	Co. I	21	-	6/28/1863	Mason's Island, VA	-
Jackson, Hamilton	Pvt.	Co. E	17	Laborer	7/3/1863	Mason's Island, VA	Harrisburg, PA
Jackson, Henry	Sgt.	Co. D	21	Blacksmith	6/14/1863	Mason's Island, VA	Howard County, MD
Jackson, Henry	Pvt.	Co. G	21	Laborer	9/27/1864	Wilmington, DE	Washington, VA
Jackson, Henry	Cpl.	Co. H	22	Laborer	6/27/1863	Mason's Island, VA	Alexandria, VA
Jackson, Henry A.	Pvt.	Co. H	22	Hostler	6/27/1863	Mason's Island, VA	Alexander, VA
Jackson, Israel	Pvt.	Co. F	19	Waiter	6/21/1863	Mason's Island, VA	Montgomery County, MD
Jackson, John	Cpl.	Co. B	22	Hostler	5/19/1863	Washington, DC	Prince George's County, MD
Jackson, John	Pvt.	Co. B	24	Farmer	6/30/1863	Mason's Island, VA	Marlboro County, MD
Jackson, Joseph	Pvt.	Co. I	20	Laborer	6/28/1863	Mason's Island, VA	Lancaster, VA
Jackson, Lewis	Pvt.	Co. E	16	Waiter	5/17/1863	Mason's Island, VA	Winchester, VA
Jackson, Robert	Sgt.	Co. A	20	Barber	5/19/1863	Washington, DC	Troy, NY
Jackson, Samuel	Pvt.	Co. H	30	Farmer	6/27/1863	Mason's Island, VA	Woodlong, MD
Jackson, Spencer	Pvt.	Co. D	18	-	6/14/1863	Mason's Island, VA	-
Jackson, Wesley	Pvt.	Co. A	29	Farmer	5/19/1863	Washington, DC	Smithville, MD
Jackson, William	Pvt.	Co. A	19	Farmer	5/19/1863	Washington, DC	Anne Arundel County, MD
Jackson, William H.	Cpl.	Co. A	26	Fireman	7/13/1863	Mason's Island, VA	Washington, DC

Name	Rank	Co.	Age	Occupation	Date	Place	Location
Jackson, Willis	Pvt.	Co. G	20	Farmer	6/25/1863	Mason's Island, VA	Culpepper Court House, VA
Jacobs, Henry	Pvt.	Co. D	30	Fisherman	7/9/1863	Mason's Island, VA	Cape Charles, VA
James, William	Pvt.	Co. A	39	Blacksmith	5/19/1863	Washington, DC	Washington, DC
Janey, Benjamin	Pvt.	Co. K	18	Laborer	6/30/1863	Mason's Island, VA	Bladensburg, MD
Jefferson, Allen	Pvt.	Co. F	19	Farmer	6/21/1863	Mason's Island, VA	Southhampton County, VA
Jenkins, Meredith	Pvt.	Co. C	18	Farmer	6/8/1863	Washington, DC	Montgomery County, MD
Jenkins, Nichols	Pvt.	Co. B	-	-	5/19/1863	Washington, DC	-
Jennifer, John G.	Pvt.	Co. F	30	Hostler	6/21/1863	Mason's Island, VA	Prince George's County, MD
Johnson, Alexander	Musician	Co. C	23	Sailor	6/8/1863	Washington, DC	Queentown, MD
Johnson, Charles	Pvt.	Co. D	18	Laborer	6/14/1863	Mason's Island, VA	Suffolk, VA
Johnson, Charles	Pvt.	Co. E	22	Farmer	6/17/1863	Mason's Island, VA	Culpepper County, VA
Johnson, Charles	Pvt.	Co. H	20	Farmer	7/6/1863	Mason's Island, VA	Frederick City, MD
Johnson, Charles	Pvt.	Co. K	21	Laborer	6/30/1863	Mason's Island, VA	Essex County, VA
Johnson, David	Pvt.	Co. F	24	-	6/21/1863	Mason's Island, VA	Shettsburg, Bedford Co., PA
Johnson, Dennis	Pvt.	Co. E	19	Farmer	6/17/1863	Mason's Island, VA	Prince George's County, MD
Johnson, Eli	Sgt.	Co. A	23	Gardener	5/19/1863	Washington, DC	Washington, DC
Johnson, Emanuel	Sgt.	Co. A	19	Farmer	5/19/1863	Washington, DC	Page County, VA
Johnson, Frederick	Pvt.	Co. K	24	Laborer	6/30/1863	Mason's Island, VA	King George County, VA
Johnson, George	Pvt.	Co. A	19	Laborer	5/19/1863	Washington, DC	Baltimore, MD
Johnson, George	Pvt.	Co. D	18	Laborer	6/14/1863	Mason's Island, VA	Charles County, MD
Johnson, George	Pvt.	Co. E	23	Laborer	7/3/1863	Mason's Island, VA	Culpepper County, VA
Johnson, George	Cpl.	Co. H	16	-	6/27/1863	Mason's Island, VA	-
Johnson, George F.	Pvt.	Co. C	29	Laborer	6/8/1863	Washington, DC	Prince George's County, MD
Johnson, George F.	Pvt.	Co. C	-	-	-	-	-
Johnson, George O.	Pvt.	Co. D	16	Laborer	6/14/1863	Mason's Island, VA	Fauquier County, VA
Johnson, George W.	Pvt.	Co. D	18	Butcher	6/14/1863	Mason's Island, VA	Washington, DC
Johnson, Henry	Pvt.	Co. G	20	Saloon Waiter	6/25/1863	Mason's Island, VA	Warrenton Station, VA
Johnson, Issac	Pvt.	Co. C	28	Farmer	2/28/1865	Syracuse, NY	Westchester, PA
Johnson, John	Pvt.	Co. F	17	-	6/24/1863	Mason's Island, VA	Harford County, MD
Johnson, John H.	Pvt.	Co. G	18	House Servant	6/25/1863	Mason's Island, VA	Baltimore, MD
Johnson, Joseph H.	Pvt.	Co. C	21	Laborer	6/8/1863	Washington, DC	Washington, DC
Johnson, Joshua	Sgt.	Co. C	18	Farmer	6/8/1863	Washington, DC	Tioga County, NY
Johnson, Marcus	Pvt.	Co. C	22	Waiter	6/8/1863	Washington, DC	Wilmington, NC
Johnson, Reuben	Pvt.	Co. F	25	Farmer	9/22/1864	Wilmington, DE	Wilmington, DE
Johnson, Robert	Pvt.	Co. C	18	Waiter	9/30/1864	Ellicotts Mills, MD	Baltimore, MD
Johnson, Robert H.	Pvt.	Co. C	18	Laborer	6/8/1863	Washington, DC	Petersburg, VA
Johnson, Robert S.	Pvt.	Co. K	25	Waiter	6/30/1863	Mason's Island, VA	Washington, DC
Johnson, Samuel	Pvt.	Co. D	18	Laborer	6/14/1863	Mason's Island, VA	Seneca, MD
Johnson, Samuel	Pvt.	Co. H	25	Hostler	6/27/1863	Mason's Island, VA	Goose Hill, MD

Name	Rank	Company	Age	Occupation	Date	Location	Birthplace
Johnson, Samuel H.	Sgt.	Co. K	30	Barber	6/30/1863	Mason's Island, VA	Kingston, Jamaica
Johnson, Walter	Cpl.	Co. B	30	Laborer	5/19/1863	Washington, DC	Charles County, MD
Johnson, William	Pvt.	Co. E	19	Laborer	6/17/1863	Mason's Island, VA	Louisa County, VA
Johnson, William B.	Pvt.	Co. D	18	Farmer	6/14/1863	Mason's Island, VA	Baltimore, MD
Johnson, William Mundy	Pvt.	Co. K	22	Laborer	6/30/1863	Mason's Island, VA	Lancaster, PA
Johnston, Alexander	Pvt.	Co. A	27	Farmer	5/19/1863	Washington, DC	Charles County, MD
Johnston, Andrew	Pvt.	Co. A	19	Laborer	5/19/1863	Washington, DC	Georgetown, DC
Johnston, Joseph	Pvt.	Co. A	19	Waiter	5/19/1863	Washington, DC	Frederick City, MD
Johnston, Moses	Pvt.	Co. A	18	Farmer	5/19/1863	Washington, DC	Spotsylvania, VA
Johnston, William H.	Cpl.	Co. A	23	Farmer	5/19/1863	Washington, DC	Anne Arundel County, MD
Jolly, David	Pvt.	Co. A	23	Farmer	7/12/1863	Mason's Island, VA	Princess Anne County, VA
Jones, Allen	Pvt.	Co. G	25	Farmer	7/10/1863	Mason's Island, VA	Alexandria, VA
Jones, Benjamin	Pvt.	Co. B	26	Hostler	5/19/1863	Washington, DC	Fairfax County, VA
Jones, Edward	Pvt.	Co. E	38	Farmer	6/17/1863	Mason's Island, VA	Hanover Court House, VA
Jones, Edward	Cpl.	Co. I	23	Laborer	6/27/1863	Mason's Island, VA	Caroline County, VA
Jones, Henry	Pvt.	Co. D	25	Laborer	4/9/1865	Faison, NC	Marion, SC
Jones, James	Pvt.	Co. E	26	Laborer	1/19/1864	Portsmouth, VA	Suffolk, VA
Jones, Jerry	Pvt.	Co. H	24	Hackman	6/27/1863	Mason's Island, VA	Eastville, VA
Jones, Jerry	Pvt.	Co. I	21	Farmer	3/21/1864	New Berne, NC	Essex County, VA
Jones, John	Pvt.	Co. H	18	Farmer	7/6/1863	Mason's Island, VA	Maryland
Jones, Josiah	Pvt.		22	Farmer	3/11/1865	Tompkinsville, NY	Virginia
Jones, Richard	Pvt.	Co. E	-	-	6/14/1863	Mason's Island, VA	Frederick City, MD
Jones, Richard	Sgt.	Co. E	25	Butcher	6/17/1863	Mason's Island, VA	Albany, NY
Jones, Solomon	Pvt.	Co. -	18	Laborer	11/22/1864	Buffalo, NY	Montgomery County, MD
Jones, William	Pvt.	Co. G	23	House Servant	7/10/1863	Mason's Island, VA	Baltimore, MD
Jones, William	Sgt.	Co. H	21	Sailor	6/27/1863	Mason's Island, VA	Upperville, VA
Jordan, George	Pvt.	Co. D	20	Teamster	7/1/1863	Mason's Island, VA	Fauquier County, VA
Jordan, Henry	Pvt.	Co. B	20	Farmer	5/19/1863	Washington, DC	Charles County, MD
Jordan, James	Cpl.	Co. D	25	Laborer	6/14/1863	Mason's Island, VA	Howard County, MD
Joyce, John	Pvt.	Co. H	23	Farmer	6/27/1863	Mason's Island, VA	Fairfax County, VA
Kane, George Henry	Pvt.	Co. E	17	Waiter	6/17/1863	Mason's Island, VA	Hartford County, MD
Kane, William	Pvt.	Co. F	29	Sailor	6/21/1863	Mason's Island, VA	Norfolk, VA
Keeland, Edward	Pvt.	Co. B	18	Farmer	7/2/1863	Mason's Island, VA	Norfolk, VA
Keeland, Samuel	Cpl.	Co. I	18	Teamster	7/12/1863	Washington, DC	Bladen County, NC
Kelly, Michael	-	Co. E	44	Farmer	3/15/1865	Wilmington, NC	New Berne, NC
Kennedy, Charles	Pvt.	Co. H	27	Cook	9/2/1863	New Berne, NC	Oberlin, OH
Kennedy, John	Pvt.	Co. G	21	Carpenter	6/25/1863	Mason's Island, VA	Mifflin County, PA
Kennedy, William	Cpl.	Co. B	36	Laborer	5/19/1863	Washington, DC	Colburne County, MD
Kent, Washington	Pvt.	Co. H	44	Farmer	6/27/1863	Mason's Island, VA	Colburne County, MD

Name	Rank	Company	Age	Occupation	Date	Place	Residence
Kimbo, David	Pvt.	Co. D	18	Laborer	6/14/1863	Mason's Island, VA	Charles County, MD
King, Andrew	Sgt.	Co. B	21	Butcher	5/19/1863	Washington, DC	Washington, DC
King, George	Pvt.	Co. B	20	Messenger	5/19/1863	Washington, DC	Washington, DC
King, James K.	Sgt.	Co. B	18	Waiter	5/19/1863	Washington, DC	Washington, DC
King, Matthew	Pvt.	Co. B	31	Farmer	7/8/1863	Mason's Island, VA	Fauquier County, VA
King, Washington	Cpl.	Co. F		Laborer	6/21/1863	Mason's Island, VA	Unity Village, Montgomery Co., MD
King, Willis	Pvt.	Co. A	28	Laborer	7/12/1863	Washington, DC	Loudon County, VA
Kinney, George	Cpl.	Co. B	24	-	5/19/1863	Washington, DC	
Kirkendall, Richard	Pvt.	Co. H	43	Farmer	6/27/1863	Mason's Island, VA	Franklin County, TN
Krumpton, Kendall	Pvt.	Co. B	37	Farmer	3/20/1865	Wilmington, NC	Fairfield, SC
Lambkin, Nelson	Pvt.	Co. D	23	Farmer	6/14/1863	Mason's Island, VA	Northumberland County, VA
Lane, Daniel	Pvt.	Co. E	19	Laborer	9/27/1864	Baltimore, MD	Frederick, MD
Lane, Joseph	Pvt.	Co. I	24	Farmer	5/31/1864	Ft. Powhatan, VA	Surry County, VA
Langley, Samuel	Pvt.	Co. E	40	Farmer	6/21/1863	Mason's Island, VA	Perquimans County, NC
Lankford, Thomas	Pvt.	Co. K	21	Laborer	9/30/1864	Baltimore, MD	Jefferson County, VA
Lanzdel, William	-		29	Laborer	9/24/1864	Baltimore, MD	Virginia
Lawrence, Drew	Pvt.	Co. G	39	Laborer	6/25/1863	Mason's Island, VA	Blackrock, Bertie County, NC
Laws, William	Cpl.	Co. K	24	Hackman	6/27/1863	Mason's Island, VA	Middlesex, VA
Lawson, Edward	Pvt.	Co. H	19	Farmer	7/27/1863	Mason's Island, VA	Charles County, MD
Lear, John Issac	Pvt.	Co. K	25	Laborer	6/29/1863	Mason's Island, VA	Prince William, VA
Lee, Francis	Pvt.	Co. I	20	Laborer	6/28/1863	Mason's Island, VA	Baltimore, MD
Lee, Harry	Cpl.	Co. B	23	Teamster	7/3/1863	Mason's Island, VA	Lancaster County, PA
Lee, John	Pvt.	Co. A	-	-	7/12/1863	Mason's Island, VA	
Lee, Nelson	Sgt.	Co. C	40	Carpenter	6/8/1863	Washington, DC	Northumberland County, VA
Lee, Peter	Pvt.	Co. F	18	-	6/21/1863	Mason's Island, VA	Northumberland County, VA
Lee, Welcome	Pvt.	Co. G	22	Farmer	6/25/1863	Mason's Island, VA	Luconians County, NC
Lee, William	Cpl.	Co. B	29	Laborer	5/19/1863	Washington, DC	Westmoreland County, VA
Lee, William P.	Pvt.	Co. I	24	Teamster	6/28/1863	Mason's Island, VA	Howard County, MD
Levers, David A.	Pvt.	Co. A	28	Farmer	5/19/1863	Washington, DC	Charles County, MD
Lewis, Charles	Pvt.	Co. K	20	Waiter	6/30/1863	Mason's Island, VA	Portland, ME
Lewis, Henry	Cpl.	Co. K	26	Teamster	7/1/1863	Alexandria, VA	Kentucky
Lewis, James	Pvt.	Co. I	20	Laborer	6/28/1863	Mason's Island, VA	Fredericksburg, VA
Lewis, John	Pvt.	Co. C	19	Laborer	7/4/1863	Mason's Island, VA	Baltimore, MD
Lewis, John	Pvt.	Co. K	23	Laborer	6/30/1863	Mason's Island, VA	Portsmouth, VA
Lewis, Robert	Pvt.	Co. F	21	Farmer	5/19/1864	Wilson's Landing	Charles City County, VA
Liber, Henry	Pvt.	Co. D	18	Farmer	6/14/1863	Mason's Island, VA	Lancaster County, VA
Liggins, John	Pvt.	Co. C	47	Barber	6/8/1863	Washington, DC	Monroe County, VA
Liles, John E.	Pvt.	Co. K	20	Laborer	6/20/1863	Mason's Island, VA	Charles County, MD
Lincoln, Jacob	Pvt.	Co. D	31	Farmer	3/5/1865	Wilmington, NC	New Hanover County, NC

Name	Rank	Co.	Occupation	Age	Date	Enlisted	Origin
Lincoln, Lewis	Sgt.	Co. H	Shoemaker	24	6/27/1863	Mason's Island, VA	Charleston, SC
Lincoln, Richard	Pvt.	Co. H	Farmer	18	6/27/1863	Mason's Island, VA	Montgomery County, MD
Lloyd, John	Pvt.	Co. H	Farmer	23	6/27/1863	Mason's Island, VA	Prince William County, VA
Loatman, Edward	Pvt.	Co. A	Laborer	22	9/23/1864	Wilmington, DE	Baltimore County, MD
Locker, Alfred	Cpl.	Co. A	Laborer	22	6/30/1863	Wilmington, DE	Charles County, MD
Logan, Robert	Pvt.	Co. F	Laborer	20	6/21/1863	Alexandria, VA	Winchester City, VA
Lomacks, James	Pvt.	Co. I	Field Hand	36	6/28/1863	Mason's Island, VA	Middlesex County, VA
Lomacks, William	Pvt.	Co. E	-	-	6/17/1863	Mason's Island, VA	-
Lomax, John	Pvt.	Co. D	Brick Maker	32	6/14/1863	Mason's Island, VA	Washington, DC
Lomax, Ralph	Pvt.	Co. G	Laborer	24	6/25/1863	Mason's Island, VA	Culpepper Court House, VA
Loveson, Robert	Pvt.	Co. E	Farmer	18	3/15/1865	Wilmington, NC	Richmond County, NC
Lucas, Albert, Henry	Pvt.	Co. F	Servant	21	6/21/1863	Mason's Island, VA	Fredericksburg City, VA
Lucas, James	Cpl.	Co. H	Laborer	22	6/27/1863	Mason's Island, VA	Dumfshrect, VA
Lucas, Jesse	Pvt.	Co. I	Farmer	23	6/28/1863	Mason's Island, VA	Chester County, PA
Lucas, John	Pvt.	Co. E	Farmer	17	6/17/1863	Mason's Island, VA	Caroline County, VA
Lucas, Manuel	Pvt.	Co. B	Laborer	33	5/19/1863	Washington, DC	Jefferson County, VA
Lummas, Allen	Pvt.	Co. A	Butcher	15	5/19/1863	Washington, DC	Washington, DC
Mayby, Dempsy	Pvt.	Co. F	Farmer	19	7/10/1863	Mason's Island, VA	Elizabeth City, NC
Macey, Franklin	Pvt.	Co. F	Farmer	18	9/22/1864	Wilmington, DE	Wilmington, DE
Macle, Nicholas	Pvt.	Co. A	Waiter	21	5/19/1863	Washington, DC	Prince George's County, MD
Madison, James	Pvt.	Co. C	Farmer	19	6/8/1863	Washington, DC	Elizabeth City, NC
Magruder, John	Pvt.	Co. G	Farmer	22	6/25/1863	Mason's Island, VA	Hagerstown, MD
Magruder, Joseph	Cpl.	Co. I	Laborer	20	6/28/1863	Mason's Island, VA	Hampsline County, VA
Mahoney, Warner	Pvt.	Co. H	Laborer	43	7/6/1863	Mason's Island, VA	King George County, VA
Mallory, Charles	Pvt.	Co. G	Mason	20	6/25/1863	Mason's Island, VA	Norfolk, VA
Manley, Charles	Pvt.	Co. E	Farmer	19	6/17/1863	Mason's Island, VA	Aldea, VA
Manley, John	Pvt.	Co. B	Laborer	25	5/19/1863	Washington, DC	Loudon County, VA
Mann, John	Pvt.	Co. K	Laborer	30	6/20/1863	Mason's Island, VA	Pamaunkey County, VA
Mann, Thomas	Sgt.	Co. B	Barber	27	5/19/1863	Washington, DC	Luzerne County, PA
Marley, Alonzo	Pvt.	Co. E	Farmer	-	7/3/1863	Mason's Island, VA	Warrenton County, VA
Mark, Ezekiel	Pvt.	Co. A	Laborer	19	5/19/1863	Washington, DC	Murfreesboro, VA
Marks, Edward	Pvt.	Co. B	Laborer	27	5/19/1863	Washington, DC	Prince George's County, MD
Marks, Jerry	Pvt.	Co. K	Harness Maker	18	7/12/1863	Mason's Island, VA	Chatham, Canada, West
Marshall, Edward	Cpl.	Co. E	Farmer	22	6/17/1863	Mason's Island, VA	Port Tobacco, MD
Marshall, Edward	Pvt.	Co. I	-	23	6/28/1863	Mason's Island, VA	-
Marshall, Francis	Cpl.	Co. F	Teamster	27	6/21/1863	Mason's Island, VA	Henrietta County, VA
Marshall, George	Sgt.	Co. G	Farmer	22	7/7/1863	Mason's Island, VA	Prince George's County, MD
Martin, John	Pvt.	Co. I	Laborer	22	6/28/1863	Mason's Island, VA	Luray, VA
Martin, Reuben	Pvt.	Co. E	Farmer	25	6/17/1863	Mason's Island, VA	Frederick City, MD

Name	Rank	Company	Age	Occupation	Date	Enlisted	Residence
Mason, Daniel	Pvt.	Co. G	19	Farmer	6/25/1863	Mason's Island, VA	Loudon County, VA
Massey, William	Pvt.	Co. G	29	Butcher	6/25/1863	Mason's Island, VA	Baltimore, MD
Mather, Riddick	Pvt.	Co. G	25	Farmer	6/25/1863	Mason's Island, VA	Hurtfort County, NC
Matthews, William H.	Pvt.	Co. C	19	Farmer	6/8/1863	Washington, DC	Charles County, MD
McCarty, Allen	Pvt.	Co. F	19	Farmer	4/14/1865	Wilmington, NC	Robinson County, NC
McCarty, James	Pvt.	Co. F	18	Farmer	3/20/1865	Wilmington, NC	Robinson County, NC
McClanagan, Dick	-	Co. F	-	-	4/14/1865	-	-
McCoy, Dick	Pvt.	Co. G	23	Farmer	3/17/1865	Wilmington, NC	Bladen County, NC
McCoy, Duncan	Pvt.	Co. B	23	Farmer	3/17/1865	Wilmington, NC	Bladen County, NC
McCoy, Frank	Pvt.	Co. G	20	Farmer	3/17/1865	Wilmington, NC	Bladen County, NC
McCoy, James	Cpl.	Co. B	23	Laborer	5/19/1863	Washington, DC	Loudon County, VA
McCoy, Manuel	Pvt.	Co. B	25	Laborer	3/17/1865	Wilmington, NC	Bladen County, NC
McCoy, Samuel	Pvt.	Co. F	19	Farmer	3/17/1865	Wilmington, NC	Bladen County, NC
McCoy, Wallace	Pvt.	Co. F	20	Farmer	3/17/1865	Wilmington, NC	Bladen County, NC
McDowell, Andrew	Pvt.	Co. B	30	Farmer	3/17/1865	Wilmington, NC	Bladen County, NC
McDowell, Watson	Pvt.	Co. B	30	Farmer	3/17/1865	Wilmington, NC	Bladen County, NC
McFarland, Edward	Pvt.	Co. G	28	Farmer	3/3/1865	Wilmington, NC	Hanover County, NC
McKinney, Robert	Cpl.	Co. A	20	Cutler	5/19/1863	Washington, DC	Washington, DC
McNeil, Jeffrey	Pvt.	Co. F	23	Farmer	4/9/1865	Wilmington, NC	Harriet County, NC
Means, Nelson	Pvt.	Co. D	24	Laborer	7/9/1863	Mason's Island, VA	Alabama County, VA
Merrick, Ellis	Pvt.	Co. D	19	Carpenter	3/5/1865	Wilmington, NC	Wilmington, NC
Middleton, Allen	Pvt.	Co. G	19	Farmer	6/25/1863	Mason's Island, VA	Charles County, MD
Milburn, Alexander	Pvt.	Co. G	20	Farmer	6/17/1863	Mason's Island, VA	St. Mary's County, MD
Miles, George	Pvt.	Co. I	23	Brick Maker	6/25/1863	Mason's Island, VA	Culpepper, VA
Miles, Henry	Pvt.	Co. I	18	Waiter	6/28/1863	Mason's Island, VA	Washington, DC
Miles, Oliver	Pvt.	Co. F	37	Fisherman	6/21/1863	Mason's Island, VA	Alexandria City, VA
Miles, Sandy	Pvt.	Co. F	20	Chimney Sweep	6/21/1863	Mason's Island, VA	Washington, DC
Miller, George	-	-	19	Laborer	9/22/1864	Wilmington, DE	Delaware
Miller, George	Pvt.	Co. E	20	Sailor	6/17/1863	Mason's Island, VA	New Castle County, DE
Miller, Wesley	Sgt.	Co. B	21	Farmer	5/19/1863	Washington, DC	Annapolis, MD
Mills, Abraham	Cpl.	Co. K	19	Waiter	6/30/1863	Mason's Island, VA	Leesburg, VA
Mills, Joseph	Cpl.	Co. G	21	Farmer	6/25/1863	Mason's Island, VA	Fairfax, VA
Mina, John W.	Pvt.	Co. A	18	Laborer	9/27/1864	Wilmington, DE	Kent County, DE
Molesham, George	Pvt.	Co. D	21	Laborer	4/15/1865	Wilmington, NC	Charleston, SC
Monroe, George	Pvt.	Co. F	23	Farmer	3/17/1865	Wilmington, NC	Bladen County, NC
Monroe, Henry	Pvt.	Co. E	32	Farmer	3/15/1865	Wilmington, NC	Hanover County, NC
Moore, Henry S.	Pvt.	Co. B	23	Laborer	3/11/1865	Tompkinsville, NY	Jamaica, NY
Moore, James H.	Pvt.	Co. B	21	Waiter	5/19/1863	Washington, DC	Frederick, MD
Moore, Mark	Pvt.	Co. A	23	Farmer	5/19/1863	Washington, DC	Charles County, MD
Moore, Wallace	Pvt.						

Name	Rank	Company	Age	Occupation	Date	Enlistment	Birthplace
Morden, Lewis	Pvt.	Co. C	20	Farmer	6/8/1863	Washington, DC	Green County, VA
Morgan, John	Pvt.	Co. A	25	Laborer	9/24/1864	Wilmington, DE	Kent County, DE
Morgan, Joseph	Pvt.	Co. A	28	Farmer	7/12/1863	Mason's Island, VA	Caroline County, VA
Morgan, Richmond	Pvt.	Co. D	25	Farmer	3/5/1865	Wilmington, NC	Jones County, NC
Morgan, William	Pvt.	Co. E	23	Seaman	2/6/1865	Hudson City, NY	New York City, NY
Morrison, James	Pvt.	Co. D	38	Carpenter	6/14/1863	Mason's Island, VA	Fauquier County, VA
Mosely, Cornelius	Pvt.	Co. H	26	Waiter	6/27/1863	Mason's Island, VA	Dallas County, AL
Mullen, George	Sgt.	Co. I	21	Hackman	6/28/1863	Mason's Island, VA	Washington, DC
Munford, Samuel H.	Cpl.	Co. F	20	Butcher	6/21/1863	Mason's Island, VA	Georgetown, DC
Murden, Wilson	Cpl.	Co. G	19	Farmer	6/25/1863	Mason's Island, VA	Norfolk, VA
Murphy, Elijah	-	Co. E	21	Farmer	3/15/1865	Wilmington, NC	Hanover County, NC
Murray, Beverly	Pvt.	Co. I	22	Farmer	7/12/1863	Washington, DC	Fauquier County, VA
Murray, William	Cpl.	Co. H	24	Laborer	6/27/1863	Mason's Island, VA	Prince George's County, MD
Murry, Ezekial	Pvt.	Co. A	19	Laborer	5/19/1863	Washington, DC	Southampton, VA
Nash, John	Pvt.	Co. K	20	Farmer	4/15/1865	Wilmington, NC	Pittsboro, NC
Neal, Thomas	Pvt.	Co. C	24	Laborer	7/4/1863	Mason's Island, VA	Rappahannock County, VA
Nelson, Edward	Pvt.	Co. G	15	Chore Boy	6/25/1863	Mason's Island, VA	Richmond, VA
Newman, Jerome	Pvt.	Co. K	22	Laborer	6/30/1863	Mason's Island, VA	Winchester, VA
Newman, John	Pvt.	Co. H	20	Laborer	9/20/1864	Baltimore, MD	Virginia
Newton, Nelson	Cpl.	Co. C	29	Laborer	7/4/1863	Mason's Island, VA	Richmond County, VA
Nichols, Harmin	Pvt.	Co. H	26	Laborer	9/15/1864	Wilmington, DE	Delaware
Nickens, James	Sgt.	Co. F	18	Oysterman	6/21/1863	Mason's Island, VA	Lancaster County, VA
Nickens, Lewis	Pvt.	Co. H	18	Waiter	7/8/1863	Mason's Island, VA	Alexandria, VA
Nickens, Thornton	Sgt.	Co. E	21	Farmer	6/17/1863	Mason's Island, VA	Loudon County, VA
Niel, John	Pvt.	Co. B	21	Waiter	5/19/1863	Washington, DC	Georgetown, DC
Nixon, Emanuel	Pvt.	Co. A	19	Farmer	12/16/1863	Portsmouth, VA	Elizabeth County, NC
Nixon, Thomas	Sgt.	Co. F	27	Carpenter	6/21/1863	Mason's Island, VA	Perquimans County, NC
Noble, Samuel H.	Pvt.	Co. K	20	Waiter	6/30/1863	Mason's Island, VA	Washington, DC
Norton, Nathaniel	Pvt.	Co. A	20	Laborer	9/30/1864	Mason's Island, VA	Baltimore City, MD
Nubia, William	Pvt.	Co. F	19	Teamster	7/10/1863	Baltimore, MD	Near Gatesville, VA
Nutt, George	Pvt.	Co. D	30	Fisherman	7/9/1863	Mason's Island, VA	Lancaster County, VA
Oden, Clayborn	Cpl.	Co. G	24	Farmer	6/25/1863	Mason's Island, VA	Kinston, NC
Odum, George	Pvt.	Co. H	24	Laborer	6/27/1863	Mason's Island, VA	Virginia-North Carolina
Offer, John H.	Pvt.	Co. I	19	Cook	6/28/1863	Mason's Island, VA	Annapolis, MD
Overall, Amos	Pvt.	Co. K	20	Farmer	6/30/1863	Mason's Island, VA	Loudon County, VA
Paine, Issac A.	Pvt.	Co. I	18	Laborer	6/30/1863	Mason's Island, VA	Alexandria, VA
Pannell, Frank	Pvt.	Co. K	24	Waiter	6/27/1863	Mason's Island, VA	Madison County, VA
Parker, John	Pvt.	Co. H	23	Sailor	6/28/1863	Mason's Island, VA	Alexandria, VA
Parker, John	Pvt.	Co. I	28	Teamster	6/28/1863	Mason's Island, VA	Caroline County, VA

Name	Rank	Co.	Age	Occupation	Date	Place	Residence
Parker, Joseph	Sgt.	Co. D	25	Waiter	6/14/1863	Mason's Island, VA	Howard County, MD
Parker, Richard	Cpl.	Co. C	19	Waiter	6/8/1863	Washington, DC	Newport News, VA
Parker, Solomon	Pvt.	Co. D	17	Laborer	6/14/1863	Mason's Island, VA	Prince George's County, MD
Patterson, Josiah	Pvt.	Co. H	18	Sailor	9/16/1864	Baltimore, MD	Virginia
Patterson, Sandy	Pvt.	Co. K	25	Carpenter	4/15/1865	Wilmington, NC	Richmond County, NC
Patton, Abraham	Pvt.	Co. A	18	Laborer	9/21/1864	Wilmington, DE	Kent County, DE
Pauls, Thomas	Sgt.	Co. I	21	Gardener	6/28/1863	Mason's Island, VA	Ellicotts Mills, MD
Peak, James	Sgt.	Co. E	23	Cook	6/17/1863	Mason's Island, VA	St. Catherine's Canada, West
Peck, Cornelius	Sgt.	Co. F	30	Wagoning	6/21/1863	Mason's Island, VA	Washington, DC
Peck, William H.	Sgt.	Co. D	19	Laborer	6/14/1863	Mason's Island, VA	Prince George's County, MD
Pelton, Abraham	Pvt.	Co. F	25	Farmer	6/21/1863	Mason's Island, VA	Pasquotank County, NC
Pendleton, Olmstead	Pvt.	Co. E	20	Farmer	7/3/1863	Mason's Island, VA	Middlesex County, VA
Penny, Cornelius	Pvt.	Co. K	19	Waiter	6/30/1863	Mason's Island, VA	Washington, DC
Perkins, Jacob	Pvt.	Co. K	20	Teamster	4/15/1865	Wilmington, NC	Camden, SC
Perry, Bryant	Pvt.	Co. G	27	Farmer	6/25/1863	Mason's Island, VA	Hurtfort County, NC
Peters, James	Pvt.	Co. E	21	Farmer	6/17/1863	Mason's Island, VA	Loudon County, VA
Peters, William	-	Co. B	24	Laborer	7/2/1863	Mason's Island, VA	Campbell County, VA
Peterson, Richard	Sgt.	Co. C	22	Farmer	6/8/1863	Washington, DC	Alexandria, VA
Pettyjohn, N.J.	-	-	-			-	-
Phillips, Charles	Pvt.	Co. A	27	Laborer	5/19/1863	Washington, DC	Culpepper County, VA
Pierson, Crusoe	Pvt.	Co. F	28	Farmer	6/21/1863	Mason's Island, VA	South Hamilton County, VA
Pierson, James	Pvt.	Co. E	24	Farmer	6/17/1863	Mason's Island, VA	Western Virginia
Pinkins, Randolph	Pvt.	Co. H	34	Farmer	6/27/1863	Mason's Island, VA	Fairfax, VA
Pippins, John	Pvt.	Co. F	22	Farmer	6/21/1863	Mason's Island, VA	Dinwidde County, VA
Pollard, George J.	Sgt.	Co. G	32	Cotton Inspector	6/15/1863	Mason's Island, VA	Mobile, AL
Pool, Adam	Pvt.	Co. H	21	Laborer	9/20/1864	Baltimore, MD	South Carolina
Posey, James	Pvt.	Co. E	20	Farmer	3/15/1865	Wilmington, NC	Charleston, SC
Posey, Samuel	Pvt.	Co. A	28	Plasterer	5/19/1863	Washington, DC	Washington, DC
Potter, James A.	Pvt.	Co. K	-	Laborer	9/3/1864	Lodus, NY	Hillsdale, NY
Pragon, Peter	Pvt.	Co. A	19	Farmer	3/7/1865	Wilmington, NC	Hanover County, NC
Pratt, Alfred	Pvt.	Co. H	18	Farmer	9/22/1864	Baltimore, MD	Maryland
Presco, George	Pvt.	Co. D	21	Farmer	6/25/1863	Mason's Island, VA	Ellicotts Mills, MD
Price, Robert	Cpl.	Co. E	18	Clerk	6/17/1863	Mason's Island, VA	New York City, NY
Price, Robert	Pvt.	Co. I	19	Field Hand	7/12/1863	Washington, DC	Prince George's County, MD
Purdy, Thomas	Pvt.	Co. B	23	Farmer	3/17/1865	Wilmington, NC	Bladen County, NC
Quaintance, John H.	Pvt.	Co. D	25	Waiter	7/9/1863	Mason's Island, VA	St. Mary's County, MD
Quaintance, Thomas	Pvt.	Co. D	25	Farmer	7/9/1863	Mason's Island, VA	St. Mary's County, MD
Quander, John P.	Cpl.	Co. G	18	Laborer	7/7/1863	Mason's Island, VA	Fairfax County, VA
Queen, George	Pvt.	Co. E	21	Farmer	6/17/1863	Mason's Island, VA	Charles County, MD

Name	Rank	Company	Age	Occupation	Date	Place	Origin
Rainy, Henry	Pvt.	Co. B	17	Laborer	5/19/1863	Washington, DC	Norfolk, VA
Randall, Jeskin	Pvt.	Co. K	22	Laborer	6/30/1863	Mason's Island, VA	Powhatan, VA
Randolph, John	Pvt.	Co. C	20	Cook	6/8/1863	Washington, DC	Montgomery County, MD
Ravenscraw, Bishop	Pvt.	Co. I	26	Farmer	3/17/1865	Wilmington, NC	Orange County, NC
Ray, Nathan	Pvt.	Co. C	19	Laborer	7/4/1863	Mason's Island, VA	Montgomery County, MD
Ray, Theodore C.	Sgt.	Co. D	21	Sailor	6/14/1863	Mason's Island, VA	Newburg, NY
Ray, Washington	Pvt.	Co. E	20	Farmer	6/17/1863	Mason's Island, VA	Salem, VA
Reader, Jesse H.	Pvt.	Co. E	25	Farmer	6/17/1863	Mason's Island, VA	Charles County, MD
Reader, Granby	Cpl.	Co. F	35	Farmer	6/21/1863	Mason's Island, VA	Pasquotank County, NC
Ready, Samuel	Cpl.	Co. F	23	Waiter	6/21/1863	Mason's Island, VA	Norfolk City, VA
Rector, John T.	Pvt.	Co. H	18	Laborer	9/13/1864	Ellicotts Mills, NC	North Carolina
Reddick, Granby	Cpl.	Co. F	-	-	6-21-1863	Mason's Island, VA	-
Reddick, Ephriam	Cpl.	Co. C	-	Farmer	6/21/1863	Mason's Island, VA	McComas County, NC
Reddick, John	Cpl.	Co. I	21	Farmer	6/8/1863	Washington, DC	Sandy Ridge, NC
Reddick, Moses	Sgt.	Co. F	23	Waiter	6/28/1863	Mason's Island, VA	Norfolk, VA
Reddick, Samuel	Cpl.	Co. F	-	-	6-21-1863	Mason's Island, VA	-
Reid, George	Pvt.	Co. D	24	Laborer	6/28/1863	Mason's Island, VA	Washington, DC
Reed, James H.	Pvt.	Co. A	23	Laborer	5/19/1863	Washington, DC	Grafton County, VA
Reed, James	Pvt.	Co. H	18	Laborer	9/14/1864	Wilmington, DE	Maryland
Reed, Jerdin	Cpl.	Co. K	28	Farmer	3/31/1865	Warsaw, NC	Corinth, MS
Reed, William	Pvt.	Co. C	22	Waiter	6/8/1863	Washington, DC	Harrisburg, PA
Reeves, Cornelius	Pvt.	Co. D	-	Farmer	4/9/1865	Faison's Depot	Marion, SC
Reeves, George I.	Cpl.	Co. D	21	Waiter	6/14/1863	Mason's Island, VA	Charles County, MD
Regan, Robert	Cpl.	Co. K	32	Laborer	6/30/1863	Mason's Island, VA	Rockingham County, VA
Rhodes, George	Pvt.	Co. A	19	Shoemaker	9/15/1863	Portsmouth, VA	Loudon County, VA
Richardson, Charles	-	-	-	-	-	-	-
Richardson, George	Sgt.	Co. C	20	Hostler	6/8/1863	Washington, DC	Richmond, VA
Richmond, Allen	Pvt.	Co. B	18	Farmer	6/20/1864	Bermuda Hundred, VA	Prince George County, VA
Rider, Elsey	Pvt.	Co. D	20	Waiter	6/14/1863	Mason's Island, VA	Eastern Shore, MD
Rives, John	Pvt.	Co. B	39	Blacksmith	5/19/1863	Washington, DC	Kenoy County, VA
Robbins, Ammi	Pvt.	Co. H	43	Laborer	3/16/1865	Syracuse, NY	Shenango, NY
Robbins, John	Pvt.	Co. G	19	Farmer	6/25/1863	Mason's Island, VA	Warrenton, VA
Roberts, Elijah	Pvt.	Co. F	21	Farmer	6/21/1863	Mason's Island, VA	Nelson County, VA
Roberts, James	Pvt.	Co. D	24	Laborer	5/31/1864	Fort Powhatan, VA	Prince George County, VA
Roberts, James A.	Pvt.	Co. H	39	Laborer	9/20/1864	Baltimore, MD	Virginia
Robinson, Charles H.	Cpl.	Co. B	20	Laborer	5/19/1863	Washington, DC	Brookeville, MD
Robinson, Daniel	Pvt.	Co. A	26	Farmer	7/12/1863	Mason's Island, VA	Alexandria, VA
Robinson, David	Pvt.	Co. E	16	Waiter	6/17/1863	Mason's Island, VA	Washington, DC
Robinson, Henry	Pvt.	Co. K	20	Blacksmith	6/30/1863	Mason's Island, VA	Fairfax County, VA

Name	Rank	Co.	Age	Occupation	Date	Enlisted	Residence
Robinson, Jerry	Sgt.	Co. B	21	Waiter	5/19/1863	Washington, DC	Fort Monroe, VA
Robinson, Phillip	Pvt.	Co. E	27	Farmer	6/17/1863	Mason's Island, VA	Winchester, VA
Robinson, Soloman	Pvt.	Co. K	29	Sailor	6/30/1863	Mason's Island, VA	Alexandria, VA
Robinson, William	Pvt.	Co. E	20	Farmer	6/17/1863	Mason's Island, VA	Frederick County, VA
Robinson, William	Pvt.	Co. H	28	Car Hand	6/27/1863	Mason's Island, VA	King Queen, VA
Rodgers, Charles	Pvt.	Co. B	21	Waiter	5/19/1863	Washington, DC	Baltimore, MD
Roman, William, Henry	Cpl.	Co. D	20	Waiter	5/19/1863	Mason's Island, VA	Washington, DC
Ross, John	Sgt.	Co. A	36	Plasterer	6/14/1863	Washington, DC	Green County, OH
Rounds, Robert	Pvt.	Co. C	22	Waiter	5/19/1863	Washington, DC	Alexandria, VA
Russell, James	Pvt.	Co. H	25	Farmer	6/8/1863	Washington, DC	Virginia
Russell, William L.	Sgt.	Co. K	19	Waiter	9/16/1864	Baltimore, MD	Hagerstown, MD
Salter, John	Pvt.	Co. I	21	Farmer	6/30/1864	Mason's Island, VA	Bladen County, NC
Sammons, James	Pvt.	Co. C	31	Laborer	3/18/1865	Wilmington, NC	Sussex County, DE
Sampson, John	Cpl.	Co. H	25	Farmer	9/23/1864	Wilmington, DE	Craven County, NC
Sanders, Henry	Pvt.	Co. F	-	Farmer	6/27/1863	Mason's Island, VA	-
Savage, Wiley	Pvt.	Co. B	28	Laborer	5/19/1863	Washington, DC	Suffolk, NC
Sawyer, Thomas, Henry	Pvt.	Co. E	19	Waiter	6/17/1863	Mason's Island, VA	Frederick City, MD
Sayles, Robert	Pvt.	Co. E	-	-	7/3/1863	Mason's Island, VA	-
Sayles, Robert	Pvt.	Co. H	17	Laborer	9/23/1864	Baltimore, MD	Harpers Ferry, VA
Scotland, Samuel	Pvt.	Co. D	22	Farmer	5/23/1864	Wilson's Creek, VA	Charles City County, VA
Scott, George	Pvt.	Co. G	18	Butcher	7/11/1863	Mason's Island, VA	Washington, DC
Scott, George W.	Pvt.	Co. H	23	Laborer	6/27/1863	Mason's Island, VA	King William, VA
Scott, Jackson	Pvt.	Co. I	24	Laborer	6/28/1863	Mason's Island, VA	New Berne, NC
Scott, James	Pvt.	Co. D	18	Farmer	6/14/1863	Mason's Island, VA	King William County, VA
Scott, John	Pvt.	Co. I	22	Farmer	6/28/1863	Mason's Island, VA	Marlboro, MD
Scott, Pringle	Pvt.	Co. K	20	Farmer	3/20/1865	Mason's Island, VA	Sumpstersville, SC
Scott, Robert	Pvt.	Co. C	25	Laborer	6/8/1863	Wilmington, NC	Petersburg, VA
Scott, William H.	Pvt.	Co. E	16	Waiter	6/21/1863	Washington, DC	Richmond City, VA
Scroggins, David	Pvt.	Co. K	19	Laborer	6/30/1863	Mason's Island, VA	Aquia Creek, VA
Sedgwick Horace	Pvt.	Co. G	15	Chore Boy	6/25/1863	Mason's Island, VA	Montgomery County, MD
Servil, John	Pvt.	Co. I	17	Laborer	6/28/1863	Mason's Island, VA	Georgetown, DC
Seymour, Charles	Sgt.	Co. E	-	Barber	6/17/1863	Mason's Island, VA	Grass Valley, CA
Shannonhouse, John	Pvt.	Co. F	44	Farmer	6/21/1863	Mason's Island, VA	Pasquotank County, NC
Shaw, James M.	Pvt.	Co. D	30	Farmer	6/14/1863	Mason's Island, VA	St. Mary's County, MD
Shaw, Samuel	Pvt.	Co. C	22	Farmer	4/15/1865	Wilmington, NC	Bladen County, NC
Shepard, Alfred	Pvt.	Co. I	22	Laborer	5/19/1863	Washington, DC	Louisa County, VA
Sherman, John	Pvt.	Co. G	20	Farmer	6/28/1863	Mason's Island, VA	Lancaster County, VA
Shields, Henry	Pvt.	Co. G	20	Farmer	9/26/1864	Ellicotts Mills, NC	Eastern Shore, MD
Shorter, George	Pvt.	Co. H	18	Laborer	9/22/1864	Ellicotts Mills, NC	Harpers Ferry, VA

Name	Rank	Company	Age	Occupation	Enlistment Date	Enlistment Place	Residence
Shorter, William	Cpl.	Co. B	19	Laborer	5/19/1863	Washington, DC	Georgetown, DC
Shorter, William W.	Pvt.	Co. K	24	Laborer	6/30/1863	Mason's Island, VA	Rockville, MD
Sidderman, Robert	Pvt.	Co. D	18	Laborer	6/14/1863	Mason's Island, VA	Howard County, MD
Sidney, Simon	Cpl.	Co. C	28	Farmer	7/4/1863	Mason's Island, VA	Richmond County, VA
Simms, George W.	Pvt.	Co. K	20	Laborer	6/30/1863	Mason's Island, VA	Washington, DC
Simonds, John	Sgt.	Co. I	18	Farmer	2/21/1865	Syracuse, NY	Canada
Simpson, John	Pvt.	Co. H	28	Farmer	7/6/1863	Mason's Island, VA	Molby, MD
Sippey, William	Pvt.	Co. C	19	Farmer	6/8/1863	Washington, DC	Loudon County, VA
Skinner, Frank	Pvt.	Co. F	27	Brick Mason	6/21/1863	Mason's Island, VA	Perquimans County, NC
Skinner, John	Pvt.	Co. C	21	Sailor	6/8/1863	Washington, DC	Norfolk, VA
Small, Thomas	Pvt.	Co. F	18	Waiter	7/18/1863	Mason's Island, VA	Perquimans County, NC
Smallwood, John	Pvt.	Co. B	18	Farmer	5/19/1863	Washington, DC	Charles County, MD
Smith, Albert	Pvt.	Co. I	22	Laborer	6/28/1863	Mason's Island, VA	Fairfax County, VA
Smith, Andrew	Pvt.	Co. I	18	Farmer	3/3/1865	Wilmington, NC	Robinson County, NC
Smith, Charles	Pvt.	Co. E	23	Farmer	7/3/1863	Mason's Island, VA	Louisa County, VA
Smith, Charles	Sgt.	Co. K	24	Farmer	6/30/1863	Mason's Island, VA	Falmouth, VA
Smith, Charles	Cpl.	Co. K	30	-	6/27/1863	Washington, DC	Rochester, NY
Smith, Edward	Cpl.	Co. G	23	Farmer	6/25/1863	Mason's Island, VA	Fairfax, VA
Smith, George	Pvt.	Co. A	20	Laborer	5/19/1863	Washington, DC	New Brunswick, NJ
Smith, George	Pvt.	Co. D	18	Waiter	6/14/1863	Mason's Island, VA	Baltimore, MD
Smith, James	Pvt.	Co. B	19	Laborer	5/19/1863	Washington, DC	Alexandria, VA
Smith, James	Pvt.	Co. C	21	Farmer	6/8/1863	Washington, DC	Loudon County, VA
Smith, James	Pvt.	Co. I	33	Laborer	6/28/1863	Mason's Island, VA	Howard County, VA
Smith, James E.	Pvt.	Co. H	18	Laborer	9/19/1864	Baltimore, MD	North Carolina
Smith, John C.	Pvt.	Co. B	20	Laborer	5/19/1863	Washington, DC	Alexandria, VA
Smith, John H.	Pvt.	Co. B	20	Laborer	5/19/1863	Washington, DC	Baltimore, MD
Smith, John H.	Cpl.	Co. K	25	Blacksmith	6/30/1863	Mason's Island, VA	Charles County, MD
Smith, Malachiah	Cpl.	Co. F	21	Gin Wright	6/21/1863	Mason's Island, VA	Hedgefield District, SC
Smith, Manuel	Pvt.	Co. K	18	Waiter	6/30/1863	Mason's Island, VA	Fredericksburg, VA
Smith, Miles	Pvt.	Co. A	22	Laborer	5/19/1863	Washington, DC	Louisa County, VA
Smith, Moses	Pvt.	Co. G	21	Farmer	6/25/1863	Mason's Island, VA	Birkley County, Western VA
Smith, Nathaniel	Cpl.	Co. A	22	Hostler	5/19/1863	Washington, DC	Burlington, ND
Smith, Richard	Sgt.	Co. A	23	Brick Maker	5/19/1863	Washington, DC	Washington, DC
Smith, Robert	Pvt.	Co. K	22	Sailor	7/3/1863	Alexandria, VA	Fredericksburg, VA
Smith, Robert	Pvt.	Co. D	19	Farmer	7/30/1863	Mason's Island, VA	Matthews County, VA
Smith, Samuel	Pvt.	Co. H	22	Farmer	6/27/1863	Mason's Island, VA	Calvert County, MD
Smith, Vincent	Cpl.	Co. G	21	Waiter	7/8/1863	Mason's Island, VA	Chambersburg, PA
Smith, Whitehall	Cpl.	Co. D	18	Laborer	6/14/1863	Mason's Island, VA	Washington, DC
Smith, William	Musician	Co. B	20	Waiter	5/19/1863	Washington, DC	Portsmouth, VA

Name	Rank	Co.	Age	Occupation	Date	Enlistment Place	Birthplace
Smith, William	Pvt.	Co. D	21	Farmer	6/14/1863	Mason's Island, VA	Woodville, MD
Smith, William	Pvt.	Co. K	23	Laborer	6/30/1863	Mason's Island, VA	Stafford County, VA
Smith, William E.	Pvt.	Co. K	23	Laborer	6/30/1863	Mason's Island, VA	Stafford County, VA
Smith, Willis	Pvt.	Co. C	28	Farmer	4/9/1865	Faisons Depot	Robinson County, NC
Smithers, Thomas	Pvt.	Co. C	18	Farmer	6/8/1863	Washington, DC	Northumberland County, VA
Snyder, Charles H.	Sgt.	Co. I	25	Laborer	6/28/1863	Mason's Island, VA	Pennfield, NY
Snyder, William	Pvt.	Co. C	35	Blacksmith	6/8/1863	Washington, DC	Howard County, MD
Socks, Thomas	Pvt.	Co. H	19	Farmer	6/27/1863	Mason's Island, VA	Liberty, MD
Soyle, Robert	Pvt.	Co. D	24	Farmer	7/9/1863	Mason's Island, VA	Northumberland County, VA
Spence, Washington	Pvt.	Co. C	27	Farmer	7/4/1863	Mason's Island, VA	Richmond County, VA
Spencer, John	Pvt.	Co. A	22	Sailor	5/19/1863	Washington, DC	Philadelphia, PA
Spriggs, Jefferson	Pvt.	Co. B	19	Farmer	7/3/1863	Mason's Island, VA	Charles County, MD
Stanley, Henry	Cpl.	Co. B	19	Farmer	5/19/1863	Washington, DC	Westchester, PA
St. Dana, James	Pvt.	Co. F	27	-	9/20/1864	Brooklyn, NY	Canada West
Stevenson, Edgar	Cpl.	Co. G	-	Farmer	6/25/1863	Mason's Island, VA	Rappahannock County, VA
Stevenson, Moses	Sgt.	Co. G	-	Farmer	6/25/1863	Mason's Island, VA	Loudon County, VA
Steward, Emmet	Pvt.	Co. K	20	Laborer	6/30/1863	Mason's Island, VA	Warrenton, VA
Steward, Charles	Pvt.	Co. G	17	Laborer	6/25/1863	Mason's Island, VA	Washington, DC
Steward, Charles	Pvt.	Co. H	21	Laborer	9/13/1864	Ellicotts Mills, MD	Virginia
Stewart, George	Pvt.	Co. A	21	Farmer	5/19/1863	Washington, DC	Harpers Ferry, VA
Stewart, Gibons	Pvt.	Co. B	19	Laborer	5/19/1863	Washington, DC	Madison County, VA
Stewart, John	Pvt.	Co. H	23	Waiter	6/27/1863	Mason's Island, VA	Philadelphia, PA
Stewart, Robert	Pvt.	Co. E	21	Farmer	6/17/1863	Mason's Island, VA	Cockeysville, MD
Stewart, Robert	Pvt.	Co. H	28	Waiter	6/27/1863	Mason's Island, VA	Georgetown, DC
Stewart, Thomas	Pvt.	Co. D	20	Laborer	6/14/1863	Mason's Island, VA	Prince George's County, MD
Stockett, Elias	Pvt.	Co. D	26	Farmer	6/14/1863	Mason's Island, VA	Anne Arundel County, MD
Stoneman, Henry	Pvt.	Co. D	18	Blacksmith	6/14/1863	Mason's Island, VA	Howard County, MD
Stoval, Lewis	Pvt.	-	37	-	1/26/1865	Poughkeepsie, NY	-
Strong, Manuel	Pvt.	Co. K	30	Laborer	6/30/1863	Mason's Island, VA	Carolina, VA
Strother, William	Sgt.	Co. I	20	Blacksmith	6/28/1863	Mason's Island, VA	Berkeley County, VA
Summers, Peter	Sgt.	Co. I	22	Umbrella Maker	6/28/1863	Mason's Island, VA	Philadelphia, PA
Sutton, Austin	Pvt.	Co. A	17	Cook	5/19/1863	Washington, DC	Northumberland County, VA
Sweden, Noble	Cpl.	Co. A	24	Laborer	5/19/1863	Washington, DC	Charles County, MD
Swindle, William	Pvt.	Co. H	-	Farmer	6/27/1863	Mason's Island, VA	Hyde County, NC
Sykes, Samuel	Pvt.	Co. I	27	Farmer	3/25/1865	Wilmington, NC	Fairfield County, SC
Symmes, George	Pvt.	Co. D	21	Farmer	7/9/1863	Mason's Island, VA	Anne Arundel County, MD
Syone, Solomon	-	Co. E	18	Farmer	3/15/1865	Wilmington, NC	Bladen County, NC
Talbot, John	Cpl.	Co. B	24	Waiter	5/19/1863	Washington, DC	Washington, DC
Tarleton, Phillip	Pvt.	Co. K	26	Laborer	7/3/1863	Alexandria, VA	St. Mary's County, MD

Name	Rank	Co.	Age	Occupation	Date	Enlisted	Birthplace
Tasco, Charles	Pvt.	Co. C	28	Laborer	6/8/1863	Washington, DC	Fredericksburg, VA
Taylor, George	-	-	22	Laborer	9/16/1864	Baltimore, MD	Virginia
Taylor, George	Pvt.	Co. F	21	Waiter	7/10/1863	Mason's Island, VA	Baltimore City, MD
Taylor, Issac	Pvt.	Co. D	21	Waiter	6/14/1863	Mason's Island, VA	Annapolis, MD
Taylor, James	Pvt.	-	22	Boatman	10/12/1864	Buffalo, NY	Canada
Taylor, James	Pvt.	Co. C	23	Laborer	6/8/1863	Washington, DC	Stafford County, VA
Taylor, James	Pvt.	Co. G	29	Waiter	6/25/1863	Mason's Island, VA	Hanover County, VA
Taylor, John	Cpl.	Co. E	19	Farmer	6/17/1863	Mason's Island, VA	Rappahannock County, VA
Taylor, Joseph	Sgt.	Co. K	21	Sailor	6/30/1863	Mason's Island, VA	Westmoreland, VA
Taylor, Walter	Pvt.	Co. C	19	Laborer	6/8/1863	Washington, DC	Lancaster County, VA
Taylor, William	Pvt.	Co. G	20	Saloon Waiter	6/25/1863	Mason's Island, VA	Alexandria, VA
Taylor, William	Cpl.	Co. H	29	Carpenter	8/19/1863	Washington, DC	Hampton, VA
Tennyson, Albert	Pvt.	Co. C	28	Waiter	6/8/1863	Washington, DC	Fauquier County, VA
Terry, William	Cpl.	Co. C	30	Cook	6/8/1863	Washington, DC	Carroll County, VA
Thomas, Aaron	Cpl.	Co. E	23	Farmer	6/17/1863	Mason's Island, VA	St. Mary's County, MD
Thomas, Benjamin	Pvt.	Co. K	21	Laborer	7/4/1863	Mason's Island, VA	Prince George's County, MD
Thomas, Charles	Pvt.	Co. B	21	Cook	5/19/1863	Washington, DC	Norfolk, VA
Thomas, Charles H.	Sgt.	Co. K	44	Marine	7/1/1863	Alexandria, VA	Sack Harbor, NY
Thomas, Daniel	Pvt.	Co. D	28	Laborer	6/14/1863	Mason's Island, VA	Charles County, MD
Thomas, Edward	Pvt.	Co. G	48	Carpenter	6/25/1863	Mason's Island, VA	Baltimore, MD
Thomas, Enoch	Cpl.	Co. G	21	Farmer	7/10/1863	Mason's Island, VA	Loudon County, VA
Thomas, George	Cpl.	Co. A	22	Farmer	7/12/1863	Mason's Island, VA	Augusta, GA
Thomas, George	Pvt.	Co. F	19	Farmer	6/21/1863	Mason's Island, VA	G_____ County, VA
Thomas, Henry	Pvt.	Co. H	23	Farmer	6/27/1863	Mason's Island, VA	St. Mary's County, MD
Thomas, Henry	Pvt.	Co. K	21	Laborer	6/30/1863	Mason's Island, VA	Harrisburg, PA
Thomas, James H.	Musician	Co. F	16	Teamster	6/21/1863	Mason's Island, VA	Schenectady City, NY
Thomas, John	Pvt.	Co. K	24	Laborer	6/30/1863	Mason's Island, VA	Prince George's County, MD
Thomas, Lewis	Pvt.	Co. A	25	Farmer	5/19/1863	Washington, DC	Charles County, MD
Thomas, Moses	Pvt.	Co. B	23	Waiter	5/19/1863	Washington, DC	St. Mary's County, MD
Thomas, Oliver	Pvt.	Co. G	23	Blacksmith	7/10/1863	Mason's Island, VA	Anne Arundel County, MD
Thomas, Robert	Pvt.	Co. H	24	Farmer	6/27/1863	Mason's Island, VA	Maryland
Thomas, Sanford	Pvt.	Co. G	19	Farmer	7/10/1863	Mason's Island, VA	Loudon County, VA
Thomas, Tobias	Pvt.	Co. A	26	Farmer	5/19/1863	Washington, DC	Prince George's County, MD
Thomas, William	Pvt.	Co. C	26	Farmer	6/8/1863	Washington, DC	Prince George's County, MD
Thompson, Andrew	Pvt.	Co. D	37	Farmer	6/14/1863	Mason's Island, VA	King George County, VA
Thompson, Archey	Pvt.	Co. B	22	Farmer	5/19/1863	Washington, DC	Fort Monroe, VA
Thompson, Benjamin	Cpl.	Co. K	21	Laborer	7/4/1863	Mason's Island, VA	Prince George, MD
Thompson, Cornelius	Pvt.	Co. C	32	Farmer	6/8/1863	Washington, DC	Prince George's County, MD
Thompson, Daniel	Pvt.	Co. F	20	Laborer	9/13/1864	Frederick City, MD	Ellicotts Mills, MD

Name	Rank	Co.	Age	Occupation	Date	Place	Place
Thompson, Daniel James	Pvt.	Co. F	20	Farmer	9/21/1864	Baltimore, MD	Virginia
Thompson, David	Cpl.	Co. F	30	Farmer	6/21/1863	Mason's Island, VA	Perquimans County, NC
Thompson, George	Sgt.	Co. H	29	Waiter	6/27/1863	Mason's Island, VA	Prince William County, VA
Thompson, George	Pvt.	Co. H	21	Huckster	7/17/1863	Mason's Island, VA	Baltimore, MD
Thompson, James	Cpl.	Co. F	19	Laborer	6/21/1863	Mason's Island, VA	Charles County, MD
Thompson, Thomas	Pvt.	Co. D	43	Farmer	6/14/1863	Mason's Island, VA	Washington County, MD
Thompson, Thomas	Pvt.	Co. F	20	Farmer	6/21/1863	Mason's Island, VA	Hertford County, NC
Thompson, William I.	Pvt.	Co. E	35	Farmer	8/24/1864	Brooklyn, NY	Canada
Thompson, Zedekiah	Pvt.	Co. E	31	Farmer	6/17/1863	Mason's Island, VA	Rockville, MD
Thornton, Harrison	Pvt.	Co. E	36	Farmer	6/17/1863	Mason's Island, VA	Prince William County, VA
Thoroughgood, Demby	Sgt.	Co. F	18	Farmer	7/10/1863	Mason's Island, VA	Princess Anne County, MD
Tibbet, Allen	Pvt.	Co. C	40	Laborer	6/8/1863	Washington, DC	Prince George's County, MD
Tibbs, Charles	Sgt.	Co. B	27	Farmer	5/19/1863	Washington, DC	Westmoreland County, VA
Tibbs, Elias	Pvt.	Co. H	23	Farmer	6/27/1863	Mason's Island, VA	Falkear County, VA
Timber, Rhoga	Pvt.	Co. A	23	Laborer	5/19/1863	Washington, DC	Fredericksburg, VA
Tipsico, John Henry	Pvt.	Co. G	-	Farmer	6/25/1863	Mason's Island, VA	Fauquier County, VA
Tolson, William	Pvt.	Co. C	20	Farmer	6/8/1863	Washington, DC	Northumberland County, VA
Tompkins, Edwin	Pvt.	Co. I	22	Farmer	12/31/1864	Ft. Powhatan, VA	Sussex County, VA
Toodles, Richard	Pvt.	Co. C	18	Farmer	6/8/1863	Washington, DC	Anne Arundel County, MD
Townsand, John	Pvt.	Co. B	22	Farmer	5/19/1863	Washington, DC	Elizabeth City, NC
Travis, William	Pvt.	Co. F	18	Teamster	6/21/1863	Mason's Island, VA	Salem Westmoreland County, VA
Tucker, Beverly	Pvt.	Co. A	22	Waiter	5/19/1863	Washington, DC	Williamsburg, VA
Tunnia, John R.	Sgt.	Co. K	38	Barber	6/30/1863	Washington, DC	Warrenton, VA
Turner, Addison	Pvt.	Co. A	19	Farmer	11/24/1863	Portsmouth, VA	Washington, DC
Turner, Dennis	Pvt.	Co. B	20	Farmer	3/4/1865	Wilmington, NC	Sampson County, NC
Turner, Frank	Sgt.	Co. G	23	Blacksmith	6/23/1863	Mason's Island, VA	Culpepper County, VA
Turner, James	Pvt.	Co. F	21	Laborer	9/16/1864	Baltimore, MD	South Carolina
Turner, Joseph	Pvt.	Co. D	29	Hostler	7/9/1863	Mason's Island, VA	Georgetown, DC
Turner, Samuel	Pvt.	Co. K	21	Laborer	6/30/1864	Mason's Island, VA	South Hampton, VA
Turner, Thomas	Pvt.	Co. H	24	Barber	6/27/1863	Mason's Island, VA	Philadelphia, PA
Tuxon, Joseph	Cpl.	Co. D	18	Teamster	7/9/1863	Mason's Island, VA	Washington, DC
Tyler, Frank	Pvt.	Co. D	18	Laborer	6/14/1863	Mason's Island, VA	Howard County, MD
Tyler, Sewell	Pvt.	Co. G	21	House Servant	6/25/1863	Mason's Island, VA	Fauquier County, VA
Tyler, Stephen	Pvt.	Co. F	27	Sailor	9/22/1864	Baltimore, MD	West Indies
Tyler, William	Cpl.	Co. H	17	Farmer	6/27/1863	Mason's Island, VA	Howard County, MD
Underhill, James	Pvt.	Co. C	18	Farmer	6/8/1863	Washington, DC	Westchester County, NY
Van Horn, Fenton	Cpl.	Co. A	22	Blacksmith	5/19/1863	Washington, DC	Loudon County, VA
Van Will, Julius	Pvt.	Co. F	18	Farmer	6/21/1863	Mason's Island, VA	Newbern City, NC
Veney, John	Pvt.	Co. F	19	Farmer	7/4/1863	Mason's Island, VA	Richmond County, VA

Name	Rank	Company	Age	Occupation	Date	Enlisted	Birthplace
Vigil, Charles	Cpl.	Co. A	23	Butcher	5/19/1863	Washington, DC	Washington, DC
Walker, Charles	Pvt.	Co. H	18	Waiter	6/27/1863	Mason's Island, VA	Washington, DC
Walker, Donas	Pvt.	Co. A	18	Laborer	5/19/1863	Washington, DC	Wilmington, NC
Walker, Frank	Pvt.	Co. I	23	Farmer	6/28/1863	Mason's Island, VA	Harpers Ferry, VA
Walker, Thomas	Pvt.	Co. G	16	Servant	6/25/1863	Mason's Island, VA	Chalittsville, Western VA
Wallace, Joseph	Pvt.	Co. A	31	Barber	5/19/1863	Washington, DC	Caroline County, VA
Walter, Hugh	Pvt.	Co. K	18	Laborer	6/30/1863	Mason's Island, VA	Port Tobacco, MD
Ward, Joseph	Sgt.	Co. D	20	Blacksmith	6/14/1863	Mason's Island, VA	Loudon County, VA
Ward, William	Pvt.	Co. E	23	Barber	6/17/1863	Mason's Island, VA	Beauford, NC
Warfield, George	Cpl.	Co. C	23	Huckster	6/8/1863	Washington, DC	Montgomery County, MD
Warner, Frank	Pvt.	Co. A	21	Laborer	5/19/1863	Washington, DC	Frederick County, MD
Warner, Reuben	Cpl.	Co. C	28	Farmer	6/8/1863	Washington, DC	Montgomery County, MD
Warner, William H.	Pvt.	Co. E	21	Cigar-Maker	7/5/1863	Mason's Island, VA	Philadelphia, PA
Warren, Moses	Pvt.	Co. F	28	Farmer	6/21/1863	Mason's Island, VA	Chowan County, NC
Warren, William	Pvt.	Co. G	17	Laborer	6/25/1863	Mason's Island, VA	Washington, DC
Washington, Anthony	Pvt.	Co. B	20	Farmer	7/2/1863	Mason's Island, VA	St. Mary's County, MD
Washington, Beverly	Pvt.	Co. A	18	Farmer	5/19/1863	Washington, DC	Fauquier County, VA
Washington, Frank	Cpl.	Co. D	19	Sailor	6/14/1863	Mason's Island, VA	Baltimore, MD
Washington, George	Cpl.	Co. B	39	Laborer	5/19/1863	Washington, DC	Prince George's County, MD
Washington, George	Pvt.	Co. B	22	Farmer	6/14/1863	Mason's Island, VA	Norfolk County, VA
Washington, George	Pvt.	Co. F	19	Teamster	6/21/1863	Mason's Island, VA	Pasquotank County, NC
Washington, George H.	Pvt.	Co. B	27	Laborer	5/19/1863	Washington, DC	Hanover County, VA
Washington, George H.	Cpl.	Co. E	27	Farmer	6/17/1863	Mason's Island, VA	Berkley County, VA
Washington, George O.	Pvt.	Co. D	18	Barber	6/14/1863	Mason's Island, VA	York, PA
Washington, Harrison	Cpl.	Co. E	23	Farmer	6/17/1863	Mason's Island, VA	Loudon County, VA
Washington, Henry	Pvt.	Co. C	23	Laborer	6/8/1863	Washington, DC	Charles County, MD
Washington, Henry	Pvt.	Co. D	28	Hostler	6/14/1863	Mason's Island, VA	Baltimore, MD
Washington, John	Pvt.	Co. E	21	Farmer	6/17/1863	Mason's Island, VA	Charles County, MD
Washington, John	Musician	Co. K	28	Bricklayer	6/30/1863	Mason's Island, VA	Columbia, SC
Washington, Lawrence	Cpl.	Co. I	21	Waiter	6/28/1863	Mason's Island, VA	Sheppardstown, VA
Washington, Paul	Pvt.	Co. F	41	Tobacconist	6/21/1863	Mason's Island, VA	Annoracker County, VA
Washington, Warner	Pvt.	Co. H	22	Farmer	6/27/1863	Mason's Island, VA	Northumberland County, VA
Washington, Wesley	Pvt.	Co. C	21	Hostler	6/8/1863	Washington, DC	Warrenton Court House, VA
Washington, William	Cpl.	Co. B	28	Laborer	5/19/1863	Washington, DC	Jefferson County, VA
Washington, Willis	Pvt.	Co. B	22	Teamster	5/19/1863	Washington, DC	King George County, VA
Watters, Charles G.	Sgt.	Co. E	24	Cook	5/17/1863	Mason's Island, VA	Charles County, MD
Watters, Henry	Pvt.	Co. G	20	Farmer	6/25/1863	Mason's Island, VA	Anne Arundel County, MD
Waters, Joseph W.	Sgt.	Co. B	21	Waiter	5/19/1863	Washington, DC	Montgomery County, MD
Waters, William	Pvt.	Co. I	19	Field Hand	6/28/1863	Mason's Island, VA	Prince George's County, MD

Name	Rank	Co.	Age	Occupation	Date	Location	Birthplace
Watkins, Daniel	Pvt.	Co. F	-	-	6/10/1863	Mason's Island, VA	Charles City County, VA
Watkins, Robert A.	Cpl.	Co. C	-	Farmer	5/16/1864	Wilson's Landing	Baltimore, MD
Watkins, Samuel	Pvt.	Co. B	18	Waiter	7/1/1863	Mason's Island, VA	Drummondtown, VA
Watson, Henry	Pvt.	Co. E	21	Sailor	6/17/1863	Mason's Island, VA	Washington, DC
Watts, Henry	Pvt.	Co. D	18	Waiter	6/14/1863	Mason's Island, VA	Caroline, VA
Watty, Annanias	Pvt.	Co. F	21	Laborer	9/17/1864	Baltimore, MD	Michigan
Waugh, James H.	Sgt.	Co. K	21	Barber	6/30/1863	Alexandria, VA	Washington, DC
Waugh, James S.	Cpl.	Co. K	17	Cooper	6/30/1863	Mason's Island, VA	Alexandria, VA
Weaver, Dennis	Pvt.	Co. D	19	Waiter	6/14/1863	Mason's Island, VA	-
Webb, Archey		Co. C	-	-	-	-	-
Webster, Daniel	Pvt.	Co. C	21	Laborer	6/8/1863	Mason's Island, VA	Washington, DC
Webster, Henry	Pvt.	Co. C	43	Laborer	7/4/1863	Mason's Island, VA	Richmond, VA
Webster, William Alexander	Pvt.	Co. I	25	Boatman	6/28/1863	Mason's Island, VA	Westmoreland, VA
Weeves, James	Pvt.	Co. A	19	Laborer	5/19/1863	Washington, DC	Fauquier County, VA
Weekes, Thomas	Pvt.	Co. A	19	Laborer	5/19/1863	Mason's Island, VA	Fredericksburg, VA
Weldon, Thomas	Pvt.	Co. H	25	White Washer	7/6/1863	Mason's Island, VA	Prince George's County, MD
Wellmore, James	Pvt.	Co. G	30	Baker	6/25/1863	Mason's Island, VA	Baltimore, MD
Wells, John	Pvt.	Co. H	14	Farmer	6/27/1863	Mason's Island, VA	Howard County, MD
Wells, Simon	Cpl.	Co. B	37	Farmer	5/19/1863	Washington, DC	Berkley County, VA
West, James	Pvt.	Co. I	45	-	6/28/1863	Mason's Island, VA	-
West, William J.	Pvt.	Co. -	32	Farmer	10/12/1864	Buffalo, NY	Canada
White, Issac	Pvt.	Co. K	20	Stevedore	4/15/1865	Wilmington, NC	Onslow County, NC
White, Lewis	-	-	31	Farmer	9/21/1864	Baltimore, MD	Howard County, MD
White, Phillip		Co. I	21	Teamster	6/28/1863	Mason's Island, VA	Henri County, VA
Whitehead, Joseph	Pvt.	Co. H	26	Waiter	6/27/1863	Mason's Island, VA	Hillsboro, NC
Whiters, Miles	Pvt.	Co. F	27	Farmer	6/21/1863	Mason's Island, VA	Pasquotank County, NC
Whiting, Frank	Pvt.	Co. B	21	-	5/19/1863	Washington, DC	-
Whittegan, Benjamin	Pvt.	Co. A	46	Gardener	5/19/1863	Washington, DC	Washington, DC
Wiggins, George	Pvt.	Co. E	17	Farmer	6/17/1863	Mason's Island, VA	Nansemond County, VA
Wiggins, Issac	Cpl.	Co. F	42	Cook	6/21/1863	Mason's Island, VA	Martin County, NC
Wiggins, William Daniel	Pvt.	Co. F	12	None	6/21/1863	Mason's Island, VA	Martin County, NC
Williams, Albert	Pvt.	Co. F	22	Farmer	5/16/1864	Wilson's Landing	Charles City County, VA
Williams, Benjamin	Pvt.	Co. H	16	Farmer	6/27/1863	Mason's Island, VA	Fauquier County, VA
Williams, Charles	Pvt.	Co. C	20	Coachman	6/8/1863	Washington, DC	Prince George's County, MD
Williams, Daniel	Pvt.	Co. H	18	Farmer	6/27/1863	Mason's Island, VA	Prince George's County, MD
Williams, Daniel	Sgt.	Co. K	37	Barber	6/30/1863	Mason's Island, VA	Port Au Prince, West Indies
Williams, Decatur	Pvt.	Co. F	50	Farmer	6/21/1863	Mason's Island, VA	Gates County, NC
Williams, George	Pvt.	Co. A	19	Farmer	7/12/1863	Mason's Island, VA	Frederick, MD
Williams, George	Pvt.	Co. F	16	Hostler	6/21/1863	Mason's Island, VA	Warren County, VA

Name	Rank	Company	Age	Occupation	Date	Enlistment Place	Birthplace
Williams, Henry	Pvt.	Co. B	21	Laborer	2/3/1865	Washington, DC	Louisiana
Williams, Henry	Pvt.	Co. C	26	Laborer	6/8/1863	Washington, DC	Washington, DC
Williams, Henry	Pvt.	Co. F	29	Blacksmith	6/21/1863	Mason's Island, VA	Fauquier County, VA
Williams, James	Pvt.	Co. G	21	Farmer	7/7/1863	Mason's Island, VA	Washington, DC
Williams, John	Pvt.	Co. C	21	Laborer	6/8/1863	Mason's Island, VA	Fairfax, VA
Williams, John	Pvt.	-	36	Laborer	12/2/1863	Albany, NY	Buffalo, NY
Williams, John	Pvt.	Co. D	18	Farmer	6/14/1863	Mason's Island, VA	Montgomery County, MD
Williams, John T.	Pvt.	Co. F	20	Laborer	9/12/1864	Ellicotts Mills, MD	North Carolina
Williams, John A.	Cpl.	Co. H	20	Boatman	7/6/1863	Mason's Island, VA	Eastern Shore, MD
Williams, Joseph	Pvt.	Co. D	19	Hostler	6/14/1863	Mason's Island, VA	Alexandria, VA
Williams, Larkin	Pvt.	Co. C	26	Laborer	6/8/1863	Washington, DC	Washington, DC
Williams, Oliver	Pvt.	Co. F	21	Laborer	9/17/1864	Baltimore, MD	Virginia
Williams, Wesley	Pvt.	Co. F	20	Farmer	5/16/1864	Wilson's Landing	Charles City County, VA
Wilson, George H.	Pvt.	Co. G	17	Barber	6/25/1863	Mason's Island, VA	Winchester, VA
Wilson, George	Cpl.	Co. D	21	Laborer	7/1/1863	Mason's Island, VA	Claiborna County, SC
Wilson, Joseph	Pvt.	Co. F	19	Baker	6/21/1863	Mason's Island, VA	Norfolk City, VA
Wilson, Lewis	Pvt.	Co. A	30	Farmer	7/12/1865	Mason's Island, VA	Montgomery County, VA
Wilson, Peter	Cpl.	Co. F	28	Farmer	6/21/1863	Mason's Island, VA	Norfolk County, VA
Wilson, William	Pvt.	Co. A	31	Laborer	7/12/1863	Mason's Island, VA	Fairfax County, VA
Wilson, William	Cpl.	Co. F	19	Farmer	7/10/1863	Mason's Island, VA	Frederick City, MD
Winkfield, William	Fifer	Co. A	35	Laborer	5/19/1863	Washington, DC	Norfolk, VA
Winn, William	Sgt.	Co. B	19	Blacksmith	5/19/1863	Washington, DC	Richmond, VA
Winston, Felix	Pvt.	Co. E	25	Laborer	6/17/1863	Mason's Island, VA	Wayne County, NC
Winston, Nelson	Pvt.	Co. B	19	Farmer	5/19/1863	Washington, DC	Louisa County, VA
Wood, Freeman	Pvt.	Co. D	24	Farmer	6/14/1863	Mason's Island, VA	Goochland County, VA
Wood, Samuel	Pvt.	Co. C	36	Farmer	6/8/1863	Washington, DC	Newbern, NC
Woodroe, Charles	Pvt.	Co. F	25	Laborer	6/21/1863	Mason's Island, VA	Hertford County, NC
World, Luke	Pvt.	Co. D	27	Farmer	6/14/1863	Mason's Island, VA	Piscataway, MD
Wright, Peter	Pvt.	Co. B	20	Farmer	5/19/1863	Washington, DC	Gales County, NC
Wright, Presley	Pvt.	Co. C	38	Carpenter	4/15/1865	Wilmington, NC	Sampson County, NC
Wright, Rufus	Pvt.	Co. B	26	Farmer	5/19/1863	Washington, DC	Lancaster County, VA
Wright, William	Pvt.	Co. G	23	Farmer	7/25/1863	Mason's Island, VA	Edenton, NC
Wright, William H.	Musician	Co. K	18	Printer	3/17/1865	Wilmington, NC	Bladen County, NC
Wumble, John	Pvt.	Co. I	21	Hostler	7/12/1863	Washington, DC	Sussex County, VA
Yelloty, Gloster T.	Pvt.	Co. F	-	-	-	-	-
Young, Daniel	Cpl.	Co. E	26	Farmer	6/17/1863	Mason's Island, VA	Salem, VA
Young, Hazard	Pvt.	Co. D	20	Laborer	6/14/1863	Mason's Island, VA	Richmond, VA
Young, Henson	Pvt.	Co. H	19	Laborer	9/22/1864	Baltimore, MD	Virginia

Young, John W.	Pvt.	Co. B	22	Laborer	5/19/1863	Washington, DC	Charles County, MD
Young, Phillip	Pvt.	Co. K	21	Laborer	6/30/1863	Mason's Island, VA	Caroline, VA
Young, William	Pvt.	Co. F	21	Laborer	9/19/1864	Baltimore, MD	Washington, DC

Selected Bibliography

Ames, Mary Clemmer. *Ten Years In Washington.* Hartford: A.D. Worthington and Company, 1874.

Angell, Stephen Ward. *Bishop Henry McNeal Turner.* Knoxville: University of Tennessee Press, 1992.

_____. *Social Protest Thought in the African Methodist Episcopal Church.* 1862-1939. Knoxville: University of Tennessee Press, 2000.

Aptheker, Herbert. *And Why Not Every Man?* New York: International Publishers, 1970.

_____. *To Be Free.* New York: International Publishers, 1969.

Armstrong, Mary Frances Morgan. *Hampton and Its Students.* New York: G.P. Putnam's Sons, 1874.

Bailey, Thomas A. *The American Pageant.* Lexington: D.C. Health. Vol. 1, 1975.

_____. *The American Spirit.* Lexington, D.C. Health and Company. Vol. 1, 1991.

Barnett, Joseph H. *Life of Abraham Lincoln.* Cincinnati: Moore, Wilstack and Baldwin, 1865.

Bennett, Jr., Lerone. *Forced Into Glory: Abraham Lincoln's White Dream.* Chicago: Johnson Publishing Company, 2000.

Berlin, Ira (ed). *Freedom,* Series II. Cambridge: Cambridge University Press, 1992.

Berry, Mary Frances and Blassingame, John. *Long Memory.* New York: Oxford University Press, 1982.

Blackett, R.J.M. Thomas Morris Chester. *Black Civil War Correspondent.* New York: Da Capo Press, 1989.

Bracey, John H. Meier & Rudwick, Elliott. *Black Nationalism in America.* Indianapolis: The Bobbs-Merrill Company, Inc., 1970.

Bradford, Sarah H. *Harriet, The Moses of Her People.* New York: J.J. Little and Company, 1901.

Brockett, L.P. *Woman's Work in the Civil War: A Record of Heroism, Patriotism and Patience.* Philadelphia: Zeigler, McCurdy and Company, 1867.

_____. *The Camp, The Battlefield, The Hospital.* Philadelphia: National Publishing Company, 1866.

Brodie, Fawn M. *Thaddeus Stevens, Scourge of the South.* New York: W.W. Norton and Company, 1959.

Brown, William Wells. *The Negro in the American Rebellion.* Boston: Lee and Shepard, 1867.

_____. *The Rising Son.* Boston: A.G. Brown, 1874.

_____. *The Black Man, His Antecedents, His Genius, and His Achievements.* New York: Thomas Hamilton, 1863.

Butler, Benjamin. *Speech of Major General Benjamin Butler, Upon the Campaign for Richmond.* Boston: Wright and Potter, 1865.

Campbell, Robert A. *The Rebellion Record.* Kalamazoo: R.A. Campbell, 1866.

Coffin, Levi. *Reminiscences of Levi Coffin.* Cincinnati: Western Tract Society, 1876.

Cornish, Dudley Taylor. *The Sable Arm.* Lawrence: University of Kansas Press, 1987.

Crotty, Daniel G. *Four Years Campaigning In The Army of the Potomac.* Grand Rapids: Dygert Brothers and Company, 1874.

Draper, John W. *History of the American Civil War.* 3 Vols. New York: Harper and Brothers, 1867-1870.

Duyckinck, Evert A. *National History of the War for the Union.* New York: Johnson, Fry and Company, 1861.

Evelyn, Douglas E. and Dickson, Paul. *On This Spot.* Garrett Park: On This Spot Productions, 1992.

Fishel, Edwin C. *The Secret War for the Union.* Boston: Haughton Mifflin, 1996.

Fishel, Jr, Leslie H. and Quarles, Benjamin. *The Black American.* Glenview: Scott, Foresman and Company, 1970.

Fitzpatrick, Sandra. Goodwin, Maria. *The Guide to Black Washington.* New York: Hippocrene Books, 1990.

Fox, William F. *Regimental Losses.* Albany: Morningside Bookshop, 1974.

Gilbert, Olive. *Narrative of Sojourner Truth.* Battle Creek: For the Author, 1878.

Gladstone, William A. *United States Colored Troops.* Gettysburg: Thomas Publications, 1990.

Glatthaar, Joseph T. *Forged In Battle.* New York: The Free Press, 1990.

Glazier, Willard. *Battles for the Union.* Hartford: Dustin, Gilmar and Company, 1875.

Greeley, Horace. *The American Conflict: A History of the Great Rebellion in the United States of America 1860-65.* Hartford: O.D. Case, 1866.

Green, Constance M. *The Secret City.* Princeton, New Jersey: Princeton University Press, 1967.

Greenberg, Martin H. and Waugh, Charles G. *The Price of Freedom.* Vol. 1. Nashville: Cumberland House, 2000.

Guthrie, James M. *Campfires of the Afro-American.* Philadelphia: The Afro-American Publishing Company, 1899.

Jones, William J. *Personal Reminiscences, Anecdotes, and Letters of General Robert E. Lee.* New York: D. Appleton and Company, 1875.

Kettell, Thomas Prentice. *History of the Great Rebellion.* Hartford: L. Stebbins, 1866.

Leech, Margaret. *Reveille in Washington 1860-1865.* New York: Grosset and Dunlap, 1941.

Lerner, Gerda (ed.). *Black Women in White America.* New York: Vintage Books, 1973.

Logan, Rayford, Winston, Michael (eds.). *Dictionary of American Negro Biography.* New York: W.W. Norton and Company, 1982.

Long, E.B., Long Barbara. *The Civil War Day By Day.* New York: Da Capo Press, 1971.

Long, Richard (ed.). *Black Writers and the American Civil War.* Secaucus: The Blue and Grey Press, 1988.

Lord, Francis. *Civil War Collectors Encyclopedia.* Harrisburg: The Stackpole Company, 1965.

Lyle, William W. *Lights and Shadows of Army Life.* Cincinnati: R.W. Carroll and Company, 1865.

Mansfield, Edward D. *A Popular and Authentic Life of Ulysses S. Grant.* Cincinnati: R.W. Carroll and Company, 1868.

May, Samuel. *Some Recollections of Our Antislavery Conflict.* Boston: Fields, Osgood and Company, 1869.

Melder, Keith. *City of Magnificent Intentions.* Washington, D.C.: Intac, Inc, 1997.

McCabe, James D. *Behind the Scenes in Washington.* New York:

Continental Publishing Company, 1873.

McElroy, John Harmon. *The Sacrificial Years.* Jaffrey: David R. Godine, 1999.

McPherson, Edward. *A Political Manual for 1866.* Washington, D.C.: Philip and Solomons, 1866.

_____. *The Political History of the United States During the Period of Reconstruction.* Washington, D.C.: Solomons and Chapman, 1875.

McPherson, James M. *The Negro's Civil War.* New York: Vintage Books, 1965.

Northrup, Solomon. *Twelve Years A Slave.* Auburn: Derby and Miller, 1853.

Ochs, Stephen J. *A Black Patriot and a White Priest.* Baton Rouge: Louisiana State University Press, 2000.

Quarles, Benjamin. *Allies for Freedom: Blacks and John Brown.* New York: Oxford University Press, 1974.

_____. *Frederick Douglass.* New York: Atheneum, 1974.

Raymond, Henry J. *The Life and Public Services of Abraham Lincoln.* New York: Derby and Miller, 1865.

Redkey, Edwin S. *A Grand Army of Black Men.* Cambridge: Cambridge University Press, 1992.

Richardson, William A. *Speech of Honorable W.A. Richardson.* Philadelphia: Ringwalt and Brown, 1860.

Ridgel, Alfred Lee. *Africa and African Methodism.* Atlanta: Franklin Printing and Publishing Company, 1896.

Robertson, Jr. James I. *The Concise Illustrated History of the Civil War.* Yorktown: Eastern Acorn Press, 1981.

Rosenberger, Francis Coleman (ed.). *Records of the Columbia Historical Society.* Vol. 50. Washington, D.C., 1980.

_____. *Records of the Columbia Historical Society.* 1971-1972. Vol. 48. Columbia Historical Society. Washington, D.C., 1973.

Rubin, Jr. Louis D. *Virginia, A History.* New York: W.W. Norton and Company, 1984.

Ruffin, Edmund. *Anticipations of the Future.* Richmond: J.W. Randolph, 1860.

Schmucker, Samuel. *The History of the Civil War in the United States.* Philadelphia: Jones Brothers and Company, 1865.

Scott, Henry Lee. *Military Dictionary.* New York: D. Van Nostrand, 1861.

Seraile, William. *Fire in His Heart: Benjamin Tucker Tanner.* Knoxville: University of Tennessee Press, 1999.

Simmons, William. *Men of Mark.* Cleveland: Geo. M. Rewell and Company, 1887.

Smith, Rev. David. *Bigraphy of Rev. David Smith.* Xenia: Xenia Gazette, 1881.

Spence, Mary L. and Jackson, Donald. *The Expeditions of John Charles Fremont.* Chicago, IL: University of Illinois Press, 1973.

Stampp, Kenneth M. (ed.). *The Causes of the Civil War.* New York: Touchstone, 1991.

Stanton, Robert L. *The Church and The Rebellion Against the Government of the United States.* New York: Derby and Miller, 1864.

Stepp, John W. and Hill, I. William. *Mirror of War.* Washington, D.C.: Castle Books, 1961.

Talbert, Horace. *The Sons of Allen.* Xenia: Aldine Press, 1906.

Trefousse, Hans L. *Thaddeus Stevens.* Chapel Hill: University of North Carolina Press, 1997.

Trudeau, Noah Andre. *Like Men of War.* Boston: Back Bay Books, 1998.

Wayman, Alexander W. *My Recollections.* Philadelphia: A.M.E. Book Concerns, 1881.

Weist, Jacob R. "The Medical Department in the West." *In Sketches of War History.* (Mollus, OH, Vol 2). Cincinnati: Robert Clarke, 1888.

Wesley, Charles and Romero, Patricia. *Afro-Americans in the Civil War.* Corwell Heights: Association for the Study of Afro-American Life and History, 1976.

Williams, George Washington. *A History of the Negro Troops.* New York: Harper and Brothers, 1888.

Wilson, Joseph T. *The Black Phalonx.* Hartford: American Publishing Company, 1890. Reprint 1994 Da Capo Press Inc.

Winter, William C. *The Civil War in St. Louis, A Guided Tour.* St. Louis: Missouri Historical Society Press, 1994.

Woodson, Carter G. *The Negro Church.* Washington, D.C.: The Associated Press, 1921.

Wilson, Joseph T. *The Black Phalonx.* Hartford: American Publishing Company, 1890. Reprint 1994 Da Capo Press Inc.

Winter, William C. *The Civil War in St. Louis, A Guided Tour.* St. Louis: Missouri Historical Society Press, 1994.

Woodson, Carter G. *The Negro Church.* Washington, D.C.: The Associated Press, 1921.

Periodicals

Douglass, Frederick, "An Appeal to Congress for Impartial Suffrage." *Atlantic Monthly,* January, 1867, pp. 112-117.

Hawthorne, Nathaniel, "Chiefly About War Matters" *Atlantic Monthly,* July 1862.

Armstrong, S.C. (et al), "The Future of the Negro," *The North American Review,* July 1884.

Henderson, George W., "History of Negro Citizenship", *AME Church Review,* January 1899.

Cunningham, James L., "Black Militia Companies at the National Drill, Washington, D.C., 1887, *Military Collector and Historian."*

Bennett Jr., Lerone, "Did Abraham Lincoln Really Free the Slaves," *Ebony* Magazine, February 2000, pps. 54-60.

Gibbs, C.R., "First Regiment, U.S. Colored Troops," *The Hill Rag,* January 23, 1984.

Roy, Joseph E., "Our Indebtedness to the Negroes for their Conduct During the War," *New Englander and Yale Review,* November 1889, pps. 353-365.

Brooks, Walter, "The Evolution of the Negro Baptist Church," *Journal of Negro History,* January 1922, pps. 11-22.

Archambault, Alan and Gero, Anthony, United States Colored Troops, Enlisted Men, Infantry, 1864-1865, *"Military Collector and Historian,"* Summer 1995, pps. 88-89.

Smith, W.F., "General W. F. Smith of Petersburg," *The Century,* August 1897, pps. 636-638.

Index

Givens, John V., 191.
Goldsboro (NC), 99, 101, 179.
Gooding, James Henry, 83.
Gordon, Mrs. Charlotte, 114.
Gordon, Sandy, 97.
Grand Army of the Republic, 188, 192.
Grant, Gen. Ulysses S., 50, 76, 78, 96, 100, 129, 131, 168, 186, 194.
Greek, 109.
Greeley, Horace, 28, 54.
Greely, Mrs. Augusta A., 207.
Greely, Pvt. Horace, 97, 207.
Green, Henry, 43.
Greene, J.E., 38.
Greer, David, 104.
Greer, Hannah, 104.
Greyson, James, 66.
Grinfer, Henry, 66.
Gurley, Phineas, 25.

Haiti, 26, 43.
Half Moon Battery, 97.
Hampton General Hospital, 81, 82.
Hampton National Cemetery, 184.
Hampton Roads, 64.
Harewood Hospital, 57, 182.
Harford County, 87.
Harper's Weekly (Newspaper), 22, 24, 60, 84.
Harris, Edward, 90.
Harris, Sen. Ira, 25.
Harris, William, 72.
Harrison, Samuel, 71.
Harrison, Rev. Samuel, 122.

Harrison's Landing, 88.
Hartford (CT), 18.
Hatteras Inlet, 101.
Hatton, George, 31, 38, 39, 71, 82, 83, 172, 191, 192, 197.
Hebrew, 109.
Hedgeman, Buck, 66.
Henderson, Charles, 194.
Henderson, Julia, 35.
"Herman Livingston," 96.
Hertford (NC), 68, 150.
Hilton Head, 115.
Hincks, Gen. Edward W., 70, 76, 80, 81, 151.
Hinton, Thomas, H.C., 32, 117.
Holman, Col. John, 2, 48-50, 60-62, 64, 66, 68, 69, 72, 78, 80, 82, 85-88, 90-94, 100, 101, 122, 130, 150, 151, 162, 166, 172, 173, 174, 176, 177, 179, 195, 198, 199, 201, 204, 205.
"Home Place," 144, 146, 152, 159, 160.
Hone, Philip, 11.
Honey Hill, 22.
Hopkins, Robert, 194.
House of Representatives (U.S.), 10, 11, 12, 38, 140, 187.
Howard University, 110.
Howe, Sen. Timothy O., 185.
Howells, J.C., 31.
Hunter, Gen. David, 118.

Idaho, 31.
Illinois, 22, 52, 113, 122.
Iowa, 19.

C.R. Gibbs

 Mr. C.R. Gibbs is an author, freelance writer, lecturer, and exhibitor of historical information and artifacts. His many accomplishments include video or television scripts on Black History for the Washington, DC Public Schools Educational Media Center, WETA-TV, and WHUR FM Radio. He served as assistant technical advisor to the Frances Thompson Company on a film entitled *American Years,* and as a consultant to the DC Public School System, Georgetown University, the Smithsonian Institution, and Maryland Public Television. He researched, wrote, and narrated, *Sketches in Color,* a 13-part companion series to the PBS series *The Civil War* for the Howard University TV station. He was the featured plenary speaker at the November 2000 Civil War Teachers and Scholars Conference at Howard University.

In February 2001, he was part of a panel of scholars that discussed "African American History and the Confederacy" at Howard University. This event was broadcast on C-Span. Mr. Gibbs is a popular Smithsonian Institution lecturer and study leader on local tours dealing with the black experience during the Civil War. He has also published several articles on African Americans and the Civil War. He is a member of The Company of Military Historians. A DC Humanities Council Scholar, Mr. Gibbs has also appeared on the History Channel. Mr. Gibbs returned recently from leading 26 people on a transcontinental crossing of Africa, from South to North. The nearly 5,000-mile journey included study stops in South Africa, Zimbabwe, Zambia, Kenya, and Egypt. Mr. Gibbs is also an honorary paramount chief of the Vai people of Liberia, West Africa.

WWW.3dpublishing.com/crgibbs/

Also by C.R. Gibbs

The Afro-American Inventor

Friends of Frederick Douglass

Black Explorers

Black Inventors: From Africa to America

Black Georgetown Remembered (with Kathleen Lesko and Valerie Babb)

Illustrations

Asa Gordon Collection: 74.

C.R. Gibbs Collection: 13, 21, 42, 63, 77, 95, 119, 178, 196.

Frank Wood (The Picture Bank): 142.

Lawrence Jackson: 190.

Library of Congress: 17, 37, 48, 86, 165, 169.

Moorland Spingarn Research Center (Howard University): 51, 98, 183, 188.

National Archives: 9, 56, 89, 121, 149, 153, 155.

Three Dimensional Publishing: 145, 158.

Three Dimensional Publishing: Cover Design.